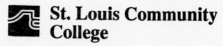

Religious Radicalism and Politics in the Middle East

SUNY Series in Near Eastern Studies
Said Amir Arjomand, Editor

A publication of the Harry S. Truman Research Institute
The Hebrew University of Jerusalem

Religious Radicalism and Politics in the Middle East

Edited by

Emmanuel Sivan and Menachem Friedman

State University of New York Press

Published by
State University of New York Press, Albany

©1990 State University of New York

For information, address State University of New York
Press, State University Plaza, Albany, NY 12246

Library of Congress Cataloging in Publication Data

Religious radicalism and politics in the Middle East / edited by
    Emmanuel Sivan and Menachem Friedman.
        p.   cm. -- (SUNY series in Near Eastern studies)
    Bibliography: p.
    Includes index.
    ISBN 0-7914-0158-8. -- ISBN 0-7914-0159-6 (pbk.)
    1. Islam--Middle East. 2. Islam--20th century. 3. Judaism-
-Israel. 4. Islam and politics--Middle East. 5. Judaism and
politics. 6. Middle East--Politics and government--1945-
7. Israel--Politics and government. I. Sivan, Emmanuel.
II. Friedman, Menachem. III. Series
BP63.A4M537 1990
296.3 '87--dc19
                                                            89-4235
                                                              CIP

10 9 8 7 6 5 4 3 2 1

Published in cooperation with
The Harry S. Truman Research Institute
for the Advancement of Peace
The Hebrew University, Jerusalem

TABLE OF CONTENTS

LIST OF CONTRIBUTORS

Aviezer Ravitzky: Associate Professor of Jewish Thought, The Hebrew University, Jerusalem

Emmanuel Sivan: Professor of History, The Hebrew University, Jerusalem

Charles S. Liebman: Professor of Political Science, Bar-Ilan University, Ramat Gan

Amatzia Baram: Lecturer in Islamic History, University of Haifa

Menachem Friedman: Associate Professor of Sociology, Bar-Ilan University, Ramat Gan

Thomas Mayer: Visiting Professor, Atlantic University, Boca Raton, Florida

Gideon Aran: Lecturer in Sociology, The Hebrew University, Jerusalem

Martin Kramer: Senior Research Fellow, Dayan Center, Tel Aviv University

The editors wish to express their warm thanks to Norma Schneider, Judith Roumani and Cheryl Beckerman, of the Harry S. Truman Research Institute for the Advancement of Peace, for their devoted efforts invested in the preparation of this volume for publication.

Introduction

Emmanuel Sivan

Religious radicalism, sociologists teach us,[1] is a mode of thought and action that entails, first of all, the rejection of those surrounding cultural forms and values perceived as nonindigenous (or inauthentic) to the religious tradition. And in order to bolster this rejection, certain key components of the tradition have to be reinvigorated and intensified. While the essence of extremism is excess, the notion that "the more the better," it is never excess for its own sake but for a higher goal: the defense of a tradition deemed to be under siege. Extremism, then, is linked inextricably to the nature of the specific religious tradition as well as to the character of the challenge. Extremists may very well differ from the rest of the believers of a religion because of the emphasis that they place on certain aspects of the tradition, even as they continue to share with the others a world view or system of meaning. They also differ from others, of course, in their perception of the danger lurking either within or without.

The study of extremism, therefore, is part and parcel of the comparative study of religion. To study the extremist forms of one religion alongside (or, if possible, in comparison with) those of another may enable us to highlight both the similarities and differences between the two.

With these aims in mind, the editors of this book embarked upon a pioneering effort in the study of the waves of religious extremism that unfurled in the Middle East over the last two decades: from the rise of Gush Emunim (GE) in Israel to the 1979 Revolution in Shi^{c}ite Iran, from the expansion of the ultra-Orthodox (*haredi*) movements in Judaism to the spread of radical groups in Sunni Islam, culminating in the assassination of Egyptian President Sadat. The salience of the phenomenon in the Middle East is undeniable, as is its unmistakable impact on politics; for example, the Israeli settlements on the West

1

Bank or the Khomeini regime. But is it really the same phenomenon everywhere? Do not the various traditions involved produce movements that, although structurally quite similar, are different in certain key aspects? And, furthermore, are all extremist movements which are generated by one religion essentially the same?

Intrigued by these questions, the editors have invited six authors to join them in setting forth the gist of their expertise on the movements they know best. Almost all the essays deal with more than one type of radicalism within a given religion. The eight essays were discussed in a colloquium and then rewritten to incorporate insights gained from hearing about analogous movements in the Middle East, be they Islamic or Jewish.

We have concentrated upon Islam and Judaism, while ignoring extremist Christian movements in the Middle East (e.g., the Egyptian Coptic militancy inspired by Patriarch Shanuda, the Guardians of the Cedar among the Maronites in Lebanon) to preserve both unity of space (the Middle East region) and affinity of tradition. For, after all, Judaism and Islam share a basic affinity, having as a central goal the shaping of human behavior rather than belief; hence, the primacy of law (*Sharīᶜa* in Islam, *Halakhah* in Judaism) over theology, whereas the obverse is true of Christianity. It is small wonder that expanding the scope, detail, and strictness of religious law, or at least certain parts of it, is the ultimate aim of the various Jewish and Islamic movements prevalent in the contemporary Middle East. Moreover, both Judaism and Islam have strong messianic components, and the interplay between these two elements — the legal and the messianic — influences how the Islamic and Jewish religions in general and their forms of extremism in particular converge and differ.

The eight essays in this book deal with the varieties of religious extremism in the Middle East in the light of their authors' shared insights and, thus, aim to provide the reader with a map of this complicated field. It is a field rendered all the more complex by the inner-directedness of the various movements within each camp. For, since the first priority of these movements is the moral regeneration of their respective religious communities through battling the "forces of apostasy" within their communities, they have little interest in external enemies. This results in each movement being determined by the conditions specific to the country that spawned it. Only rarely are the extremists of one religion even interested in extremists of another.[2]

The unique, therefore, is highlighted more often than what is common (though the latter occurs too, as we have said, thanks to insights gained by the authors from hearing about other types of extremism). The authors, especially Ravitzky, Liebman, Mayer, Kramer and myself, also endeavored to account for what unifies and differentiates forms of extremism within each of the two religious traditions. It would be presumptuous on our part to claim that a comparative framework for the analysis of Jewish and Islamic extremism can be proposed as a result of this undertaking. Still, it may be useful to sketch some outlines for such a framework as they emerge from the eight essays.

The essential impulse shared by all movements described here might be termed, following Said A. Arjomand,[3] "revolutionary traditionalism;" that is, a political radicalism born out of a religious tradition, which transcends that tradition in an attempt to preserve its authenticity in the face of contemporary challenges. The tradition so defended is not a matter of dessicated bookish lore nor a marginal component (or set of long-forgotten precedents) in the history of that religion. In all the cases analyzed here, we deal with a *living* tradition, transmitted from one generation to another by scholars, mystics, or other religious activists; a tradition that is part of the *mainstream* of that religion. Sunni and Shi^cite radicalism was born of an antiaccommodative attitude toward political power that had always existed within these two strands of Islam. This attitude (as Chapters 2, 4, 6, and 8 make clear) was much more important in Shi^cite Islam, given its persecuted stance throughout history. But, even among the Sunnis, who are more accommodative on the whole, there had always been a legitimate, vigilante-type alternative that was defiantly antiaccommodative and was perceived as within the pale, an integral part of Sunni political lore. Some of this vigilante lore has been covered by historical dust (e.g., the writings of the school of Ibn Hazm in Muslim Spain), but other variants continue to this day (namely, the neo-Hanbalite school founded by Ibn Taymiyya in the fourteenth century). When in the 1960s modern Sunni extremists looked for a tradition to build upon they naturally turned to Ibn Taymiyya (see Chapter 2, pp. 49). Neither here nor in Shi^cite Islam does the phenomenon in any way represent a revival of ancient heresies, outside the pale of the legitimate religious discourse. All attempts made by the post-1952 Egyptian regime to brand the extremists as heretics inevitably failed.

Heresy likewise is definitely not the essence of Jewish extremism. The ultra-Orthodoxy of the Haredim and Neturei Karta, as Chapter 5 argues, is a successor to a long tradition of Jewish exclusionary existence in an exilic phase of history, a tradition that until the Age of Enlightenment and secular nationalism (nay, even up to the Holocaust) was *the* major living tradition of Judaism, resigned to life outside of history (and politics) as long as God had not performed the miracle of messianic redemption. As for Gush Emunim (Chapter 7), they build upon the minor but legitimate tradition of Jewish activist messianism — exerting oneself to hasten the arrival of the Messiah and not passively waiting for him — a tradition that had played a key role in certain historical moments as late as the seventeenth century (with the mass movement of Shabtai Zvi which had deep roots in the Kabbalah). These medieval kabbalistic concepts were revamped by Rabbi Zvi Yehuda Kook in the 1950s to answer questions raised by the establishment of the State of Israel, in a manner no different in essence from the one used by Sunni thinker Sayyid Qutb to reinterpret Ibn Taymiyya's political theory for the needs of the twentieth century. In a slightly different fashion (see Chapter 2, p. 50), this also is what Khomeini did with the *usuli* notion of ulama hierarchy and social responsibility. It should be stressed that the different traditions they build upon explain the divergent paths of Sunni and Shi°ite religio-political movements today. Despite all the "ecumenical" attempts at rapprochement (see Chapters 6 and 8), these paths are likely to remain as divergent as ever.

The divergence of opinion between Gush Emunim and the Haredim is not so much a matter of basic concepts — both accept the distinction between "normal," diasporic time and miraculous, messianic time — as a matter of diagnosis. While GE believes that the messianic Age of Redemption actually dawned in 1948, the Haredim believe that they still live in a diasporic age, the establishment of the "apostate" State of Israel having changed nothing.

Their strong base in the religious tradition goes far to explain the initial appeal that all these movements have for "true believers." This base also makes the believers' task of transcending the living tradition while remaining true to it so complex and daunting. For, despite their deep roots in tradition, these cannot be called conservative movements, as they spring from a radical political mythology designed to galvanize people into political action aimed at delegitimizing and eventually scuttling the political or social orders.[4] In the case of "revolutionary traditionalism," the intellectual and affective justification for the myth — a dramatic story based on past or future events, true or fictional — is found not in a long-extinguished or brand-new set of values, but in values still cherished by at least parts of the society.

These values provide the extremists with a set of criteria for judging the present state of affairs as nefarious; nay, even irreligious, apostate. This is their most crucial function, for the primordial impulse of all these extremist movements is one of religiosity in a state of siege; that is, a defensive initiative designed to thwart the demise of either Judaism or Islam, undermined from within by "nominal (hypocritical) believers," who are in fact Hellenized (*mityavnim*, in Hebrew), Westoxicated (*gharbzada*, in Persian). Both terms, and their plethora of synonyms, refer in Sunni, Shiᶜite, and Jewish ultra-Orthodox militancy to the same phenomenon: people captivated by the ideals of the Age of Enlightenment in the broadest sense of the term (human-centered, progress-minded, scientific, rationalist, etc.). In the case of Gush Emunim, the modernity that is rejected is of a more constricted type: secular Zionism with its "defeatist propensity" for compromise over immutable values such as the sanctity of the Land of Israel, a propensity "laid bare" after the 1973 War. (GE, it should be stressed, was founded in the wake of the 1973 war and the resultant pessimism, not after the 1967 war with its messianic euphoria.)

In all four movements, however, the tools of modernity are accepted (media technology, military hardware, and so forth); rejection refers to goals and values rather than the means.

As befits religions predicated upon Divine Law, the Jewish and Islamic extremist militants deduce these goals and values from the *Halakhah* and the *Shariᶜa*. And the Divine Law also provides guidelines for the construction of the future order: "a *Halakhah* state" or "a *Shariᶜa* state." These slogans, heralded by Haredim as well as by Sunnis and Shiᶜites, refer to an ideal polity in which the religious code covers the public as much as the private realm, and usually according to the most rigorous exegesis, the obverse of the lenient one resorted to by modernist reformers. Here again, Gush Emunim differs from the rest: it concentrates the application of *Halakhah* on one major issue, the incorporation of the "still unredeemed" parts of *Eretz Israel* (the Land of Israel) in the territories governed de facto by the Jewish state. As Chapters 3 and 7 make clear, this characteristic is closely associated with the unique diagnosis GE believes in (see pp. 83; 165–166). The interplay between the legal and the messianic is quite evident here. For Jews, the Jewish state can be achieved only outside the historical time-frame. This is why the ultra-Orthodox who do not see the End of Days on the horizon (Chapters 2 and 5) deny the legitimacy of the State of Israel and aspire to reestablish the exilic type of closely knit, *Halakhah*-governed, autonomous community that had existed in the Eastern

European shtetl. The past they are fixated on (that is their "founding myth" in anthropological parlance) is the seventeenth and eighteenth centuries, when the shtetl flourished, well before the onslaught of enlightenment, assimilation, and secularism. This is why they dress in the black garb so common in eighteenth-century Poland.

The Gush Emunim ultra-nationalists (see Chapter 3) legitimate the State of Israel precisely because they believe that the very existence of the state is proof that the process of Redemption has begun and that we are therefore already operating outside history. But, the ultra-nationalists continue, Israel can retain its legitimacy only if certain conditions related to messianic requirements — for example, settlement of the Land of Israel, which is the theater of Redemption — are met. Thus, the activity of these Jewish radicals is geared mainly toward furthering the process of Redemption by settling in the entire land. Their "founding myth," accordingly, is fixated on a completely different past: the First and Second Jewish commonwealths (thirteenth to sixth centuries B.C.; second century B.C. to second century A.D.), which prefigure the Third Commonwealth now being created through the "pangs of the messianic Redemption." It is no sheer coincidence that GE activists are dressed in an unabashedly contemporary Israeli garb, with a dash of a pioneering, military accoutrement. The skullcap and ostentatiously worn prayer shawl are the sole vestmental signs of their messianic obsessions. They speak modern Hebrew while the Haredim prefer Yiddish, the day-to-day language of the shtetl (Hebrew being the sacred language of ritual and Law). Gush Emunim followers choose fancy biblical names for their offspring and settlements; the Haredim opt for common "diasporic" ones.

The interplay between messianism, legal ideals, and myths of the past is operating along other lines in extremist Islam. The messianic element is tightly held in abeyance in almost all Sunni groups, the only exception being the *Takfir wa-Hijra* Sunni sect in 1977 Egypt, which declared its leader (who was later executed) as *Mahdi* (Messiah and caliph). But, unlike the ultra-nationalist Gush Emunim, this sect was antinomian in that it also rejected most of the *Shari^{c}a* as evil, because its evolution throughout Islamic history always had been contaminated by collusion with the powers that be. The exception proves the rule: the messianic element on the whole is quite irrelevant to the Sunni discourse on delegitimation. Sunni extremists hold that the present order must be toppled in "normal" (nonmessianic) historical time and a new legitimate order established without awaiting the Messiah (or *Mahdi*).

As explained in Chapter 2, this perception on the whole is true for Shi^{c}ite extremists as well, but only on the intellectual level. On the affective level, whereas Sunnis are nonmessianic, the Shi^{c}ites retain a powerful eschatological undercurrent that is especially prominent in the popular manifestations of the Karbala myth, an ancient vehicle for Shi^{c}ite sensibility of persecution and victimization, which was transformed in this century into a pivotal means for articulating revolutionary aspirations.[5] Nevertheless the *Shari^{c}a* myth, with its clearcut orientation toward the past, definitely reigns supreme even among Shi^{c}ites, especially as the interpreters of the Divine Law, the ulama, lead the Shi^{c}ite extremists and, in fact, constitute the revolutionary cadre (see Chapters 2 and 4).

It follows, then, that the Sunni, Shi^{c}ite, and Jewish ultra-Orthodox myths are essentially past-oriented, in that they focus upon eras in which the Divine Law was effectively applied in "normal" historical time: the seventh century for Muslims and the seventeenth-eighteenth-century shtetl for the Jews. The ultra-nationalist Jewish myth is oriented toward both the past (the two Jewish commonwealths) and the future of the Jewish state, insofar as it applies the law (*Halakhah*) in accordance with tradition.

The functions of political myths are not merely cognitive and hermeneutic — interpreting past, present, and future and thereby defining group identity — but also behavioral; in other words, myths are supposed to lead to action. But as the eight case studies presented in this book show, whether that action will be directed toward drawing away from the corrupt present order into a state of internal or physical exile or toward taking the initiative to change the present state of affairs by whatever means are at hand — including violence — depends on circumstances. Still, here again, there is a broad common denominator between Jewish ultra-nationalists, most Sunni, and all Shi^{c}ite radicals — all three rely on deliberate intervention in the sociopolitical arena to bring about change in the "apostate" rulers and civil society of their own camp and, if necessary, in foreign powers as well. Ultra-Orthodox Jews, on the other hand, defer all structural change to messianic times, and the few Sunni sects (such as the Samawiyya in Egypt) that despair of ever being able to defy the all-powerful modern nation-state retire into a self-imposed seclusion designed to save their own souls even if they cannot save the "apostate," hostile and alien environment in which they are fated to live. But, whether they choose withdrawal or activism, both Jewish and Islamic extremists endeavor to preserve their own versions of the tradition they cherish by constructing "counter-societies"[6] predicated upon values and patterns of behavior alien and inimical to their respective civil societies. These counter-societies serve two purposes. They are designed to serve as models for a future society based on the rigorous application of either *Shari̇̄a* or *Halakhah*. And, in the case of the more "interventionist"-minded extremists, they also view themselves as potential tools for subverting and toppling the present order.

This accounts for the sustained effort by the Haredim to maintain their distance from the "Zionist apostate state," relying on funding from sympathizers in the Diaspora in order to maintain their own network of services; especially education, health, and welfare but also in internal policing, using services of the accursed state only in extremis (e.g., for external security). In like fashion, the Sunni extremists in Egypt, Tunisia, and Sudan, chastened by the recent failure of their revolutionary attempts, today rely more and more on developing near their mosques, outpatient clinics and educational establishments (including preschools, a novelty in Arab lands). Through these institutions, as well as through Islamic banks where usury is prohibited, they hope to minimize their followers' contact with the state and prove that Islamic ideals of social justice and moral probity can be implemented in a modern setting.

The toppling of the present order remains the goal—however remote and elusive—of all the extremists surveyed in this volume. For the interventionist-minded this involves the possibility of active martyrdom, while passive martyrdom is all that can be envisaged for those who practice withdrawal, be they Sunnis or ultra-Orthodox Jews. The underlying motivation for both modes of behavior is an alienation that, although it is to some extent intellectual, is mainly emotional. It is this alienation that extremists not only aspire to but have generally succeeded in disseminating among both their own hard core followers and their ever-expanding periphery. That is how they come to exercise effective cultural hegemony in their respective societies. The spread of Jewish settlements in the West Bank, the growing impact of religious law in Israel (notably in personal status, leisure, and the closing down of state economic enterprises on Shabbat) are prominent examples in the Jewish sphere. Among Muslims, not only is the Iranian regime still in power, despite the setback in the war with Iraq, but Sunni extremists (some of them pro-Khomeini—see Chapter 6) launched the Intifada (uprising) in Gaza and the West Bank and continue to play a prominent role in it. Despite the tarnished image of Iran's revolutionary message (see Chapter 8), Shi̇̄ite extremist groups, notably

Hizballah, are very active in Lebanon.[7] The Sunni extremists are at the forefront of most social protest movements (in Tunisia in summer and fall 1987; in Algeria in October 1988). They have forced even secularist regimes like the Ba^cth in Syria, to make *Shari^ca* the major source of all legislation. They brought about the application of the *Shari^ca* by the state in Sudan (under Numeiri) and in Pakistan (under Zia ul-Haqq). In Egypt, Morocco, and the Arab Gulf emirates they had an impact on the school curriculum and television and radio programs as well as on public mores (women's dress, men's beards, high fertility among educated women, lower median age at marriage for both genders, etc.). It is indeed, above all, in setting the terms and priorities for debate in public affairs in Middle Eastern societies, rather than in the distant possibility of their seizing power, that all these Jewish and Islamic extremist groups play an important role in the future of this part of the world.

Chapter One

Religious Radicalism and Political Messianism in Israel

Aviezer Ravitzky

In 1899 Rabbi I. J. Reines, the founder of Mizrachi (the religious Zionist movement), made the following statement in favor of Zionism:

> There is nothing in this ideology that relates to the idea of messianic Redemption. . . . In none of the acts or aspirations of the Zionists is there the slightest allusion to future Redemption. Their only intention is to improve the conditions of life of Israel, to uplift their honor and to accustom them to a life of happiness . . . how then can one compare this idea with the [traditional] idea of Redemption?[1]

The following year Rabbi Reines was joined by other rabbis, who declared that

> those who think that the Zionist idea is somehow associated with future Redemption and the coming of the Messiah, and who therefore regard it as undermining our Holy Religion, are mistaken. . . . And if some preachers, while speaking of Zion, also mention Redemption and the coming of the Messiah, and thus let the abominable thought enter people's mind that this idea encroaches upon the territory of true Redemption, only they themselves are to blame, for it is their own wrong opinion they express.[2]

These words were intended to move the heated discussion of Zionism in Orthodox circles as far away as possible from the question of messianic Redemption: the Zionist idea does not replace messianic expectations nor does it wish to realize them, oust them, or be their heir. Zionism offers a partial and relative solution, *hic et nunc*; it operates in an unredeemed world and does not encroach upon the territory of the absolute and the whole, or of final Redemption.[3] The attempt to provide religious sanction for the Zionist idea led these rabbis, and

11

others with them, to make a clear distinction between the sphere of human history, to which Zionism relates, and the sphere of "the anticipated miraculous Redemption"[4] at the end of days, "the sphere of pure faith, the faith in the Messiah."[5] There is no point of contact between the two spheres. Just as some (nonreligious) Zionist spokespersons distinguished between the two spheres in order to "defend" Zionism against messianic tendencies and absolute supra-historical demands,[6] to leave room for secular political efforts without apocalyptical speculations,[7] the religious Zionists distinguished between these spheres from the opposite direction—if only for apologetic reasons. They did so to "protect" messianism from Zionism and to ensure the integrity and purity of the belief in the days of the Messiah and of the vision of Redemption in the fact of the historical, human, natural, and partial Zionist fulfillment to which they lent their support. For the historical, topical task does not trespass into the domain of the utopian vision of the future.

Such a separation of domains, however, did not prove tenable in the later developments of religious views and tendencies. It became neither the highway of religious Zionism nor influential in sanctioning Zionism among the non-Zionist Orthodox. On the contrary, religious polemics about Zionism—and subsequently about the position and future of the State of Israel—increasingly focused on the messianic question, so that diametrically opposed standpoints were formulated in connection with this question, even on issues that were not directly related. On the one hand, too many elements of the Zionist vision and its realization touched upon the sphere of messianic expectations—ingathering of the exiles, liberation from foreign bondage, social justice, "the trees of [the Land] of Israel bringing forth their fruits"[8] — for religious consciousness to insist on the methodical separation of the two spheres. On the other hand, too many other elements challenged the classical messianic belief—the severance of Redemption from religious repentance, secular activity, earthly and natural processes, the "breach of oaths" [not to force the end prematurely][9] — for religious consciousness to avoid the question, What is the relationship between the historical and the utopian, between the natural and the miraculous, the political and the spiritual, the secular enterprise and religious Redemption? Is it the beginning of the messianic era or the work of Satan?

It should be emphasized here that the Jewish messianic idea as such has always been a matter of internal tension and contradictory views. The profound differences in this matter were already reflected in talmudic and midrashic literature on such questions as What is the connection between Redemption and human activity? Will Redemption come step by step, gradually, or suddenly, unexpectedly? What is the relation between Redemption and repentance? The controversy, sometimes touching upon the very essence of the messianic idea, ranges from the expectation of cataclysmic changes in nature — "new heavens and a new earth"[10] in the literal sense — to the confinement of messianic hope to the national-social sphere alone, to the political liberation from bondage. The issue has become no less thorny in the course of the generations.[11] Scholars, preachers, prophets, and apocalyptic visionaries have always discovered new aspects. When all these facets are considered in light of contemporary historical events and ideological positions, they assume a new vitality. But, as often occurs with polemical literature, the reader may well wonder what it is all about, whether these are strictly scholarly discussions of the halakhic and aggadic sources or heated ideological debates on the burning questions of the time.

To sum up, when the debate about the State of Israel and its future touches upon messianic expectations, the tension becomes twofold: (1) that between the partial, contingent, uncertain historical present and the perfect, absolute, utopian messianic future; and (2) the internal tensions and even contradictions within the messianic idea itself.

Zionism as an Anti-Messianic Undertaking

The two diametrically opposed radical religious conceptions of the status and future of the State of Israel appear to be deterministic: the future is given and fixed; revealed and known in light of the messianic promise. Human deeds may hasten or delay future destiny, straighten the path toward it, or place obstacles in its way, but the trend of the historical process — and with it the future of Zionism — is determined and foreseen for better or worse. Both conceptions consider Zionism from the standpoint of messianic belief, both deny the legitimacy of any Jewish political sovereignty in the Land of Israel that is not complete in nature, ultimate and final. One view regards Zionism and the establishment of the state, per definition, as an antimessianic process conceived and born in sin, a hopeless enterprise doomed from the beginning, regardless of our deeds. The second view regards Zionism and the establishment of the State of Israel, per definition, as a messianic fulfillment, conceived and born in a holiness that guarantees complete future success and final Redemption, future spiritual repentance and return. The common denominator of these two standpoints is that both infer the end of the Zionist enterprise, for good or for evil, from its very beginning, according to its inherent religious value.[12]

The first view is most strongly developed in the circles of Neturei Karta, the Edah Haredit in Jerusalem, and the Satmar Hassidim.[13] According to this conception, Zionism reflects the Jewish people's betrayal of its destiny, nature, and essence; it is a manifestation of Israel's secession from faith in Divine Providence and future Redemption, of its betrayal of the covenant. Aspiring toward normalization of the Jewish people, even in the worldly political sphere alone, deliberately challenges the miraculous ways of Jewish history, the ways in which Divine Providence has placed the people of Israel outside the natural laws of causality, subjecting them instead to different laws: those of punishment and reward, of exile and Redemption. "Unless the Lord builds the house, its builders labor in vain. Unless the Lord watches over the city, the watchman keeps vigil in vain" (Psalms 127:1). Passive Jewish expectation of a miraculous, supra-natural and supra-historical Redemption, entirely unrelated to worldly activities and human political work, embodies the faith of the Jew, the Jew's acceptance of the Kingdom of God, of the truth of prophetical promises for a miraculous return, of the unique character of the chosen people, and of messianic Redemption:

> Whoever doubts that this Redemption will come miraculously, rejects the principle of our belief in the Torah. . . . the very fact of taking it upon oneself to hasten Redemption prematurely is an act of infidelity, Heaven forfend. . . . It is not possible for a man to adhere to these two convictions—belief in this state [the State of Israel] and belief in our Holy Torah—for they are each other's absolute opposite, and they cannot wear one crown. (Rabbi Yoel Teitelbaum, the Satmar Rebbe)[14]

The Jewish people had been sworn to quietism. They were adjured, according to the Midrash, not to return to the Land of Israel by force, not to hasten the End and not to rise up against the nations of the world.[15] The attempt to integrate the eternal people into the history of the nations; the initiative to return through physical power to the sphere of political—and military—history was a collective revolt of the people of Israel against the Kingdom of Heaven, an aggressive aspiration to overstep their boundaries into the realm reserved for the Holy One, Blessed be He, as did the generation of the tower of Babel:

It was forbidden to Israel to attempt to free themselves by their own strength and power; Israel should trust in the Lord, await salvation from the hands of the Lord and Redemption through the coming of the righteous Messiah. . . . these Zionists came to our Holy Land to build their national home and destroyed religion and uprooted our Holy Torah and our faith in our true Salvation through the coming of the Messiah; and their leaders raised the banner of revolt against the Kingdom of Heaven . . . and they induced the people of Israel to break the oath to which the Lord has sworn Israel, and they have caused terrible bloodshed in Israel. (Rabbi Amram Blau)[16]

Just as the political passivity of the Jewish people in its exile has theological as well as historical significance, and is a duty imposed by the Torah and by faith, the Zionist enterprise has not only historical, political significance but belongs as well to the sphere of demonology. It is a satanic, antimessianic revolt, the last attempt of the forces of evil to mislead the people before the true, final Redemption.[17] In other words, opposition to the State of Israel is not opposition to the specific character of the society itself, to its secular leadership, laws, or ways, but opposition to the very existence of the state; an a priori not an a posteriori opposition. Any political Jewish entity in the premessianic era is rejected in principle. There is no hope for it apart from the hope that it may vanish. Even if the *Halakhah* (Jewish religious law) were to become the law of the state, even if Israel's citizens were to repent and return to the Torah, this would not affect the essence of the state in the least because it is rooted in the original sin of its establishment. In the last instance, such concepts as "Torah-true state" or "halakhic state," as human created, are considered self-contradictory, for they imply fulfillment of the Torah through revolt against the Kingdom of Heaven, obeying a commandment by committing a greater sin. Hence the deterministic logic of the attitude towards the State of Israel:

Even if the members of the Knesset were righteous and holy men, it would still be a terrible crime to hasten Redemption and rule independently before the time has come, for it is clear that the oath and the prohibition against anticipating the End applies to the whole of Israel, even to the most righteous of men. . . . Even if all the members of the government were beloved and selected men, even if they were like the talmudic sages, if they take the government and freedom in their own hands before the time has

come, they defile the Holy Torah. The kingdom of Bar-Kosiba
was also a kingdom true to the Torah . . . the men of his generation were also righteous men . . . and they were severely punished
because their work was an anticipation of the End, before the
time had come.[18]

In other words, what has been distorted, by definition, cannot be
repaired, except by Israel's collective forsaking of the political act, of
the illegitimate freedom it has given itself.

Moreover, as we learn from some of the most far-reaching expressions of this school of thought, there is no way for the Zionists to repent religiously; such repentance is undesirable! The spheres must be
demarcated clearly, the borders defined, and the wall between sacred
and profane, between light and darkness, between Israel and the State
of "Israel" raised even higher. For there is no hope, for either the state
or the individual! The fact that the individual has revolted and become
lawless can never be undone! The sinful outcome testifies to the sinful
root, for from the very beginning "his soul is not rooted in Israel, but
in the spirit of Amalek. . . . They descended from the rabble that
came from Egypt, and do not belong to the people of Israel" (Rabbi
Y. A. Z. Margulis).[19] There is, as it were, an ontological gap between
the "guardians of the walls" and the Zionist camp, and every attempt
to narrow this gap is nothing but an attempt to blur the demarcations
and confuse the issues. Let them go on and defile themselves. Good
and evil, pure and unclean are finally separated on the eve of Redemption, and "when these are wiped out from Israel, the Son of David [the
Messiah] will come."[20] In the last instance, social isolationism symbolizes metaphysical separation as well. It is true that these and similar
extreme expressions are exceptional, but they come from within.[21]

The social and political consequences of this view are clear: social
isolation from *Klal Israel* (the people of Israel), in order to defend
She'erit Israel (the remnant of Israel), and political isolation from the
State of Israel: a total boycott of elections, taxes, national insurance,
and other institutions of the state. Such radicalism finds its expression
in the complete withdrawal into the insular community, in the refusal
to participate in the Jewish people's return to history, in the total con-
centration on waiting for the supra-historical.

That the number of people who hold these views is small is entirely
irrelevant to this small minority group. In its own view, its members
are the real people of Israel, the true elite. There is no doubt that the
question of responsibility toward the whole of Israel concerns the rabbis

and scribes who are its spiritual leaders. However, the examples in the history of Israel of the few who kept the flame burning and stood up against the many who broke the covenant—from the biblical examples of the Levites against those who worshipped the golden calf, or of the prophet Elijah against the priests of Baal,[22] to the more recent struggle of Rabbi Jacob Sasportas against Shabtai Zvi and his followers—are very much alive in their consciouness: "For if the few who knew the truth had feared the dangers of their generation, and had followed the many in their deviations, the remainder of Judah would, Heaven forbid, have been lost; but they who fought for the truth, even though they were the smallest of minorities, they saved their generation."[23]

These groups exhibit features typical of ideologically radical minority groups that are deeply convinced of their own mission: as members of a minority, destined to live in the present as dissenting, exceptional individuals, they are the true representatives of tomorrow.[24] They who live at the fringes of history in the present are the messengers of the promise and determine the fulfillment of history; they are the remnant of Israel destined to mold the whole of Israel anew. In other words, they who are faithful to the word of the Lord, the guardians of the wall, are not merely faithful to the past but also are the loyal avant-garde of a future that will be built on the ruins of the present.

> For it is clear, without the slightest doubt, that all the buildings erected in our Holy Land by heretics and atheists will be burnt and destroyed by the King Messiah, and no remnant of them shall survive. . . . And in their place the Holy One, blessed be He, shall erect for us other, entirely holy buildings. And then shall all the nations know that "I the Lord have built up the broken-down [places]" [Ezekiel 36:36], and they are not like unto the first buildings that were destroyed. (Rabbi Y. Teitelbaum)[25]

Zionism is a stumbling block on the path toward the predestined goal of history;[26] as such it cannot escape the inevitable judgment of deterministic messianism.

Zionism as Messianic Fulfillment

The opposite religious standpoint regards the history of Zionism and the State of Israel ex the history of the realization of the messianic vision, "the revealed signs of the End." This applies to the past and present reality that we witness as well as to the expected and dreamt-of future: "the state as the embodiment of the vision of Redemption."

Those who adhere to this view of "redemptionist" Zionism, the disciples of Mercaz ha-Rav Yeshivah and the ideological leaders of Gush Emunim, search for signs of the realization of the prophetic vision and exceptions in the concrete reality of our time; they seek traces of the process of Redemption in current historical events. Such a religious response to historical events does not regard messianism as the antithesis of reality, as a hope of its future perfection, but as integrated in it, rooted and embodied in reality. "Our reality is a messianic reality." "True Redemption, which is revealed in the progress of settlement of the Land, the revival of Israel in its Land, and in the continuing renewal of this settlement by the ingathering of the exiles . . . in the possession of the Land . . . in our public devotion to its holiness" (Rabbi Z. Y. Kook).[27] The return to Zion and Jewish political sovereignty are intrinsically sanctified since they embody a human response to a divine call. Whereas according to the logic of Neturei Karta and the Satmar Hassidim, the original sin is rooted in the very existence of the Jewish state and cannot be corrected or purified, according to the logic of the messianic approach, the holy essence of the state cannot be damaged or destroyed.

Therefore, the Zionist enterprise will inevitably lead to repentance and redemption: once the process has started, there is no return. We are at the height of an irreversible progress, the very beginning of which guarantees its outcome. The Midrash said: "The third Redemption will not be interrupted"[28] (unlike the redemption from Egypt and the building of the second Temple). And these words apply to us, to our generation, to the future that the historical process we witness will lead to with certainty. Events are guided by preordained historical and supra-historical laws, which are implemented through human work:

> The special compulsion of life goes its certain and only way in strength and faithfulness . . . towards its determined, true destiny, towards its perfect and unshakable realizaton. This is an "historical necessity" and a "cosmic inevitability" that exists by the grace of the divine covenant that cannot be shaken . . . from this supreme and inner command of life the absolute certainty of the process of our return and of our being built here is derived and clarified . . . and without an alternative, without fluctuations, it

determines, assigns, captures and lightens the one, clear and certain way, the way of life and of building, the way of resurrection and Redemption. (Rabbi Z. Y. Kook)[29]

It is within our power to accelerate this process or to delay it; to remove obstacles in its path or to erect them. But nothing can alter the preordained direction. The ups and downs do not alter the determined destination. A favored metaphor is that of a traveller on a train who can assist or hold back the engine's progress, but who is powerless to change the course of the tracks or the journey's final destination. These have been laid in advance by the Cause of all causes, to lead toward repentance and redemption.

The significance of contemporary events, of the return to Zion, interpreted as the fulfillment of messianic promises, is not confined to the national sphere — the ingathering of exiles, possession of the land, and the peace of Israel — but also is perceived as an aspect of a cosmic, universal process of messianic fulfillment, of Redemption of the world and of humankind. Historical necessity is anchored in cosmic, supra-historical necessity, and therein lies the guarantee for the future of the building. Nor is this vision confined to the ideological and theological spheres. It relates as well to an alternative Zionist historiography and an alternative Zionist historiosaphy.

This historiography assigns a different beginning to modern Zionism, tending to emphasize events that others do not consider central to historical development. For example, it teaches that the process in which we are involved did not start with the beginning of political Zionism nor with the first Zionist *aliyah*, or wave of immigration. The "beginning of Redemption" started in the early nineteenth century when the followers of Rabbi Eliyahu of Vilna immigrated to the Land of Israel. At that time a group of Jews, led by Rabbi Menahem Mendel of Shkelov, immigrated to the Land of Israel in order to hasten Redemption by rebuilding Jerusalem. These immigrants were guided by their concrete expectation, based on ancient traditions and allusions in the Zohar, that the coming of the Messiah would occur in the year 1840. Their concept of Redemption was activist in nature: we are living in the time of grace, but the Jewish people must first wake up, both by spiritual return and by going up to Eretz Israel to rebuild it; awakening in this world will lead to heavenly awakening. The next phase in this version of the historical process was in the mid-nineteenth century, with the rise of "Mevasrei Zion" rabbis Kalisher and Alkalay, who taught that Redemption is not a sudden event, but a gradual process that must be preceded by human preparation and building in the worldly and natural sphere. *Teshuvah*, the return to God that the rabbinic sages considered a precondition for divine Redemption, was interpreted as a physical return to the Land of Israel. Therefore, in the contemporary messianic conception of Zionism and the State of Israel, people like rabbis Kalisher and Alkalay are granted an outstanding historical status; they are described not only as the harbingers of Zionism, but as its very instigators. In the following text, however, we shall turn our attention mainly to the historiosophical principles that underlie this vision, leaning heavily on the teachings of Rabbi Abraham Isaac ha-Cohen Kook.

At the turn of this century Rabbi Kook developed a complex dialectical structure that allocated to Zionism and the contemporary return to Zion a crucial place in the vision of Redemption and in the messianic process. Such an ideological construction faced two objections: with regard to the first question, that of "breach of the oath" not to force the End, one had to ask whether the Jewish people do indeed have the right to break into history with worldly activity drawn from human sources, whether they have the right to replace the passive expectation of miraculous Redemption with ordinary human deeds.

The second question deals with cooperation with secular Zionism: assuming that human, national awakening as such is allowed or even laudable, are we free and entitled to participate in and be coresponsible for the work of those who break the covenant and openly desecrate Jewish religious laws, the work of Jews who have declared their enterprise in revolt against the practices and traditions of their parents and grandparents, against the Kingdom of Heaven? In other words, can good results be brought about by the guilty and can the Holy Land be built by a process of secularization?

Rabbi Kook's answer to these questions and objections involves a series of distinctions he made in his search for the hidden, inner meaning of the historical process; he distinguished between the visible and the hidden, the subjective and the objective, and the conscious and the unconscious.

First of all, Rabbi Kook regarded Zionism as a response to a call from Heaven, to a divine move not stemming from human sources. He viewed what appears outwardly to be a daring initiative of the people as nothing but human response on the hidden level, the answer to an awakening above and beyond human understanding. The Jew acts, yet does not create. "This wonder is performed before our eyes, not by the work of man or by his machinations, but by the miraculous ways of Him who is perfect in knowledge, the Lord of War, who bringeth forth salvation. This is certain—the voice of the Lord is heard."[30] This is not a hastening and premature anticipation of the time; it is the fortunate moment, the hour of grace, of "the revealed signs of the End." (In accordance with the Talmudic word: "There are no better revealed signs of the End than these, as it is written [Ezekiel 36:8]: But ye, O mountains of Israel, ye shall send forth your boughs, and your fruit shall ye bear for My people Israel, for they are near at hand to come.")[31] In other words, the fulfillment as such, the gradual success as such are proof of the religious legitimacy of the work; the national revival testifies to the divine source from which it springs. Thus Zionism is interpreted as a worldly awakening stemming from a Heavenly awakening.[32]

According to Rabbi Kook, one should also clearly distinguish between the subjective intentions of the individuals acting in history and the objective outcome of their deeds, between trend and result. A person may play a role in the course of certain events, assist in the advance of a historical process, fight for it, and hasten it, without even being aware of the real meaning of these events or the eventual results and repercussions of the process. In fact, the latter may be alien to that individual's own intentions. Thus a Zionist who regards Zionism as an entirely secular enterprise and whole-heartedly opposes the world of the Torah, the commandments, and religious Redemption may in the last instance turn out to be someone who has taken part in a historical, cosmic process that differs entirely from his or her own objectives and goals. For that person lays the foundation for religious messianic redemption without having a clear notion of it. (The relation of this view to the Hegelian concept of "cunning historical Reason" is clear.)[33] This is "the irony of history": "Even those who do not know the ultimate goal of the building can carry the bricks. And not only can they carry the bricks, they may even direct the work, but when the inner and real purpose of the building is revealed, all becomes clear."[34]

Parallel to the distinction among the different levels of the historical process—between visible and hidden, between subjective and objective—Rabbi Kook also distinguished among the different levels of awareness of the actors in the drama of history, between conscious and unconscious inclinations, between proclaimed and secret intentions. He undertook to give an interpretation of the intentions of the secular Zionist that went beyond the latter's own recognition and self-declaration, arguing that in the last instance it appears that the builders are not entirely unaware of the purpose of the building, of the true source and objective of their work; in the last instance the Return to Zion, the national revival, the pioneering work, and the social reforms appear to be parts of the process of Return to the source, parts, that is, of an unconscious process of religious return, repentance. "Truly, in the awakening desire of the entire nation to return to its Land, to its substance, to its spirit and true nature, shines the light of repentance."[35] "They do not know themselves what they want."[36]

This insight proceeds from fundamental philosophical and mystical assumptions on which we cannot elaborate in this context. Rabbi Kook perceived religious faith as human natural inclination, the yearning for God as an original and natural tendency of the human being: "Man's devotion to God is his most natural desire."[37] Moreover, he believed in the unique immanent, religious nature of the people of Israel, in the existence of a given, permanent affinity that makes it impossible for the bond between the people and its God to be severed entirely: "A covenant was made with Knesset Israel which cannot be entirely defiled. The spirit of the Lord and the spirit of Israel are one."[38] This conviction underlies Rabbi Kook's unshakable belief that Jewish national togetherness and the search for national revival spring from a sacred source.[39] The very return of Israel to its Holy Land, to its holy tongue, to its collective Jewish life, will be revealed as a return to its God.[40] Although the concepts of faith, repentance, and holiness apply to deeds and steps that originally were not performed consciously for the sake of Heaven, their outcome will clarify the true significance of their beginning: "We do not regret that social justice is pursued without the divine Name being mentioned, for we know that the very aspiration for justice, in whatever form, is in itself a token of the most enlightening divine influence."[41]

All this is said, of course, in relation to the paths that lead toward Redemption, rather than to future final Redemption itself, for the latter demands complete religious consciousness; it demands that the "natural" attribute of Israel be raised to the level of free choice. But this does not apply to the dialectical course toward Redemption, to the steep paths leading to it, which do not necessarily pass through the conscious recognition of every individual.

What is the significance of Rabbi Kook's principal assumptions and expectations when they are interpreted and applied to concrete contemporary reality and to the State of Israel? Does this vision of Redemption promise and ensure a certain, revealed, and known future for this concrete reality and this concrete state, "without alternatives or fluctuations"? (See the words quoted earlier, of his son, Rabbi Z. Y. Kook.) To what degree do our deeds—earthly political and spiritual-religious—determine our faith, for good and for evil?

There is no doubt as to how Rabbi Kook's teachings have been interpreted by the second generation of his disciples: their reading renders his belief and expectation into certainty and knowledge. Our time is the final, irreversible messianic time, the time of the "revealed signs of the End" whose beginning guarantees its outcome. Its realization is not dependent on human work and behavior. Although it is within human power to hasten or delay the process by taking part in it or holding aloof, by removing obstacles or placing them, none of this can change the course of the last phase, to which the revealed historical events are leading. This course is set and determined, whether we desire it or not. Even withdrawals and deviations from the way are in the last instance parts of this course:

> We are living in the last phase of history . . . the Redemption of Israel in our days is not dependent on Israel's deeds. . . . Divine guidance in our time does not reckon with the deeds of Israel in general, but is in accordance with the plan of the world . . . none of the processes of Redemption in our days—true and faithful Redemption from which there is no return—are dependent on our deeds. (Rabbi Eliyahu Avihayil)[42]

Everything is foreseen. Not only the very existence of such a "plan of the world" but also its substance and moves are revealed and known. Contemplation of the historical reality that evolves before our eyes, on the one hand, and study of the prophetical promises, on the other, give us both faith and knowledge.

With regard to the contemplation of historical reality:

> People ask us: where do you get your certainty that you understand the divine plan? Isn't it presumptuous to pretend that one understands divine reality? It is true, we cannot know precisely the divine plans . . . but when the events are happening and the Holy One, blessed be He, performs His deeds before our eyes, we must be blind if we do not see what is happening . . . this is not presumptuous, it is rather a look at the world with open eyes. (Rabbi Eliezer Waldman)[43]

And with regard to the study of prophetical promises: "Yes, we have communication ["behind the curtains," secretly]. The prophets of Israel are in communication with what is to happen in the future, and they have handed down to us the "secret of their communication" (Rabbi Shlomo Aviner).[44] This "secret prophetical communication" refers, of course, to the concrete future of the concrete State of Israel and not to a hoped-for future whose appointed time is unknown.[45] It refers to the messianic conclusion of contemporary, topical, visible events.[46]

Whether this deterministic interpretation of messianic hope follows necessarily from the teachings of Rabbi A. I. Kook has recently become the subject for a crucial discussion in certain circles. Those who found in Rabbi Kook's teachings other aspects making future redemption conditional on human deeds, who found a warning in addition to a promise, were regarded as unfit for Torah teaching.[47] Even quotations from the words of Rabbi Kook himself pointing at such aspects were suspected of being the product of an unfit editor! The attempt to interpret the vision of Rabbi Kook as one whose realization depends upon adherence to the Covenant as a possibility or a choice, but not as a necessity, has shaken the ideological roots of these circles.

It should be stressed here that the writings of Rabbi Kook reveal a complex standpoint in this matter, one that is not merely the result of changing times and the vicissitudes of historical events. On the one hand, there are many expressions in his writings reflecting hope, yearning, and a deep faith in the future of "the beginning of Redemption," of which we are the witnesses. His view reveals and exposes both divine and human activity in the events of his generation. It is a view that certainly awaits realization, fulfillment, elevation to the level on which God and His people respond to each other completely. Moreover, Rabbi Kook's teachings reflect a clear historical and cosmic optimism, a faith in the continuous uplifting of human nature and desire for the good: "Human nature and human will were much more savage in the past than they are now. And in the future they will be more civilized than in the present."[48]

A view such as this naturally implies a belief in progress and betterment, not in withdrawal and lapses. This optimistic hope concerning the universal, human sphere becomes even stronger with regard to the national, particular sphere, given Rabbi Kook's understanding of the Jewish people's Return to Zion. For this return unites and combines two holy essences, two unique qualities: that of the People of Israel and that of the Land of Israel. This is a fruitful encounter that, by its very nature, bears the promise of spiritual elevation, of the liberation of hidden powers, rather than of crisis and decline. There is no doubt that the events of Rabbi Kook's time—the Balfour Declaration, the growing strength of the *yishuv* and its moral position—caused him to rejoice: "Every day brings us the encouragement and certainty of approaching salvation, of the light of life and of supreme purity."[49]

Yet, there is a second aspect to Rabbi Kook's views, one in which Redemption is not confined to the historical, external process or realization of the worldly political dream alone; it is also believed to bring about an upheaval in the consciousness of the individual in which hidden repentance becomes open repentance, unconscious recognition becomes conscious. And, parallel to this, Redemption demands fulfillment in terms of free choice, of actual individual decision, beyond the potential quality inherent in the people as a whole. "Moral qualities demand continuous development; they do not grow naturally and automatically."[50]

Changes toward the level of consciousness and free will, by definition, are not part of the objective, predestined, and foreseen order of things. Their very nature asks for human free response. Men and women have been given the keys that open the door between profane and sacred:

> To the same degree that we succeed in revealing what is hidden, we can climb to this great spiritual height, when sacred and profane meet . . . to the same degree we can turn our little work in the fields of national revival and of building Eretz Israel in the present into a stepping stone towards the Revealed End, into the key to complete Redemption.[51]

Rabbi Kook does not refrain from voicing explicit conditions and warnings: "Only on the quality of the entire nation's link with the source of life, with the Torah of the Lord, does the success and strength of Zionism depend, now and in generations to come. But if we abandon the Torah there is no hope, and every flower will wither and every root will turn into dust."[52] The first level, the unconscious level of Israel's hidden election, indeed guarantees that the whole of Israel shall not fall, that "Knesset Israel" shall not be "defiled entirely." But the last phase of the process, the conscious realization, the open repentance, are the concern of every individual and depend on free decision and efforts, on conscious knowledge of the inner purpose of the building.

Two generations after Rabbi Kook formulated his vision and teachings, his expectations in the secular-political domain have been realized to a much greater degree than those in the spiritual-religious sphere: the *yishuv* has grown tenfold, political independence has been achieved, large portions of the Land of Israel are in Jewish possession, "the trees of Israel yield their fruits." Even if one considers this survey of the events highly selective, it must nevertheless be obvious that these developments provide the believers with firm ground on which to stand. On the spiritual-religious level, however, we are confronted with a different reality: a majority of the population has not responded to the religious call, has not admitted that its national identity springs from the source of Torah, faith, and repentance. And even with regard to the general moral level of our generation, some expectations and hopes have been frustrated. One might say that the revealed physical return has become increasingly revealed, whereas the hidden spiritual return has become more and more hidden. This gap between the two levels must leave its mark on the consciousness of those followers of Rabbi Kook who try to apply his teachings in a concrete manner to the present generation.

Indeed, the earthly-political achievements of the State of Israel in many fields have contributed to the development of a firm and conscious conviction that finds traces of messianic fulfillment in contemporary history and concentrates its efforts on exposing signs and tokens of "the Revealed End":

> Throughout the generations the sages of Israel have analyzed Israel's history with open eyes in the light of the Torah, and with unwavering faith in the guiding hand of God. Only on this basis, said Rabbi Abba in the Talmud, shall we know the End by two clear signs: the ingathering of exiles and the abundance of fruits yielded by the Land of Israel. To these signs we are the witnesses, and there is no longer room for doubt and questions that challenge our joy and our feelings of gratitude to the Redeemer of Israel. (Rabbi Zephanya Derori)[53]

True, Maimonides taught that the days of the Messiah are unknown to us until they come.[54] However, "the question is: what will happen when they come; and you close your eyes and say; nothing; we see nothing" (Hanan Porat).[55] The Six-Day War and its repercussions gave a dramatic momentum to this consciousness.

On the spiritual-religious level, the frustration because collective repentance has remained hidden and the expected religious revival has tarried also has helped transfer the focal point of religious consciousness to historical fulfillment in the real, earthly sphere, where it can be seen by all, and to make less of religious revival as a condition for the Redemption of Israel.[56] This sometimes goes so far that the people's behavior – political, moral, or religious – is entirely severed from its destiny and future,[57] to the point where one can hear such utterances as: "Redemption is imposed on us, *in spite of* our deeds." Others who do not go that far will nevertheless go to any length to impress an a priori forecast on present reality. This reality, willy-nilly, is one of return and repentance, however reluctant it may be: "A return to the Land of Israel, to the People of Israel, to the nation's heroism, to work and to agriculture, a return to social justice."[58] Revealed historical reality, by definition, is a religious return, and why should one complain?

Although expressions such as these are rooted in the teachings of Rabbi A. I. Kook, the rabbi hoped for a gradual rapprochement between the revealed and the hidden, the inner and the external, the soon-to-come unification of worldly historical salvation and conscious and voluntary religious recognition. He was fully convinced that secular Zionists, once they attain their worldly goals, which are of a positive nature as such, would realize that from the onset they were really seeking something beyond these goals. In other words, Rabbi Kook expected that the two levels – matter and spirit, Land and Torah – would be linked one to the other. But as this unification tarried, and the gap widened instead of narrowing, the "revealed signs of the End" have become increasingly visible, while the "hidden, spiritual return" becomes hidden more and more deeply within. Rabbi Kook's disciples therefore were forced to reinterpret reality on the basis of a priori conceptions. They were forced to diminish the gaps, the deficiencies of the reluctant reality, and to endow them with the illuminating aspect of their vision. Thus, messianic vision no longer serves as a critical and normative standard for empirical historical reality, demanding the betterment of its ways; rather it provides a protective and sheltering model to justify and defend historical reality as it is. It no longer is the criterion by which reality is judged and evaluated but a brief for the defense. "Our reality is a messianic reality and a reality of repentance."[59] An honest person does not protest against messianic reality nor criticize something that is essentially repentance. On the contrary, the person should be rooted in it and should scrutinize his or her own ways in its light. The two aspects of the ideological responses to reality – one that severs our deeds from our destiny and future, and the other that reinterprets reality in light of the ideal – ensure the unwavering progress of messianic determinism, from which there is no return.

Finally, beyond the physical and spiritual domains of national fulfillment, Rabbi Kook expected a universal perfection of human qua human, the perfection of good intentions and the realization of social and international reforms. The Redemption of Israel is anchored in the betterment of the world: "The building of the nation and the revelation of its spirit are one, entirely united with the building of the world . . . Abraham's blessing of all the nations of the earth begins its working with might and openly, and on this foundation the Land of Israel will be built again."[60]

Rabbi Kook regarded the events and crises of World War I as the birth pangs of a new humankind, as awakening, catharsis and cleansing; and he regarded the new social revolutions as harbingers of radical reform. There were justifications for such expectations in the favorable circumstances of the time, for it seemed that the nations of the postwar period were really beginning to turn their swords into plowshares. But these expectations were crushed under the boots of the regimes and their armies, and in the wake of the defilement of once-promising social revolutions. The face of the "post modern" period does not smile like that of the "modern era."

Confronted with this situation, and believing in the "revealed signs of the End," the followers of Rabbi Kook had two ways of responding (parallel to the two responses to the delayed appearance of religious repentance). On the one hand, they could abandon the universal aspect of the vision of Redemption as a focal point of religious consciousness[61] and concentrate totally on the Redemption of Israel; and on the other, they could reinterpret the current situation of humankind to endow it with an a priori optimistic aspect in light of the redemption of Israel. Both alternatives were fully exploited.

Determinism and Human Activity

The history of modern social and political movements shows that historical, deterministic views should not be identified with the passive attitudes of merely sitting and waiting for future developments without doing anything to bring them about. Indeed, the opposite is true, as is shown by precisely those movements that believe in iron laws of historical development that will lead mankind toward predestined goals.[62] Those who know these laws wish to be the harbingers of tomorrow, the avant-garde who act in accordance with the inevitable logic of history, taking part in it and advancing it. Their numbers are totally irrelevant, for they *know* that they are the real representatives of the forces of historical development. Determinism is not manifested by refraining from active interference, but by the certain knowledge of the final, predestined outcome.[63] Paradoxically, precisely this certain knowledge of the future, which will come as either a perfection of current reality or on the heels of its ruin, offers the motivation for feverish activity, for whole-hearted devotion to work for the advancement of the "true" historical trends. For the person who has deciphered the secret meaning of events is called upon to remove the obstacles, to hasten the radical upheavals.[64] That person therefore should take part in the trends of the time deliberately and knowingly, for they represent the future and anticipate, in the midst of history, the end of days.

All this is demonstrated by the messianic and topical interpretation of Jewish sources and contemporary events. For example, the Talmud mentions two possible factors that may bring about the Redemption of Israel: merit and the determined hour. "I the Lord will hasten it in its time" (Isaiah 60:22): "It is written: 'in its time', and it is written 'I will hasten.' If they deserve it – 'I will hasten'; if they do not deserve it – 'in its time'."[65] In the course of the generations, these words were interpreted to mean: if Israel repents, Redemption will be hastened and will come before the predestined time, before the last of days; but if Israel does not repent, the End of Days will come in any case. In other words, Israel wil be redeemed in the future to come whether the people deserve it or not.

Many of those who seek the revealed signs of the end of our days tend to interpret contemporary events as "Redemption in its time" and not in terms of "I will hasten." It therefore might have been expected that, as their religious consciousness increasingly focuses on the signs of the increasingly evident Redemption that will inevitably come, they would tend to adopt a passive attitude. For the serenity of those who await the inevitable would not seem to leave any room for human activity. However, here, too, as in the secular messianic ideologies, the opposite conclusion is drawn: Redemption that comes "in its time" demands feverish activity. If Israel had "deserved" it, Redemption would have come in a miraculous way, suddenly, as a heavenly move ("I will hasten") that requires no active human interference. But, since Israel does not "deserve" it, Redemption comes in a natural way, gradually, through worldly activity, through the human work of building (and this is the meaning of "in its time"!).[66] Here, too, it is precisely the certainty of the predestined and expected outcome that provides the motivation and incentive to act: "The Revealed End – its beginning is in the hands of man, its end in the hands of Heaven" (Rabbi Uzi Kalcheim).[67]

On the one hand, consciousness of the Revealed End expands the scope of human responsibility, namely that of national Jewish activity. A proper human response, one befitting the greatness of the time, may not confine itself to the spiritual sphere, the sphere of Torah study, but must expand to encompass the domain of worldly history, of natural and material building. On the other hand, consciousness of the Revealed End reduces the domain of human responsibility. For the Jewish people are "in charge" only of the beginning of the historical process; of the awakening toward the ingathering of the exiles, settlement of the land, and military struggle, whereas Providence guarantees the outcome of the process. It is obvious that such a view will have repercussions in the sphere of such political behavior as settlement and military activity. For, because "the end is in the hands of Heaven," the certainty of the outcome allows daring activity and taking of risks.

Opposites Meet

In spite of their opposing approaches to the contemporary Jewish state, the two radical religious views just described share some significant theological assumptions. Both impart inherent religious significance (in one case positive, in the other, negative) to the very existence of the State of Israel. Both react to historical events through the messianic perspective. And both deny the possibility of any Jewish return or Jewish political independence in the Land of Israel that is not messianically complete in nature, final and total. Both also share an explicitly deterministic conception of the historical process: they know that final Redemption is at hand and that it will be revealed shortly, either on the ruins of the Zionist state, as its negation and denial (the view of Neturei Karta), or as the direct culmination of the Zionist enterprise, as its full realization and fulfillment (the contemporary interpretation of Rabbi Kook's writings).

Opposing political conclusions are drawn from these two views. However, opposites sometimes meet. Those who adhere to the Neturei Karta view of radical religious anti-Zionism deny the very nature of the present political and worldly return. This is reflected in their complete withdrawal from the historical process, their social withdrawal from the people, and their political withdrawal from the state; by their ban of parliament and national elections and their rejection of the laws of the state. Those adhering to the neo-Kookian view of radical religious Zionism share the belief that there can be no return that is not complete and final. For the divine act, by definition, is complete and whole. Consequently, there is no return other than that to the whole land; that is, complete and undivided. No human being may compromise on Divine goals. Compromises, half- and quarter-way solutions are for the political sphere not for the theological sphere—and they are certainly not for the messianic era.

The concept of peace, too, is interpreted in light of the perfect biblical promise, the prophetic and ultimate vision. As such it is dis- cussed exclusively in a utopian framework. But, if we translate this consciousness into political terms, paradoxically, it may neutralize every concrete, historical effort toward political, down-to-earth, peace settlement. For such a contingent achievement does not remove all the tensions, does not beat swords into plowshares, or create an ideal state of harmony. It may appear as nothing but an illusion, for real peace belongs in the realm of the absolute and final.[68] Thus, the exalted status assigned to peace may lead, paradoxically, toward the rejection of every concrete form of peace in the political context of our time. For, because such a peace is based on interests and on the balance of power rather than on true love and total commitment, it is merely a temporary contingent, whereas we are marching confidently toward the realization of the ultimate world order.

Moreover, there lurks the danger that the enemy will no longer be depicted as a foe. For this still is the enemy of the messianic, heavenly plan, the last obstacle on the path toward Redemption; the enemy is not a mere temporary enemy of the people Israel, but the eternal enemy of the Lord, Satan himself, standing in the way of national, human, and cosmic fulfillment. With such an enemy, one does not compromise nor reconcile, one fights to the bitter end.

At this point, the extremist representatives of the two conflicting views on the Zionist state are likely to meet. Whenever the gap widens between expectation and fulfillment—that is, between absolute vision and its partial and fragmented realization—the concrete state with its laws and institutions may lose legitimacy and authority. This applies especially to the most extreme representatives of the messianic inter- pretation of Zionism and of the State of Israel. From now on, only a State of Israel that constitutes "the foundation of the heavenly throne on earth" (in the words of Rabbi Kook)[69] has any claim on our fidelity and not the shadowy figure that we encounter. The pure Idea is the true, sovereign authority and not its compromising, faulty, illegiti- mate reflection. Again, paradoxically, the supreme significance bestowed upon the "State of Israel" imagined by the believer is apt to empty the actual state of its substance and validity. When the real polity is in contravention of its destiny, whether by unfaithfulness to the integrity of the land or the Torah, the sovereignty of that polity loses its legitimacy. In this respect, the whole is no longer viewed as the perfection of the partial but as its adversary and enemy, exactly as it is viewed by anti-Zionist Orthodoxy. For the Holy One is present only in the whole, otherwise He hides His face; there is no middle road between complete Exile and complete Redemption. Thus, here the messianic era may once again stand as the sharpest denial of the historical era. It is at their roots that opposites sometimes meet.

Outburst and Clash

Today, a new and different phenomenon — Kahanism — is being manifested by those at the margin of both religious and nonreligious Jewish society. As the roots of this new development, its consciousness and political reality, demand a separate study, the remarks that follow are limited to the role and function of the radical elements analyzed earlier in the mind-set and ideology of Meir Kahane.

In each of the preceding, polarized ideologies, anti-Zionist ultra-Orthodox radicalism and Zionist political messianism, two factors operate side by side: one acts as a moderating influence and a second leads to extremism, militancy, and clashes. In the radical ultra-Orthodox perception, confrontation is the product of a negation, the sharp rejection of the secular Jew and the very existence of a Jewish state in premessianic times. Thus, the potential for outburst and clash is found in an uncompromising rejection of the "other" Jews and their institutions.

But this very same perception also constitutes the machinery for holding back and limitation. As this is a time of exile and not of redemption, we are living in an age of nonfulfillment, of imperfection, of "broken vessels," and not in an age of totality, of ultimate messianic realization. Hence, the meaning of our actions is not a total meaning nor does it approach the borders of the absolute and eternal. This awareness has a sobering, restraining effect: we must not try to hasten the advent of the Messiah, of ultimate redemption. Jews in exile have always known how to accept their fate, wait patiently, survive under foreign rule, and bend under adversity. Even here, in the Holy Land, we have not yet been redeemed from our spiritual exile (and we do not recognize political redemption without spiritual redemption.) It is thus in the nature of things that nonfulfillment, faulty performance, and partial solutions abound. Everything does not hang in the balance awaiting final and absolute decisions.

Proponents of the extreme messianic-political perception act radically for exactly the opposite reasons. For them, radicalism is produced by the consciousness of redemption, the consciousness of the ultimate fulfillment from which there is no turning back. Their sense of urgency, of a unique opportunity, and of the certainty of pioneers leading their society toward inevitable redemption contain the seeds of social collision. For they view the present as a time of final reckoning from which there is no retreat, a time that permits and even calls for the drive for perfection to be unleashed in order to accomplish the long-awaited breakthrough toward totality, which reaches its climax in attempts to blow up the shrines on the Temple Mount and the like. The logic of the era of the End of Days, of a messianic order of things, leaves no room for acceptance or adaptation of partial and faulty phenomena. Thus, this conception threatens to burst all sorts of dams and throw off encumbrances imposed by the realities of history.

This same perception, however, also carried within it the potential for restriction and restraint: as the members of this group have adopted Rabbi A. I. Kook's doctrine on the role of the secular Zionist as a partner, one who lays the groundwork for religious redemption and is a potential penitent, a head-on collision has been side-stepped, at least on the ideological level. For the renewal of the Jewish body politic, in its own land, draws its validity and its authority from the will of the Jewish community as a whole and not from that of small isolationist factions. Thus, while the assumption of a leadership role in this renewal is a worthy endeavor, one must refrain from stepping so far out that one risks cutting oneself off from the rest of the camp. Although recent phenomena like the Jewish underground show that these ideological principles do not provide an iron-clad guarantee against subversion and the complete break-down of barriers, it is no coincidence that opponents of subversion within the group itself have been criticizing such acts on the basis of Jewish peoplehood, Jewish sovereignty, and love for one's fellow Jews.[70]

With the appearance of Meir Kahane, however, the most radical aspects of the opposing camps have been combined: a militant confrontation within the Jewish ranks, on the one hand, and a sharp messianism, on the other. Kahane has managed to free himself of the restrictions imposed by "love for one's fellow Jews," in the style of the messianic Zionist camp, as well as from the fear connected with premature redemption, in the style of the anti-Zionist ultra-Orthodox camp. And in the process, all constraints have been removed.

Kahane calls for a frontal clash with the "Hellenists," a label that he does not shrink from applying to assimilationist Jews influenced by Western culture:

> a country crawling with Hellenism . . . [with] Hebrew-speaking *goyyim* [gentiles, assimilationist Jews] whose self-hate—the spoiled fruit of the cancerous "I"—drives them to reject Judaism and trample it underfoot. . . . Hellenists running wild in God's Temple. . . . On the day that Judaism was separated from Zionism, the latter became just another form of ugly nationalism. . . . Jews versus Hellenists: that is the real battle![71]

In fact, it is quite clear that if the problem of the external clash, the confrontation with the Arabic-speaking *goyyim*, were to be "resolved," Kahane's militant zeal would be directed full force at the internal clash, at confronting the "Hebrew-speaking *goyyim*." For, "this is a war, no less a war between two philosophies of life that cannot coexist, that are destined to do battle with each other unto death."[72] Thus, the constraints imposed by the dictum, "love for one's fellow Jew," do not apply here.

And as for leaders of the Israeli Left, no holds at all are barred. Indeed, Kahane's writings contain explicit references to people of this stripe deserving to die:

> It is this foreign body, this malignancy of gentilized foreign culture, concepts and values, that must be dealt with and erased from our midst. . . . These are born-by-accident Jews who are riven with schizophrenia over their identity. . . . The truth is that they—not the PLO—represent the real threat to the Jewish state and people. . . . They corrupt the country from within. . . . What to do? How do we fight this? How do we *urgently* act? . . . The answer lies in ridding ourselves of the *extremist* version of "love of Jews." . . . Indeed, the rabbis of the Talmud bring down the verse, "And thou shalt love thy fellow Jew as thyself," in order to explain why we must kill the Jew who is deserving of death in a humane way ["Bror lo mitah yafah"—Psachim 75].[73]

Nevertheless, the Messiah is just around the corner: "It is crystal-clear that Almighty God is prepared, on this day, to lead us to the full and final redemption, and that the initial phase of this redemption is already in full swing. We have arrived at the historic moment of redemption."[74] Moreover, "time is running out"; the end is approaching. And, in the true style of the "reckoners of the end of days," Kahane knows the precise time that has been allotted us from on high: "forty years" (the title of the detailed pamphlet he has devoted to this forecast). "An extension of forty years—God's last hope that, perhaps, His final warning might be heard. The countdown has begun—the countdown of forty years—our last chance."[75] We no longer live in an age of exile, adaptation, and patience, waiting for the storm to pass; rather, it is an age of mastery and pride. Nor is it a time of partial, gradual fulfillment and renascence but one of decision—total, final, overwhelming. There are no fears, therefore, of "prematurely induced redemption," as with the ultra-Orthodox.

Finally, in addition to the radicalizing factors just cited, Kahane creates yet another radicalization with his prognostication of catastrophe: his warning of an approaching disaster to be brought down by God's wrath. And this applies to Diaspora Jewry as well as to the Jews of the State of Israel.

The Diaspora Jews face a disaster and destruction worse than the Holocaust of European Jewry. Their countries of residence are moving toward collapse, total devastation; and Jews will be hit hardest. For they will experience a double fall: once as part of the general population of the United States or Europe; and again as Diaspora Jews, scapegoats for the nations of the world, targets for their slings and arrows, suitable objects for obloquy—as has always been the case.[76]

Only the Jews of the State of Israel have been granted a reprieve, but one that is limited to an allotted period of time, during which our fate will be decided: if we perform our duty, if we pass the test, the full redemption will come about without crisis or catastrophe; however, if we hestiate or hold back, if we miss our opportunity, the full redemption will be accompanied by tragedy, and its course marked by devastation and ruin, as set forth in the Scriptures that depict "the great and terrible day of the Lord."

On what, then, does Kahane say our fate depends? What does he consider the supreme test? The clash with the gentiles, which he translates to mean the removal of the Arabs from the country (or in some cases, their subjugation and the negation of their civil rights). This removal will bring about the solution of the demographic problem of miscegenal mingling, the problems of terror and a potential fifth column. Above all, however, it means cleansing the Holy Land of the desecration of the Divine Name brought about by the presence of gentiles:

The redemption could come upon us at once, and in shining glory, if we act in accordance with what we have been commanded by God; or else it may come in the wake of a terrible tragedy, if we refuse [to so act]. A major criterion for true Jewish faith in this decisive era is our willingness to set aside our fear of man in favor of the fear of God and the removal of the Arabs from Israel. . . . Let us remove the Arabs from our midst, so as to bring about the redemption.[77]

Truly, in contradistinction to the two precedent radical trends, this mind-set has no firm ideological and historical root in the Israeli religious consciousness. Yet, it combines every possible element of radicalization—confrontation with the gentiles as the focus of Jewish identity, intra-Jewish confrontation, precipitous messianism, and the threatening catastrophe—in one political focus.

Epilogue

These ideas were presented at an international colloquium on Religious Radicalism and Politics in the Middle East, held in Jerusalem in 1985. Therefore, the focus is almost exclusively on radical Jewish trends, rather than on majority sectors of the Israeli society or on more moderate religious positions. Developments in Israel since 1985,[78] point even more clearly to the same processes of radicalization and polarization at the extremes and, at the same time, to the restraining role of the religious centrist groups.

In the past few years, an ideological split has occurred within Neturei Karta, and the most militant faction no longer accepts the authority of its traditional rabbinical court (BaDaṢ). It is this small faction which has not only denied the very legitimacy of the State of Israel but has explicitly called for political cooperation with the PLO. At the same time, at the fringes of the opposite religious-political camp, some voices have proclaimed that the historical phase represented by the State of Israel has reached its end and we are thus entering the final messianic phase which calls for the establishment of a purely halakhic Kingdom. (There is some evidence that this mind-set is also relevant to a new phenomenon, the "Sicarii underground"). Parallel to this, a group of religious ultra-nationalists has declared its symbolic dissent from the secular and democratic state of Israel, "establishing" the new, religious "State of Judah" in the occupied territories, in order to prevent, by all means, any future attempt by the government to lead the Jewish people to a territorial withdrawal.

Meir Kahane's Kach party has lost its parliamentary seat and much of its political presence on the Israeli scene—the Israeli Central Election Committee disqualified it on charges of racism and undermining the democratic character of the state. But it has retained its influence in street demonstrations, often of a violent nature.

As we saw earlier ("Opposites Meet"), when the gap widens between expectation and fulfillment—between absolute vision and its partial and fragmented realization—the concrete state may lose legitimacy and authority.

To be sure, the above are all peripheral groups. In contrast, the involvement of the majority of the ultra-Orthodox circles in Israeli political life has intensified significantly in the past few years. Winning more than ten parliamentary seats in the 1988 elections, these circles have been propelled from the margins of the Israeli political arena to positions of major responsibility. These developments have taken them, if only de facto, far from their old separatist position, toward a more pragmatic adjustment to the concrete historical situation.[79] Simultaneously some religious Zionist voices have directly confronted the ultimate messianic interpretation of Zionism, trying to restore the classical religious ideas and pragmatic approaches which originally characterized the Mizrachi movement. Recently, moreover, a few leading adherents of the messianic outlook have also made significant efforts to formulate a more moderate, less deterministic conception of the nature of the State of Israel and the course of Jewish history.

Nevertheless, the theological conceptions and the social power of the religious "Redemption" Zionist camp are still crucial to any serious attempt to analyze the contemporary ideological and political scene in Israel. It was perhaps to be expected that at the beginning of the Palestinian intifada, a comprehensive article would appear (written by Rabbi Zalman Malamed, the influential head of the *yeshivah* of the settlement of Beth-El), seeking to define the specific role of the intifada as an additional stage in the inevitable process of Redemption.[80]

Chapter Two

Islamic Radicalism: Sunni and Shi^c^ite

Emmanuel Sivan

Sunni radicalism began to develop long before the Iranian revolution of 1978. It arose out of conditions specific to Arab countries and the manner in which those faithful to the Sunna reacted to these conditions. In the quarter century between the appearance of the ideas of Sayyid Qutb, the father of Sunni radicalism, and the end of the 1970s, not only were the Sunni radical movements devoid of Iranian-Shi^c^ite influence, but almost no reference was made in these movements to the fact that Iranian Islam simultaneously was undergoing a process of radicalization. A mixture of ignorance and apathy predominated. The most one can find are several references to the organizational lessons of the *Fidaiyan al-Islam*, an Iranian phenomenon of the early 1950s; it seems that whatever inspiration the radical Sunni movements in Arab lands sought from the outside came from Sunni circles in India and Pakistan.

The reason for this was partially linguistic: although a significant number of radical Sunni works had been translated from Arabic into Persian, including three books by Sayyid Qutb, only a small amount of material had been translated from Persian into Arabic, perhaps for lack of translators. By contrast, some English translations of Indian-Pakistani thinkers were available to the Arab Sunnis, as were translations from Urdu into Arabic by the Indian Abu-l-Hasan Nadvi, a popularizer of Maudoudi's thought and a diligent student of Arabic.

The language barrier, however, does not provide a full explanation for the lack of Iranian influence on the Sunnis. This becomes evident from the fact that there was no intellectual influence in the reverse direction either, despite the greater number of translations; radical Sunni thought, whether Arabic or of the Pakistani Maudoudi school, did not affect parallel Iranian-Shi^c^ite thought. One possible exception is the limited influence of Sayyid Qutb's social thinking, but this came in the late 1940s, before he underwent radicalization. By contrast, Qutb's thought of the 1950s and 1960s left a clear mark in Turkey, a

39

country that is not Arabic-speaking but which has a Sunni majority. In Pakistan his important works have been translated into Urdu, and in Malaysia a series of classical writings of the Sunni revival (including Qutb's) has been published recently.

It is also clear that the extreme radicalization undergone by Iranian Islam between the ᶜAshura' demonstrations in 1963 and the revolution was completely unknown to Sunni zealots. Even after the revolution, when some Arabic translations of the writings of Iranian ayatollahs finally appeared, this was through the auspices of radical Shiᶜite movements in Iraq and Lebanon or through leftist Arabic circles. *The Islamic Government*, Khomeini's basic work, written in 1971, was published in two Arabic translations in 1979: one by *Dar al-Taliᶜa*, a leftist publishing house in Beirut, and the other in Cairo by Hasan Hanafi, an independent leftist thinker with Islamic leanings (whose stand towards Khomeini was somewhat critical).

Against this background, it is amazing to ascertain from the writings of revolutionary Shiᶜite thinkers such as Khomeini, Taleghani, Mutahhari, and Mudarresi just how similar their philosophy is to that of the standard-bearers of Sunni radicalism[1] with respect to the diagnosis and cure of today's problems.

Diagnosis

Islam in the twentieth century is facing a danger to its existence far beyond the scope and seriousness of any it has known in the past. This time the danger is internal; it comes from Muslim public figures and movements that, despite being sincere in their concern for the welfare of their people, have willingly allowed themselves to be captivated by the enchantment of Western ideas of nationalism, socialism, liberalism, economic development, democracy, and so on. Those stricken by love of the West, the "Westoxicated" (*gharbzadaha* in the Persian expression popularized by Jalal Al-e Ahmad), therefore are Muslims in appearance only. They make use of the latest in audio-visual aids to instill their ideas in the subconscious minds of Muslims and to stimulate Westoxication; in other words, to further modernity and the "good life," which they promote through various and sundry publicity techniques. A necessary result of all this is that the Muslim world is in a state of apostasy, an especially dangerous condition because it is unconscious. In Sunni terms, *Dar-al-Islam* therefore has returned to a state of *jahiliyya* even worse than the one that preceded the appearance of the prophet Muhammad in Arabia.

The Cure

Those faithful to Islam must return to the political arena, from which they have been absent for so long. They must issue systematic and severe criticism of modernity in its Muslim version and heighten the consciousness of the masses, above all of the avant-garde (*tali͑a*) intellectual youth. These young people require the most urgent attention for they hold the key to liberation from the fetters of Westoxication. However, systematic criticism alone stands no chance of inducing the regimes in power to change from within because of the authoritarian, ruthless nature of these regimes and their deep commitment to the modern *jahiliyya*. Radicals, therefore, should not shrink from drawing the unavoidable conclusion: the existing regimes must be delegitimized.

Application of the Cure

Delegitimization of such powerful regimes will necessitate, after a preparation stage, an armed uprising and seizing the governments by the avant-garde of political Islam; only this will enable the establishment of a state in which the *Shari͑a* is applied. That Sunni and Shi͑ite thinkers reached such similar assessments independently is explained by the fact that the radicals in the 1960s and 1970s acted in the most developed nations in the Middle East — Iran, Egypt, Syria, and Lebanon — where (at least in the first three), by dint of its monopoly on economic life and the means of coercion and persuasion, the state was turned into an effective tool of modernity. However, if this is so, the Shi͑ite and Sunni movements' mutual ignorance is even more perplexing. And the situation did not change significantly following 1978, for even after the Iranian revolution broke out Shi͑ite influence in the Arab world was quite limited; it did not ordinarily extend beyond Shi͑ite areas in Iraq and Lebanon. The relationship of this revolution with the Sunni radicals, as we shall see later, was laden with tensions and ambiguities.

Still, the similarity in the messages of these two movements is extremely impressive. Does this not bolster the claims made by a good number of Sunni thinkers in the last half-century that the historic differences between Sunnism and Shi͑ism have now grown irrelevant? But, if this is the case, then why did the rise of radicalism fail to strengthen the tendencies toward ecumenism, compromise, and a narrowing of the gap between the Islamic sects?

The Historic Heritage

In order to answer these questions, it is best to begin with a review of the four major areas of controversy between Sunnism and Shiʿism and their influence on revolutionary thought. These points of contention, in ascending order of importance, are jurisprudence, historic viewpoint (or "foundation myths"), political theory, and messianism (or "eschatological myths").

Jurisprudence

The differences in this area are the least significant. Although Shiʿite laws on temporary marriage (*mutʿa*), the right of the husband to initiate divorce, the relative portion of male and female family members in inheritance, disqualification of people in several "inferior" professions from giving testimony, and so forth, differ from those of the four Sunni schools (*madhahib*), these differences are no more important than the numerous areas on which the four schools differ among themselves. It therefore was natural for the "ecumenical" Muslim thinkers concentrated in this area to declare that the Shiʿites are a fifth *madhhab*, and to call this school *madhhab Jaʿfari* (after Jaʿfar, the sixth Shiʿite Imam), just as each Sunni school was named after its main religious teacher. In a famous *fatwa* (responsum) issued in 1959, Muhammad Shaltut, then rector of al-Azhar University, gave official authorization to the trend toward rapprochement by introducing "Jaʿfari law" into the study curriculum of this institution. The move received the warm blessing of Shiʿite advocates of ecumenism, including the Lebanese thinker Muhammad Jawad Maghniya and the Iranian Muhammad Taqi al-Qummi.[2]

Because the Islamic state to which the radicals aspire must be based on the *Shariʿa*, it is clear that normative Shiʿite law is of definite relevance to the Sunni radicals. Indeed, the few Sunni radicals to take a positive stand on the Iranian revolution[3] use the substantial similarity between Sunni and Shiʿite normative law as a central argument. The vast majority of radical Sunni thinkers maintain complete silence on the issue of law. But, the fact that they do not raise the issue in a reproachful manner seems to imply that they, too, accept the ecumenical theses with regard to jurisprudence.

The Khomeinistic propaganda in Arab countries, for its part, repeatedly mentions that the laws of the Jaʿfari school belonging to the common *Shariʿa* are being applied in Iran. Muhammad Husayn Fadlallah, the major radical Shiʿite thinker in Lebanon, goes so far as to say that the "five *madhhab*" are legitimate variations of Islam.[4] It is possible that this claim is assimilated with greater ease in Arab countries such as Iraq and Lebanon, where Sunnis and Shiᶜites live in close proximity and the tendency for many years has been to minimize the significance of the differences between Sunni and Shiᶜite normative law (*furuᶜ al-fiqh*).[5]

Even a problematic issue such as *taqiyya* (a commandment that Shiᶜites conceal their faith in a pressure situation) is far less critical than in the past, for Khomeini himself denounces the use of this principle to justify acquiescence and submission to the regime in power. Khomeini sanctioned its use only in cases of minor significance (as a sort of "white lie"); under no circumstances was it to be used in connection with basic problems related to the fundamentals of Muslim belief.

With regard to the disagreement over the methodology of jurisprudence (*usul al-fiqh*), one major stumbling block was removed as soon as the Sunni radicals accepted the principle of *ijtihad* (jurists' invocation of personal judgment in matters of religious law). This principle had been held in abeyance by Sunni Islam ever since the tenth century, whereas the Shiᶜites have always upheld it. There are still differences of opinion regarding the second of the four basic legal principles, the *Hadith* (oral law): both camps accept the six basic compilations of the *Hadith*, but whereas all the Sunni schools accept only these six, the Shiᶜites recognize other *Hadith* compilations, which rely at times on different sources (mainly from the House of the Prophet). Khomeini tries to obfuscate this divergence. When a Sunni scholar wrote to him in 1979 asking point blank what the sources are of his jurisprudence, he answered: the Koran and four Shiᶜite legal treatises based upon Shiᶜite *Hadiths*.[6] This disagreement, of course, is a function of history; that is, of the bitter struggles between the two camps in the seventh to ninth centuries. It therefore is advisable to move on to a discussion of this history.

Historic Perceptions

The source of the Sunni-Shiᶜite breach is the struggle for power between the followers of ᶜAli (the prophet Muhammad's cousin and brother-in-law) and the supporters of the first three caliphs. At first political, the struggle gradually became religious. The key events during this formative period — especially in the years between the death of the prophet in 632 C.E. and the slaughter of ᶜAli's grandson Husayn and his followers in Karbala, Iraq, in 680 C.E. — turned into the "foundation myth" (to use anthropological terms) of the Shi^ca. And these events nourish the intellectual and experiential, the elitist and popular aspects of the Shi^ca until this very day. The central feeling (or motivation) of the Shi^ca throughout the generations has been the historic injustice done to the house of ^cAli when his right to the caliphate was usurped: one must bewail this injustice, despise its perpetrators, preserve the heritage of the house of ^cAli as much as possible, and aspire to amend the historic wrong in the future.

The interpretation of this decisive half-century is naturally much less central to the historic vision of orthodox Islam, the camp that won the day. Still, the orthodox historic vision is completely opposed to that of the Shi^cites: the first three caliphs were orthodox (*Rashidun*), just as was ^cAli, and their four caliphates form the golden age of Islam, especially in the eyes of Sunni fundamentalists. Even if the Sunnis admit that several of the Omayyad caliphs, particularly Husayn's assassin Yazid, perpetrated evil in the eyes of Allah, they do not see this as negating the legitimacy of this dynasty, as the Shi^cites claim. Furthermore, to the extent that Husayn can be seen as having a reasonable claim to the caliph's throne, this is, according to the Sunna, by virtue of his personal qualities (mainly in comparison with Yazid) and not because he was an Imam; in the language of the Shi^ca, a descendant of ^cAli. According to the Sunni viewpoint, not only members of the prophet Muhammad's family but all descendants of the Arabian Quraysh tribe, including those of the Omayyad clan, have the right to be chosen as caliphs.

Khomeini himself mitigates a bit of the harshness of this historic dispute by taking a positive stand toward at least two of the first three caliphs in question, Abu Bakr and ^cUmar (632–644). For the sake of our discussion it makes no difference that Khomeini's motivation is not identical to that of the Shi^cite ecumenicists who declared these caliphs to be "orthodox" so as to enlarge the common denominator with the Sunnis. Khomeini's arguments derive specifically from his political theory. In his efforts to prove that Islamic government had existed and functioned for a considerable amount of time, he "adopted" the twelve years of Abu Bakr and ^cUmar so as not to be limited to the four years of ^cAli's caliphate (656–660). (In the eyes of contemporary Muslim radicals, the members of the Omayyad dynasty who began to rule in 660 did not establish a truly Islamic regime.)

Khomeini recognizes all twelve Imams and their mythical qualities, as do the rest of the Iranian Shi^cites (who are also called Imamites), but eleven of the twelve never rose to power and most of them lived in hiding. Although Khomeini's stand towards Abu Bakr and ᶜUmar is positive, it seems that he stops short of prohibiting the Shiᶜite custom of cursing the first three caliphs—even though this would have facilitated export of the revolution through ecumenism—because he is not willing to forgo castigating (and cursing) the third caliph, ᶜUthman, under any circumstances. He does not and cannot append the twelve years of ᶜUthman's reign (644–656) to the era when Islam actually ruled, because ᶜUthman was of the Omayyad clan and a mortal enemy of ᶜAli. As such, he deserves all vilification, in Khomeini's opinion, as do Omayyad caliphs such as Muᶜawiya and Yazid. By contrast, the Sunnis view ᶜUthman as one of the four "orthodox" caliphs. (Palestinian Sunni radicals speak of the analogy between his assassination-martyrdom and their own people's sufferings: "We are ᶜUthman's blood-soaked shirt.") On the ᶜUthman issue, therefore, Khomeini makes the demands of the revolutionary teaching yield to the historic hatred toward the Omayyads.

Ecumenical considerations, drawing closer to the Sunnis in order to facilitate export of the revolution, are certainly not foreign to Khomeini. This can be seen, for example, from the leaflet appeal the Iranians have issued to Sunni fellow pilgrims to Mecca every year since the revolution. In one of these leaflets, Khomeini states, "there is only one thing worse and more dangerous than nationalistic propaganda, and that is fomenting disagreements between Sunna and Shiᶜa and sowing hatred and dissension which harm the brotherhood of Muslims . . . therefore I appeal to those faithful to Islam to see the Shiᶜites as their precious brothers, so as to thwart these detestable devices."[7] The trend toward reconciliation undoubtedly explains when Khomeini refrains from another accepted Shiᶜite custom: cursing the Companions of the Prophet (a Sunni writer hostile to Khomeini scrutinized all of his writings but could produce only a single questionable negative contention directed toward one of the Companions).[8] The desire for conciliation may also help explain why Khomeini has mounted no attack on ᶜUthman. Still, his very unwillingness to mention ᶜUthman in the same breath as Abu Bakr and ᶜUmar is clear testimony that his faithfulness to Shiᶜite tradition places clear limits on his ecumenism. In order to meet the demands of his revolutionary doctrine, he is willing to deviate from this tradition openly, and not merely by implication as in the Companions' issue, as he did with regard to the first two caliphs; but even here he draws the line at a certain threshold. As one who was directly involved in blocking ᶜAli's right to the caliphate, ᶜUthman is closely linked to the historic trauma of the Shiᶜa and is therefore taboo. Thus, although it is likely that Khomeini and the Iranian propaganda establishment will continue to avoid attacking him for the sake of the revolution, they will certainly not grant him legitimacy.

The ^cAli-^cUthman struggle is only part of the Shi^cite political mythology. A different affair, the assassination of Husayn, is both more prominent and more widespread. In every sense, it is a political myth, as the concept is defined by anthropologists: an engaging political drama built on a detailed narrative description of events. This particular affair has a hero (Husayn), a plot (with a beginning, middle, and end), unity of time (the tenth of October 680 C.D.) and place (Karbala) and, above all, a tragic ending. The assassination of Husayn and his followers took place on the tenth day of the Muslim month Muharram, a date that was turned into the central Shi^cite holiday, a mournful holiday so characteristic of Shi^cism as a "Religion of Lament" (which it has been called by Elias Canetti).[9]

During the nine days preceding the holiday the story of the assassination is related at public and private gatherings. On the tenth of Muharram (the day is called ^cAshura'), colorful performances are put on (*ta^cziyya*), reenacting the events of the historic tragedy, and these are followed by massive mourning marches in which men stripped to the waist beat themselves to the point of drawing blood in order to express and deepen their grief. The ^cAshura' day, with its intriguing dramatic form, emotional charge, political significance, and active believer participation has always been the primary vehicle through which the myth has been dramatized, enacted, and propagated as justification for a certain manner of political behavior (rejection of the legitimacy of the Sunni caliphate, strengthening the devotion to ^cAli's house, and deepening the feeling of an injustice never righted). It is not surprising, therefore, that the gatherings and ceremonies of ^cAshura' served as landmarks in the development of the revolutionary movement in Iran, from the public assemblies of the 1963 ^cAshura', which signaled the rise of the massive protest movement against the Shah and his modernization (the "white revolution") to the more organized gatherings of December 1978 in which revolutionary ferment and fervor resulted in hundreds of thousands demonstrating against the Shah in the streets of Tehran.

In the Sunni world the ^cAshura' does not possess this content, or political content of any sort. It is a voluntary fast day, a relic of the brief period in the early days of Muhammad's prophecy when the Muslims observed "Yom Kippur" as part of a short-lived covenant with the Jews in the city of Medina. But to the Shi^cites this holiday (as well as other less important ones such as the birthdays of ^cAli, Husayn, and the Hidden Imam) is ingrained too deeply in the folk tradition to be uprooted.

The Shi^cite ^cAshura' has always been problematic in the eyes of the Sunni advocates of reconciliation because it is permeated with such a strong odor of past divisions that it is perforce at cross purposes with Muslim ecumenism. (Let us recall here that in Sunni countries such as Egypt the ^cAshura' was celebrated from the twelfth to the nineteenth century as a day of festivity and rejoicing at the downfall of the Shi^cite dynasty of the Fatimids. Moreover, the Ottomans completely banned ^cAshura' gatherings in Shi^cite communities.)

In the final analysis, ^cAshura', the holiday of the Shi^cite redeemer, Husayn's sacrifice, has proved too mystical, romantic, and emotional for the taste of the rationalistic and humanistic Sunni advocates of ecumenism, the mass participation with its manifestations of violence certainly not being to their refined, elitist taste. One Sunna ecumenist and follower of Sheikh Shaltut, who visited Nabatiyya in southern Lebanon on ^cAshura' 1960, reported finding "exactly the same disgraceful drama that one can witness on this day in Iraq, Pakistan and Iran," the spectacle causing him to "lament the state of Islam," which had degenerated to such a low level of primitivity. Another ecumenist, a Lebanese journalist, reacted in similar fashion to the celebrations that took place in Nabatiyya five years later.[10]

The Shi^cite revolutionary wave in the 1960s and 1970s only increased the saliency and centrality of the ^cAshura' in that it imparted additional political significance. Thus, compromise on this delicate issue is even more difficult today than it was in the past. For, although remembrance of the wrong done to Husayn preserves the fundamental reason for Shi^cite protest and bitterness, heightening their sense of being the oppressed, persecuted, and stigmatized part of the Muslim community, it also grants them compensation: they are the true believers (with the Sunnis only nominal Muslims) and Husayn's sacrifice will contribute to their redemption. Sunni historiography, including those segments that view Yazid as a wrongdoer and regret the death of the righteous Husayn, surely do not impart this almost cosmic significance to these events. (And, it should be added in the same vein, Sunni popular religion considers the Shi^cites heretics and not Muslims; in *One Thousand and One Nights*, for instance, the term *Muslim* is identical with Sunni, and the Shi^cites are branded as *Bafida*; i.e., apostates, rebels against legitimate authority.)

Political Thought

The ecumenists of both camps have always refrained from touching this historical area, and for a good reason: because of the political origin of the Sunni-Shiᶜite division, the gap between the positions was enormous. Ecumenists could ignore this area, at least until recently, because questions of political theory did not especially occupy the Muslim world in the half-century since the decline of the pan-Islam movement that sought to renew the caliphate of old.

As related earlier, however, things changed with the emergence of the new radicalism. Concentrating on the political realm, this movement made a deeper mark in areas of political thought than in any other area. And this holds true for both Sunni and Shiᶜite radicalism. Two out of three points of the tripartite message common to both groups ("the cure" and "the application of the cure," discussed earlier) can be vindicated only through their political theory. It is only natural, therefore, that this situation, as a sort of defensive reflex, led to a rise in the importance given political questions in the teaching of religious establishments engaged in fighting off the danger of cultural hegemony on the part of the radicals.

Although radical thought among both Shiᶜites and Sunnis reached the same conclusion — that the revolution is justified as well as urgent — the two groups arrived at this conclusion in different ways. It was an easy task for Iranian radicals to justify the right to revolt (*widerstandrecht*) since, according to Shiᶜite traditional teachings, a state that is not ruled by the descendants of ᶜAli, ipso facto, is illegitimate. It should be stressed that this theory applies to a specifically Shiᶜite (or rather Imamite) time frame: from the date of the final Occultation of the Twelfth Imam (941) to the future date of the Hidden Imam's return to earth as the *Mahdi* (Messiah). (Between 874, the date of the Imam's physical disappearance, and 941, contact with him was maintained through his four special deputies, after which all contact was lost.)

Despite (or alongside) the de jure delegitimization, the Shiᶜites developed positions of de facto accommodation with ruling governments throughout history, especially in Iran from the sixteenth century onward. Motivations ranged from preventing anarchy to enabling the state to defend itself against foreign (in particular non-Muslim) invaders. Even so, the accommodation was always strictly pragmatic. Consequently, it did not require a great intellectual effort for Khomeini to evolve the claim that when a state, such as Iran under the Shah, relinquishes part of its sovereignty to foreigners, bars the influence of Islam on public life, and even inculcate pagan traditions and symbols in several areas of life—a Sassanian, rather than Muslim calendar; use of pre-Islamic Persian symbols; the title "Light of the Aryans" granted to the Shah; celebrations commemorating 2500 years since the founding of the kingdom—there can be no form of accommodation. A policy of compromise with such a regime cannot be justified even on pragmatic grounds, for such grounds do not atone for the regime's sins. The conclusion is unavoidable: it is mandatory to rebel against and replace the "apostate" ruler. This array of claims and charges relies on *Hadiths* from Shi^cite sources and on the writings of some of the sect's thinkers in the Middle Ages.[11]

The task of Sunni radicals was immeasurably harder than that of their Shi^cite counterparts, and they had to carry it out in a different manner (with the aid of different sources and supporting evidence). First, they do not recognize the Shi^cite time framework; Sunni political theory deals with a "normal" historic time framework; from the onset of Islam to the end of days. Second and more importantly, Sunni tradition continues to view an existing Muslim regime as legitimate as long as the ruler does not publicly reject Islam; that is, by repudiating the credo (*shahadatayn*), which of course is highly unlikely. As far as Sunni theorists are concerned, even a bad Muslim ruler, who tramples upon some major and minor Islamic principles, is preferable to chaos. The believers therefore have no recognized right to rebel. This political tradition is so deep-rooted and strong that radicals like Sayyid Qutb had to delve into obscure sources and rescue from oblivion the few fourteenth-century theological texts by Ibn Taymiyya that, when interpreted creatively, enabled him to define the specific conditions under which rebellion could be justified in the framework of Sunni political theory. It is ironic—but not coincidental—that Ibn Taymiyya was an avowed enemy of the Shi^cites, as we shall see later.

The two camps are divided on other areas of political theory as well. According to modern Shi^cite revolutionary thought, in the absence of the Imam sovereignty lies in the hands of the mullahs (ulama), who are the inheritors of the twelfth (the Hidden) Imam's political and legal, but not spiritual, authority. In a situation in which it is possible to reach an understanding and accommodation with the ruler, the task of the mullahs is to preach, moralize, castigate the aberrations of the regime, and return the ruler to the right path. However, when the aberrations reach such proportions that accommodation is no longer permissible (as they did in the days of the Pahlavi dynasty), the mullahs must take the reigns of government into their own hands.

Khomeini applied this theory not only to the ulama class in general, but to certain elements of it in particular. With the victory of the *usuli* school in the mid-nineteenth century, the Iranian Shiᶜa developed a formal hierarchy of ulama, something rare in the world of Islam: above the rank and file of mullahs stand the *mujtahidun* (authorities on matters of jurisprudence), and above these the *marajiᶜ al-taqlid* ("models of imitation," prominent figures of authority). In theory, although not always in practice, members of the last group were supposed to recognize one of their rank in each generation as the supreme *marjaᶜ*, or *marjaᶜ aᶜ la*. This is the same "virtuous Jurist" (*Faqih*) that Khomeini speaks of in his revolutionary teaching, and in whose hands he sought to vest not only religious authority, as was accepted until then, but also political rule (*wilaya* or *wilaya ᶜamma*, a concept that originally referred to the authority of the Hidden Imam).

Khomeini's view was crystalized in 1970, in lectures before young mullahs in Najf, Iraq, his place of exile, and was set down in writing a year later in his book *The Islamic Government*. According to this view, the ulama — or to be more precise those ulama who did not collaborate with the Shah, and their number was substantial — were supposed to serve as the nucleus of the revolutionary vanguard to be led by the *mujtahidun* (ayatollahs), with the "Virtuous *Faqih*," Khomeini himself, at their head. These same clerics were to take power in the postrevolutionary state, each according to his rank.[12] The political action demanded of Shiᶜite Islam, therefore, was foremost that of the ulama (naturally according to their special hierarchy), who were designated to exceed the bounds of their supreme legal-spiritual authority and take direct control of government. This view was carried into effect in the prerevolutionary state and carried even further in the Islamic Republic of Iran's constitution, the fifth article of which puts political power into the hands of the *Faqih* and, in his absence or in case of controversy over succession, in the hands of a revolutionary high command composed of three or five *mujtahidun* outstanding in their generation.

All of this is foreign to the Sunni point of view; their ulama have never enjoyed any spiritual status except for that conferred by their erudition. The Shiᶜite ulama have always enjoyed a charismatic status by virtue of their attachment to the Hidden Imam, from whom they derive their authority and whom in his absence they represent as a group (at least in religious matters, although not — until Khomeini — in political matters). "The ulama are the heirs of the prophets." A well-known *Hadith*, accepted by Sunnis and Shiᶜites alike, is used by Khomeini to justify the *wilayat al-faqih*, whereas Sunni radicals resort to the *Hadith* merely to denote the ulama duty to provide moral guidance to the community.[13] Furthermore, the Sunni ulama have never enjoyed an economic independence comparable to that maintained by their Shi^cite counterparts, thanks to donations and contributions consecrated to them as a sort of material acknowledgment of their holiness. This independence has enabled the Shi^cites to be audacious in their attitude toward the powers that be.

The Sunni sages, one should also stress, have always been imbued with a feeling of subservience toward the state. This results from an ideology that posits the prevention of anarchy as an important goal. It is no wonder, then, that radicalism did not spring from their midst and that Sunni radicals tend to loathe the whole ulama stratum. This being the case, there was no ideological or practical reason to let the ulama lead the revolutionary movement or to set aside a respectable role for them in the state of the future. With the exception of Sheikh Sa^cid Sha^cban, leader of the *al-Tawhid al-Islami* movement in Tripoli, Lebanon, and Sa^cid Hawwa, ideologist of the Syrian Muslim Brethren today, the few ulama playing leadership roles in the Sunni revolutionary organizations usually have acted as rubber stamps, who lent religious approval to decisions of the revolutionary vanguard. Sheikh ^cUmar ^cAbd al-Rahman of the Jihad group that assassinated Sadat was of this ilk, as is Sheikh Bayanuni of Syria's Islamic Revolutionary Front. The "Islamic Tendency Movement" in Tunisia included two religious sages among twenty-five leaders, but they did not belong to the secretariat, and when the leadership was brought to trial in 1983, it was characteristic that these two men, both of them very old, were acquitted.[14] Similarly, religious figures did not play prominent roles in the middle and lower echelons of Sunni radical movements. Further, theology students are rare in the university groups, which are particularly active.

The absence of ulama from the ranks of Sunni radicals partially explains the decentralized structure of the movement, just as the ulama's presence on various levels helps to explain the centralization and hierarchy of the Shi^cite movements. If the ulama are not important to Sunni radicals in the present, why should they become important in the postrevolutionary future? The only Sunni organization that gave some thought to the Islamic state is the *al-Takfir wa-l-Hijra* movement in Egypt, which depicted a caliphate headed by Shukri Mustafa, an agronomist by profession and, like most other Sunni radical leaders, an autodidact in matters religious. At least in this sense, members of the *Takfir* were faithful to the teaching of Sayyid Qutb, who stressed that the Muslim state in the process of realizing the longed-for *hakimiya* (sovereignty) of Allah is in no way a medieval theocracy ruled by clerics.[15]

Eschatological Myths

At the far edge of the Shiᶜite frame is the *Mahdi*, who will destroy the kingdom of evil and establish a reign of justice on earth. A similar myth at the end of days exists in Sunnism, but in a different form and with different symbols and meaning. With the exception of a few Sunni messianic movements, the *Mahdi* is less central for Sunnis than for Shiᶜites. It goes without saying that the Sunni *Mahdi* does not have to be of ᶜAli's house. But for the Shiᶜites the *Mahdi* is the Hidden Imam, who will establish a govenment of ᶜAli's descendants, a rule that will be both legitimate and just in vindication of Shiᶜite suffering throughout history.

As with other eschatological myths, the *Mahdi* myth was pushed out of sight time and again, and as its importance grew less immediate and pressing to the Shiᶜite faithful, it underwent a process of ritualization that rendered it more conservative and less radical. Thus, Shiᶜite ecumenists such as Sheikh Muhammad Husayn al-Kashif al-Ghita' (born in Iraq and a resident of Lebanon) claim that since the tenet of the *Mahdi* (or *rajᶜa*, return to earth) is not fundamental but a super-erogation, the Sunnis, who do not believe in the Hidden Imam and his return to earth as they accept only five fundamentals, can be considered true believers in every sense of the word.[16]

It seems at first glance that Khomeini himself is open to such claims. After all, his criticism of the many Shiᶜites who collaborated with the authorities is based upon the premise that people must strive to achieve justice in the here and now, in this world from which the Imam is absent, and not wait "hundreds and perhaps even thousands of years" for the establishment of absolute justice by the Imam upon his return to earth. However, even if Khomeini does not stress the concept of *Imama* (or the *Mahdi*), his teaching repeatedly implies the principle[17] that forms the boundary of the time frame he works in (the fifth article of the Iranian constitution states that it will be valid "as long as the Twelfth Imam is absent"). Furthermore, Khomeini has served as *marjaᶜ* since the early 1960s, and his authority as such is defined as stemming from a delegation of authority for the sake of guardianship (*wilaya ᶜamma*) on behalf of the Hidden Imam. Only in this way could Khomeini transform the institution of *marjaᶜ* from a strictly religious function into one that is political as well.[18] Some of his disciples who are inclined to literal interpretations will even claim that Khomeini actually is a mystical emanation "issuing directly from the *Mahdi*" and serving as preparation for the *Mahdi*'s return.

It is from this concept that the title recently applied to Khomeini in Iran—*na'ib al-Imam* (vicar of the Hidden Imam)—is derived.[19] Khomeini does try to emphasize that he is not imbued with the Hidden Imam's spiritual powers (especially not with ^c*isma*, infallibility), and that since in his essence he is no different from other mortals, his rule is strictly functional (*wilaya i^ctibariyya*). Nonetheless, the frame of reference and the basis for comparison is the *Mahdi*; the regime is measured against him, and the time allotted for it to rule is delimited by him.[20] It should therefore come as no surprise that the Hidden Imam's birthday (which falls on the fifteenth of Sha^cban) has always been one of the four major religious holidays in Iran (along with the ^cAshura' and the birthdays of ^cAli and Husayn, all of which relate to the "foundation myth"). During this holiday, Khomeini extols the "return of the *Imam-Mahdi* in the end of days" in fervid speeches that receive wide media coverage.[21]

Controversies and Ecumenism

One can ascertain the importance of the above-mentioned areas of controversy and the problems they create from perusing the writings of the very few Sunni radicals who admire Khomeini. These radicals are careful to circumvent the four obstacles or to resort to casuistry in order to present them as unimportant. The Palestinian Fathi ^cAbd al-^cAziz Shqaqi utilizes Sheikh Shaltut's responsum on the *madhhab Ja^cfari*, diminishing the significance of the *Mahdi* issue as a mere symbol of justice "according to Khomeini's interpretation, which transcends the narrow bounds of the accepted Shi^cite concepts of the *Imama*."[22] Shqaqi goes on to say that in any case we must bear in mind Khomeini's call for immediate action against tyranny without waiting for the messianic period at the end of days. He quotes extensively the Kashif al-^cAta' school, according to which the *Imama* is a noncompulsory principle, but he cannot bring any proof that Khomeini supports this ecumenical approach for the simple reason that there is no shred of evidence to prove this. What makes the task of such sympathetic Sunni radicals even more difficult is that opponents of Khomeini within revolutionary Iranian Islam, such as former president Abu-l-Hasan Bani Sadr, for example, also anchor their political-social theories in the concept of the *Imama*.

Sunni-Shiᶜite relations are marked with discomfort and unresolved contradictions with regard to the *marjaᶜiyya* issue as well. Shqaqi explains the political and activistic nature of Khomeini's outlook as deriving from the character of the office he holds, as opposed to the purely spiritual and traditional office of Abu-l Qasim al-Khu'i, the *marjaᶜaᶜla* based in Najf whose authority is still widely accepted in Iraq and Lebanon. However, Shqaqi does not confront the problem that arises from Khomeini's role. For, if Khomeini is indeed the "supreme *marjaᶜ* of Iran, Pakistan, India and Afghanistan," then all Sunni Muslims who accept what Shqaqi defines as the "Islamic alternative" and who admire Khomeini's justification of "the ulama's involvement in politics" should, perforce, accept Khomeini's rule over them. But, although Shiᶜite extremists in Lebanon and Iraq indeed do so, Sunnism's strong tradition of regionalism and decentralization, and lack of any *marjaᶜ* would render accepting Khomeini as *marjaᶜ* in Sunni countries as tantamount to changing the nature of religious (or religiopolitical) authority, by injecting into it new principles of hierarchy and centralization.

Another admirer of Khomeini, Egyptian philosopher Hasan Hanafi, confronts these questions more directly: it is true that the *Mahdi* embodies the principle of justice, but relating to him as the source of a theoretical framework for justifying the rule of the Virtuous *Faqih* "introduces metaphysical aspects which not all believers will be able to accept, and which are deeply anchored in medieval Shiᶜite philosophy."[23] Hanafi is also troubled by the fact that Khomeini builds his political theory on quotes from *Hadiths* of clearly Shiᶜite extraction and character, thereby "stirring up anew ancient disputes between Sunna and Shiᶜa that cause each camp to negate the credibility of the *Hadiths* expounded by the other." Nonetheless, Hanafi still hopes it will be possible, somehow, to extricate the substance of Khomeini's revolutionary message, which he sees as relevant to the entire world of Islam, from the stocks of Shiᶜite sectarianism into which it is now locked. And he views Khomeini's rejection of the principle of *taqiyya* as offering a glimmer of hope in this direction.

The four bones of contention mentioned earlier are also the focal point of those Sunni radicals critical of the Iranian leader. Adnan Saᶜd al-Din, a member of Syria's Revolutionary Islamic Command, claims that "on the eve of the revolution, while still in France, Khomeini promised that his regime would draw its inspiration not from the extreme Shiᶜism of the Safavid dynasty . . . but from the [first] four orthodox caliphs. However, no sooner did Khomeini seize power than he began to take a blatantly Shi^cite sectarian stand in his declarations, his articles, and in the constitution of the republic." Sa^cd al-Din goes on to say that "the Iranian government attacks good Muslims for not accepting the principles of Shi^cism and denigrates the [first] three orthodox caliphs."[24] Even the ecumenically oriented Lebanese Sheikh Sa^cid Sha^cban has declared that he would support the Iranian revolution wholeheartedly if it accepted the Koran as a platform and the six (Sunni) books of *Hadiths* as a means of interpreting the Koran. "Instead of pronouncing Iran a state with a Shi^cite doctrine, they would be better off calling for Muslim unity and implementation of the *shari^ca*."[25] (As we saw earlier, Khomeini was quite adamant that his legal system be Shi^cite.) The Tunisian radicals, even during the short period in early 1979 when they admired the Iranian revolution as the spearhead of a worldwide Muslim resurgence, noted with some concern the revolution's blatant Shi^cite character (e.g., that the leader's authority stems from the Hidden Imam), although they hoped that ecumenism (in the *madhhab Ja^cfari* version) would prevail. But, as we shall see later, suspicions were to mount and these hopes were to prove false.[26]

Sunni radicals are especially sensitive to the Shi^cite undertones in Khomeini's thinking because they owe so much to the neo-Hanbalite school. The goal of this school was the eradication of dangers to the integrity of the faith in the form of both "apostates" and Sunni deviants such as the Mongols and Shi^cites. The founder of this school, Ibn Taymiyya, directed his barbs mainly against those ^cAlawites and other Shi^cite extremists whom he defined as actual heretics, but he did not hesitate to rebuke the Imamite (Twelver) and Zaydi branches of Shi^cism as well. The anti-Mongol and anti-Shi^cite aspects were so interwoven that modern radicals imbued with neo-Hanbalite ideas became particularly sensitive to "internal dangers" of the Shi^cite variety. This sort of neo-Hanbalite animosity was found as early as the 1940s and 1950s in a previous incarnation of the Muslim Brethren, primarily in countries where Shi^cites lived. For example, Dr. Mustafa al-Siba^ci, the Brethren leader in Syria who originally advocated ecumenism, became deeply disappointed with "the Shi^cite subversion and hypocrisy" during this period.[27] Anti-Shi^cite sentiment was ten times greater among new radicals whose revolutionary theory was based entirely on Ibn Taymiyya. Needless to say, they rejected ecumenical tendencies toward both Christians and Shi^cites as modernistic attempts to contaminate the unique purity of pristine Islam.[28]

The major pro-radical publishing house in Cairo, Dar al-Ansar, put out a series of books, entitled "In This I and My Comrades Believe," more than six months before the Iranian revolution. The declared purpose of the series was to establish a protective fence around religious teachings and clear lines of demarcation between authentic (Sunni) Islam and unauthentic deviant versions, especially Shi꜀a. The first book of the series dealt with the Shi꜀ite custom of denigrating the reputaton of the Companions of the Prophet, and the second one focused on the main doctrinal disputes between Sunnism and Shi꜀ism.[29]

In the introduction to the third book, published at the end of 1979, publisher As꜀ad Sayyid Ahmad related that "a few friends" advised him to stop publishing the series because it was beginning to constitute a sort of political act, a stand against revolutionary Iran, which still enjoyed a certain amount of admiration in fundamentalist circles for having taken control of the government, if not for the content it imparted to this government. Ahmad refused, disclaiming any political intention — which was undoubtedly the case, at least with regard to the first two books. He emphasized, however, that adherence to Muslim authenticity — that is, to the radical interpretation of the Sunni tradition — prohibits one from blurring differences between it and Shi꜀ism.

It was no accident that this third book revived a controversy between the radicals' mentor, Ibn Taymiyya, and a contemporary Shi꜀ite sage, over concepts of the Hidden Imam, his infallibility, Shi꜀ite obedience to him, and the return of the *Mahdi*.[30] In his introduction, Ahmad labored to bring forth further points of contention between the two camps: temporary marriages (*mut꜀a*) and the ulama hierarchy accepted by the Shi꜀a, the cursing of Abu Bakr and ꜀Umar, and the *taqiyya*; he does not seem to believe in Khomeini's conciliatory moves with regard to the two latter points.

Subsequent books in the series deal with the historic perceptions of the two camps, a critique of Shi꜀ite law (which is not taken to be a *madhhab Ja꜀fari*), and in the last and most popular of the books, a disquisition of *The Islamic Government* as a text laden with typical Shi꜀ite thought.[31]

Against this background, it is possible to understand the infuriated reactions of radical and pro-radical circles in Egypt when Khomeini delivered a speech extolling the Hidden Imam, the infallible *Mahdi*, at the Imam's birthday celebration of 1980 in Tehran. In this speech, Khomeini stressed that, upon his return to earth, the Imam will bring about all that Muhammad did not have a chance to achieve, a statement the Sunnis perceive as actual heresy because it contradicts the doctrine of the "seal of the prophets" (of Muhammad as the final and most elevated stage in the divine revelation) and because it hints at ᶜAlawite concepts of ᶜAli's superiority to Muhammad. To add insult to injury, the semiofficial Egyptian press, along with conservative publications in Jordan and Tunisia, pounced upon this and similar speeches, exploiting them to discredit radicalism in general.[32]

Characteristic of how Sunni radicals had to wash their hands of Khomeini is a statement made by the Tunisian Islamic Tendency Movement, which took a relatively sympathetic stand toward the revolution, when pressured for a statement on Khomeini at a press conference it convened in 1981:

> We indeed recognize that Khomeini's activity as a representative of the Imam greatly contributed to the success of the revolution in Iran, but we regret outright the principle of the *Imama* as part of the Imam greatly contributed to the success of the revolution a result of historic circumstances which we certainly cannot accept. We stress that it is the right of the people in every nation to choose its leader, and that the leader does not derive his legitimacy from any external, transcendental source.[33]

But the message is not always conveyed in such deferential terms. When Sunni radicals in Gaza were disturbed by pro-Khomeinist tendencies in their ranks, they resorted to unearthing historical polemics to the effect that the Shiᶜites were allies of the Mongols — in the thirteenth and fourteenth centuries. As Mongol (*tatar*) is the emotion-laden term these radicals use to denote modern-day "infidel" regimes in Islamic lands, the implication is that the distinctly Shiᶜite Khomeini is the inheritor of a tradition of hostility to the Sunna. And Khomeini's alliance with Assad — a "typical Mongol ruler" — only enhances the accusation.[34]

Idiom and Content

The question that begs asking is whether Khomeini, who was so eager to export the Iranian revolution, was aware of the repercussions that speeches such as the one he made in Tehran would have in Arab countries. For it was a crazy humor that induced him to emphasize, of all things, the *rajᶜa* (return of the Imam), though his revolutionary theory explicitly calls upon believers to act in the here and now rather than to rely on the Imam's return. And, if he were aware of the repercussions, why did he not try to dilute them or issue a clarification that could be interpreted as retraction—even if only for foreign consumption? On a broader plane, for the sake of the world Islamic revolution, why did he not try to systematically lessen the importance of the Shi^cite fundamentals in his doctrine? If he could not do so before taking power, then why not afterward? Better yet, he could have tried to develop an orderly system of revolutionary thought in the ecumenical spirit that would be acceptable to all branches of the Muslim world. And, if he really did want to export the revolution, why did he persist, until the end, in his imperviousness to the sensitivities of potential allies in the Sunni radical camp?

The answer to these questions may be partially gleaned from the earlier discussion on the neo-Hanbalite tradition as the foundation for Sunni radicalism. Khomeini, too, developed his theory in the only manner and with the only concepts he saw as authentic. In his eyes, as in the eyes of Sunni radicals, the revolutionary energy had to be drawn from the bedrock of traditionalism, which still survived despite the attrition of modernity. He rejected modernity in general and Islamic modernism in particular from the outset of his campaign in 1941. And, as an extension of modernism, ecumenism was perforce rejected as well—all the more so because it imitated a foreign (Christian) model. Thus, any true Sunni-Shi^cite ecumenism—that is, ecumenism based on mutual compromise—would damage this authenticity. In the words of one Sunni radical thinker, "Protestants and Catholics can reach a conciliation for the benefit of imperialism, but even for the sake of peace and fraternity, the Sunna cannot accept such Shi^cite fundamentals as the Hidden Imam and the *Mahdi*." (It is instructive that such an old-fashioned Shi^cite ecumenist and admirer of the Iranian revolution as the Lebanese M. H. Mafhniya criticized the governance of the Virtuous Jurist doctrine strongly in the name of a Sunni-flavored interpretation of the role of the jurists.)[35]

It should be remembered that Khomeini developed the essentials of his teaching in the prerevolutionary period, when his target audience was the Iranian masses. This meant he had to reach them through both rational and emotional claims that would play upon sensitive chords in the popular religious mentality (e.g., the Husayn martyrology; the messianic expectation). A purely abstract intellectual structure, and all the more so a structure including such completely novel ideas as Islamic ecumenism, would not have aided his cause. Some of Khomeini's close associates like Ayatollah Mutahhari refrained from stressing the element of reconciliation, even though they themselves leaned toward ecumenism (of a quite moderate sort). The revolution was to erupt from out of the tradition and its concepts—although, naturally, these concepts were carried beyond their ancient limits by the revolution. Therefore, the idiom was no less important than the content, the experiential-religious dimension no less important than the theological-juridical one; the ritualistic (or "operative") as crucial as the expressive. Conversely, when Sunni fundamentalists speak of "Islamic fraternity," they do so either in broad, general terms (*umma*, *Dar-al-Islam*) or in Sunni concepts; the problematic popular conventions of Shi^cism are nowhere mentioned.[36]

The importance of the religious idiom and the experiential-affective dimension becomes clear upon an examination of how the ^cAshura' celebrations have changed during the past twenty years. By the 1960s, it was already possible to discern a change in the character, content, and text of the plays presented on this holiday in several regions of Iran; the same is true for the speeches and slogans issued at the mass-participation parades that accompanied these plays. And, by the 1970s, anthropologists were noting that the new Husayn myth was spreading and affecting ^cAshura' celebrations throughout Iran, including the rural areas.[37] The ^cAshura' was being converted from a memorial day extolling the martyrdom of Husayn, whose sacrifice redeems the believers who mourn him, into an outraged (not mournful) birthday commemoration by believers united in communion with Husayn's heroism and willingness to sacrifice. Today, the believers are called upon not to lament Husayn but to emulate him, by following in his path and waging battle against the tyrannical Yazids of their own time. The passive, accommodating approach that accepted the reality (albeit with deep sorrow) has given way to an activist, belligerent, rebellious approach in which the medieval politico-religious myth has preserved its form but changed some of its content.

It was natural for Khomeini's followers to choose the ^cAshura' holiday to symbolize and embody in a dramatic form the revolutionary doctrine they had developed out of—but which in a certain sense transcended—the Shi^cite tradition. Only the Husayn myth, with its centrality to the Iranian Shi^ca world of belief, attitudes, view of history, and behavior, could so successfully embrace and integrate conceptions of the beginnings of Islamic history and the readiness for martyrdom: the traditional foundation stones upon which the Iranians built their revolutionary dogma. The ^cAshura' celebrations on the days immediately preceding the revolution (December 9–10, 1978) were the apotheosis of this change, which was greatly expedited by current events: the Shah's repression of demonstrations during the previous months were a concrete expression of Pahlavi tyranny, and the victims who fell in these demonstrations were viewed as emulators of Husayn. Tradition and revolution, continuity and change thus were blended smoothly to mobilize the masses. There is no way such content could have been imparted to the cAshura' in the Sunni world, with its completely different tradition regarding this day (a strictly voluntary fast day, certainly not a central holiday and myth). It goes without saying —even though the gist of the change, but not its details, would have been similar: from accommodation to revolution—that the process of change in the Sunni political tradition would have been completely different from that in the Shicite tradition because of the problems that such change entails. Both idiom and content, therefore, would have had to undergo a different metamorphosis in the Sunni world.

True, some Sunni circles in Arab countries have, since the 1950s, turned Husayn into a revolutionary myth, no doubt independent of developments in Iran. However, the people involved were either modernistic ulama or, more often, the same patently secular thinkers and historians who turned the Kharijte sect, abhorred in the Sunni tradition, into the standard-bearers of their social revolution.[38] But, with the Kharijte issue, their influence was limited to intellectual liberal-leftist circles. On a completely different track, efforts were made by modernistic, ecumenical Sunni and Shicite religious figures in Lebanon to turn the cAshura' into a holiday of rapprochement among all the communities (sometimes including the Christians), by stressing the lofty values of "justice, truth and honor" symbolized by the Husayn affair. These ecumenical efforts never took root, however, for the mental soil was saturated with too much Sunni-Shicite animosity. They were reduced to meetings of dignitaries committed to intercommunal compromise held on the eve of the cAshura' day and to historic interpretations in the small-circulation ecumenical journal, al-cIrfan (published in Sidon), and, of late, in the intellectual organ of the Sunni religious establishment in Lebanon, al-Fikr al-Islami.[39]

The deep bond between idiom and content, or between the affective and the cognitive, is apparent in the attempts to alter and renew the Husayn myth that have succeeded in various parts of the Shicite world. Activism similar to but unconnected with the Iranian brand can be found among the Shicite minority in Turkey. And, as mentioned earlier, a phenomenon of this sort took place on a much wider scale in

Lebanon. The ᶜAshura' celebrations had always enjoyed the same centrality and possessed the same martyrological-lachrymose character among the Shiᶜites in Lebanon as they did in Iran, even though the self-flagellation exhibited at these celebrations as a sign of mourning was less violent (blows to the chest and head were by fist, stone, or the dull edge of a sword, rather than by iron chains). We have already discussed the Sunni ecumenists' repugnance and abhorrence toward this ceremony in Nabatiyya in 1960 and 1965. Anthropologists observing this popular ceremony in 1966 and 1973 reported that its character had remained unchanged among the important Shiᶜite community of southern Lebanon.[40] By the end of the 1960s, however, the first signs of change could be seen. A young religious scholar, Muhammad Mahdi Shams al-Din, who later became one of the leaders of Amal, offered a new interpretation of the ᶜAshura' that evoked interest among Shiᶜite intellectual circles in Beirut. In it, Husayn was presented as an activist who refused to reconcile himself to the tyrannical regime despite its superior strength and, as such, was a source of inspiration for the actions of religious faithful in all generations.[41] It is likely that Shams al-Din, who had been a lecturer in Najf, was influenced by the several Iranian historians and religious sages who were feeling their way along a similar path during these same years.[42] But this had nothing to do with developments in the township of Bint Jubayl, on the Shiᶜite fringes of southern Lebanon, where a sociologist discerned an activistic spirit in the ᶜAshura' celebrations of 1966. The influence in this case was partly due to Palestinian refugees, for the demand for sacrifice in the present focused to some extent on the liberation of Palestine. Of greater influence were the young local intellectuals who had been educated in Damascus, where they were instilled with Baᶜth ideology, and who were now eager to integrate this ideology into their religious tradition.[43]

On this background, the Imam Musa al-Sadr, founder of the Amal movement, began a systematic transformation of the ᶜAshura' in southern Lebanon in the mid-1970s. Al-Sadr's ideology required that the Shiᶜite masses make their political stand more activist and that they stop accepting their fate (and the regime in power) as representing a divine decree to which they must reconcile themselves. He selected the ᶜAshura' celebrations of the towns and villages of southern Lebanon as a collective educational tool to impart his ideology in the form of speeches and plays. In his speech on the ᶜAshura' of 1974 in Nabatiyya, he said:

Let us not be content with ceremonies of pure mourning, and thus have them remain as external, fossilized religious manifestations through which the tyrants can camouflage their crimes, brainwash the populace, and accustom them to passivity. Do not allow ceremonies of lamentation to serve as a substitute for action. We must transform the ceremonies into a spring from which will gush forth the revolutionary fury and the constructive protest. . . . Let me ask you: if Husayn were living with us now and saw that the rights of the people, and justice were being trampled upon by the foot of pride, what would he do?

A year later in Tyre, he sounded a similar note:

It is forbidden for the *Ashura'* to be merely a historic commemoration; it must serve as a spur to action in the present and the future. . . . Husayn has three types of enemies: those who murdered him with their own hands, those like the Ottomans who wished to erase his memory and prohibited assemblies of mourning, and—worst of all—those enemies who seek to distort the goals of Husayn's rebellion, to fashion them in desiccated molds, and to reduce his historic act to laconic utterances and lamentations. The last category of enemy sought to eradicate the very essence of the Shi^c^a doctrine and replace it with redemption through mourning.[44]

This essence of Shi^c^a, al-Sadr claimed, calls for continuous revolution against tyranny, for the sake of the cluster of values Husayn defended to his last drop of blood and that, encouraged by Husayn's very death, penetrated into the souls of his followers for generations. The new doctrine had spread with the Amal movement before al-Sadr's disappearance in summer 1978, and it still appears in the ^c^Ashura' celebrations of both Beirut and eastern Lebanon. For example, at an October 1984 rally in Beirut, it was stressed that the ^c^Ashura' was not "merely folklore, or even a plain historic event to be bewailed . . . but an eternal source of lessons on doing, on acting, on defending freedom."[45]

Al-Sadr brought about changes not only in the ^c^Ashura' but also in the popular celebrations on Husayn's birthday that became a tool for promulgating the new myth. In 1974, he stated that "this day marks the rebirth of Islam, since the Prophet Muhammad had said [according to the Shi^cite *Hadith*]: 'Husayn belongs to me and I belong to him.' Islam did not descend upon the earth in order to sanctify class privileges and the glory of tyrants, but to put an end to exploitation, to redeem the oppressed, and to raise the downtrodden and the destitute from the dirt." However, the original spirit of Islam sank into oblivion with the rise of the Omayyad "caesars," oriental despots in Islamic garb, a situation that lasted "until Husayn appeared, took a stand against them, and uncovered through their words and deeds the full extent to which these rulers deviated from true Islam." Husayn observed that whereas the external manifestations of Islam—mosques and prayer—made it seem as if the religion was in good shape, when he probed more deeply and scrutinized its essence, he found that this essence had been distorted beyond measure. In al-Sadr's opinion, this is true today as well. The contemporary tyrants "wrap themselves in the mantle of freedom and democracy, but they will learn that we, like Husayn in his time, will openly castigate their sinful behavior, and will struggle to put an end to their tyranny. We, a band of Husayn's followers, are ready to pay with our lives in order to win back our honor. Not even our deaths will grant the tyrants peace and quiet."[46]

Al-Sadr was an Iranian mullah of Lebanese origin who moved from Najf to Lebanon in 1968. Thus, it is more than likely that he was aware of spiritual developments in Iran in the 1960s and 1970s. Nonetheless, there is no evidence that he acted under the direct inspiration of Khomeini and his delegates. Al-Sadr, whose aim was to revise the distribution of power in Lebanon, not to convert it into a Muslim state, focused his attention primarily on the reality and needs of Lebanon, building his theories on the indigenous development in the local Shi^cite community (the leaning toward social activism and challenging the antiquated political structure; the search for a new intellectual course by Shams al-Din and his students). His mysterious disappearance in Libya during summer 1978, a few months before the Iranian revolution broke out, leaves one to guess the stance he would have taken toward it. Still, it seems that there was an affinity between al-Sadr's basic "traditional-revolutionary" spiritual inclination and the spirit of the revolution, especially as he had been close to Mutahhari and Beheshti. When the Lebanese Shi^cite masses swore allegiance to the "dual revolutionary heritage" of Khomeini and al-Sadr at the ^cAshura' celebrations in 1978 and 1979, they were giving expression not only to a widespread popular feeling, but to a penetrating intellectual insight as well.[47]

Exporting the Revolution

The role of the cAshura' is testimony that the attraction of Khomeinism, like other movements of change, is based to a large extent on
the fact that traditional Shicite religious sensibility is an active force
among diverse strata of the population. This thesis is reinforced by an
examination of movements in Arab countries that have been attracted
to revolutionary Iran, all of which, with no exceptions, are Shicite. It
is interesting that most of them were not established by Khomeini or
his representatives (although these agents evidently aid them today
and also had a hand in setting up the Command of the Islamic Revolution, in Iraq). As a rule, these were indigenous movements that sprang
up out of local initiative in Lebanon and Iraq. Some of them, the al-
Dacwa movement and the Organization of Muslim Action in Iraq,
were founded a number of years before the revolution in Iran; others
were founded after the revolution, in part inspired by it, though to a
much greater extent in response to local conditions and events: Jund
Allah and Hizballah in Lebanon, in reaction to the civil war and the
disappearance of al-Sadr; and al-Amal al-Islami, also in Lebanon, in
reaction to the Israeli invasion; the *mujahidun* and the Association of
the Ulama by Iraqi expatriates, in reaction to persecution by the Iraqi
regime in summer 1980.

Speeches made at cAshura' celebrations are a clue to the spirit of
these organizations. In his 1982 speech, the head of the Islamic
Revolutionary Command in Iraq, Muhammad Baqir al-Hakim (son
of the *marjacacla* from Najf who invited the exiled Khomeini to teach
there), called for absolute rejection of the false concept "that Husayn's
death in Karbala was due to a divine decree that we are unable to
fathom, and that this is why we are unable to emulate his example . . .
as if the only thing we can do is mourn him, act out the scene of his
death, mutilate ourselves in public to the accompaniment of great
wailing and numerous sermons." Not that it is bad in itself "to love
Husayn and bewail his assassination," but it is forbidden to reduce the
cAshura' to this alone; it must be turned into a living symbol of the
right to rise up against tyrannical rule. Allah bestowed Husayn [and
the other eleven Imams] upon the believers as a paragon for all generations. Husayn's sacrifice was not made to redeem the faithful, but
to provide Islam with a therapeutic and purifying shock that would
transform the "oppositional stand from theory into practice, from
potential into execution . . . and into a form of truth which men—
even if they are few against many—will live by and fight for

against all who desecrate the commandments of Allah." Al-Hakim concludes that "Yazid of our generation has many names: the Shah, Saddam Husayn, etc. The believer has only one duty: to oppose him in whatever form he appears." It is no wonder, then, that al-Hakim calls the Iranian revolution "the Husayni Revolution." In fact, publications of the Iraqi Islamic Revolutionary Command and Organization of Muslim Action deal extensively with the Husayn affair, drawing an analogy between it and the struggle waged by Shiᶜite radicals, the "successors of Husayn," against contemporary tyrants. The celebrations that took place in Iraq and Lebanon on the anniversary of the death of Muhammad Baqir al-Sadr, the head of Iraq's al-Daᶜwa movement who was murdered by the regime in 1980, followed similar lines.[48]

In a proclamation issued by al-Amal al-Islami, a splinter group in Baᶜlbek that broke off from al-Amal on the background of the 1982 war, the goals of the movement are defined as follows: "We constitute a sort of huge ᶜAshura' procession; our suicide squads are as precious to Allah as are the martyrs of Karbala—members of the prophet's family and their heroic disciples."[49] The motif of martyrdom constantly reappears in pro-Khomeini circles. For example, *al-Liwa' al-Sadr*, "the organ of the Islamic Revolution in Iraq," published a letter by a mother whose three sons were killed in underground activities, in which the mother welcomes death as unavoidable and necessary, and lauds them in light of the Husayni model.[50]

The Shiᶜite quarterly *al-Hikma*, published in Beirut by Muhammad Husayn Fadlallah, the mentor of Hizballah, dealt with the topic in 1981 in a more scholarly and reflective fashion. After providing ample documentation and exegesis, the quarterly reached an operative conclusion:

> Let the ᶜAshura' become the slogan of this century, a true expression of a movement, which springs from within our nation in order to change our reality for the sake of a better future. ᶜAshura' endows us with a sense of purpose and the knowledge of how to meet challenges. On this day man feels that ideas are not merely the stuff of reading and philosophy, but forces that spur us to action, fundamentals that motivate us to confront the reality in order to alter it, to fashion it anew to the best of our ability. ᶜAshura' teaches us that all of us, young and old alike, are responsible for the welfare of the faith . . . this day expresses the affliction of the oppressed and their readiness for sacrifice in order to

change their condition. We are in great need of an cAshura' mentality to build a new man who is aware of his role and ready for
action, for we know that Allah helps only those who help themselves. It is incumbent upon man to take the initiative.[51]

The cAshura' myth is tightly interwoven with other aspects of
radical Shicite thought. In the eyes of Fadlallah, al-Hakim, and
Musawi (the leader of al-Amal al-Islami), the Iranian revolution is a
symbol of "Husaynism" in our days. The achievements of the revolution are extolled and its lessons studied in all the radical publications
of Lebanon and Iraq, where the Iranian example is used, more than
anything else, to justify violence. The "armed struggle" gained legitimacy through concepts of Shicite political theory and *Hadiths* that explain how and when it should be employed and the kind of regime that
should be established when it succeeds. It is no wonder, then, that
Shicite leaders recognize Khomeini as both *na'ib al-Imam* (vicar of the
Hidden Imam) and *qa'id al-Umma* (leader of the Muslim community),
both of whose authority is binding in all parts of the Islamic world.[52]
As opposed to Sunni radicals, whose vision, as we have seen, usually
ends at the political-national borders within which they operate, the
Shicite radicals in Iraq and Lebanon subject themselves to authority
from outside their own nation-state. In so doing they express, with
great poignancy, their rejection (common to them and Sunni radicals)
of the idea of nationalism.[53]

In 1979 Muhammad Baqir al-Sadr, leader of the Iraqi Dacwa
movement, wrote an erudite interpretation of the Iranian draft constitution, at the request of eight Lebanese Shicite sages. In it he
stresses the *wilayat al-faqih* (the Faqih, the *marjacacla*, as
supreme ruler) is the foundation stone of all political authority. This
doctrine draws its legitimacy from two principles: (1) the notion that
the ulama, in general, and the Faqih, in particular, are representatives of the Hidden Imam; and (2) the concept of the virtuous *marjaciyya*. Here, Sadr was interpreting a theory that he had helped
develop back in 1966, in which the *marjaciyya* was defined by him as
the repository of both political and religious leadership[54] — a relatively
new idea that Khomeini was to take up, elaborate, and propagate in
Iran (and not much less Iraq and Lebanon), but only after protracted
debate with those who adhered to the traditional concept of *marjac* as
religious leader only.[55]

Acceptance of Khomeini's authority — even by Sadr, who though
much younger was in a way his mentor — implied recognition of the

special role of the ulama as a class, with the *marajᶜ* and the *mujtahidun* at their head: The ulama would lead the Muslim revolution in Shiᶜite Arab countries, :and they would rule in the Islamic state; and this is dictated both by doctrine ("the *ulama* as successors to the prophets") and by the reality, in which sages play a very active role in the Shiᶜite radical organizations of Iraq and Lebanon.[56] This means that those worthy of leadership are the same ulama as those in Iran who "lived with and for the people, suffered the same persecutions, and could thus wave the banner of *jihad* not as an abstract slogan coined in an ivory tower, but as an experience they had lived and breathed long before the rest of the populace developed a similar consciousness."[57]

Thus, although Muhammad Baqir al-Sadr drew the eight Lebanese sages to him by virtue of his profound erudition and political courage in the struggle against the Baᶜth regime—a combination that turned him into a sort of counter-*marjaᶜ* *vis-à-vis* al-Khu'i (who had advocated accommodation with the regime before he became more recalcitrant)—it is characteristic of the nature of Shiᶜite radicalism that he, too, recognized Khomeini's authority, as did his successor, al-Hakim, after al-Sadr was assassinated.

It becomes clear, then, that even before the revolution in Iran, Shiᶜite radicals in Arab countries had developed common identifying features, distinct from those of the Sunni radicals, in at least two areas of Shiᶜa-Sunna controversy. Khomeini's contribution was to sharpen these distinguishing traits, especially in relation to the *wilayat al-faqih* concept. The fourth area of controversy, normative law, is hardly mentioned in Shiᶜite radical writings, a clear indication of its marginal role in the lives and thinking of the Shiᶜites. By contrast, however, the eschatological myth (the return of the *Mahdi*) and the ulama hierarchy are heavily stressed. The "foundation myth" surfaces not only through the ᶜAshura'—as vital as this day is to a movement that calls its people to deeds of sacrifice—but also through oft-repeated references to Shiᶜite *Hadiths* and articles by the Twelve Imams, reminders of ᶜAli's struggle for and right to the caliphate, the Umayyad usurpation leading to his downfall and so forth.

The question may be put differently: is the revolutionary theory that Khomeini developed to meet the needs of, and in the framework of the tradition of Shiᶜite Iran, at all capable of attracting the Sunni world? Is it possible, after the revolution, to formulate the theory in a version that will captivate non-Shiᶜites, a version somewhat different from that which attracts a significant number of Shiᶜites in Iraq, Lebanon, and the Persian Gulf states?

Khomeini's regime, which is undoubtedly interested in exporting the revolution, can (and to a certain extent indeed tries to) solve the problem by resorting to a two-track propaganda strategy: a Shi^cite vein for local consumption and an ecumenical vein for foreign consumption. However, two difficulties are involved: (1) right from the start many of Khomeini's followers in the main target countries were Shi^cites whose indigenous propaganda is (and was well before 1978) suffused with Shi^cite fundamentalism, and (2) more significantly, the Khomeini regime will not be able to maintain such compartmentalized propaganda in the long run, due to the "global village" that modern communication has created. For, messages earmarked for internal use are quickly disseminated and translated throughout the Middle East, as the furor over Khomeini's speech on the *Mahdi's* birthday in 1980 can testify.

In order to confront both these challenges, Iranian propaganda written in Arabic[58] (as well as Lebanese Shi^cite organs and Iraqi journals coming out of Tehran) employs slightly different tactics. On the one hand, to the extent that it is possible to separate content from idiom, the threefold message common to all the Muslim radical movements is stressed. Emphasis is placed on those activities of the Iranian revolution geared to actualizing theory in the economic (redistribution of income and property) and moral (status of women, drinking wine) realms. On the other hand, it attempts in several ways to reduce the importance of Shi^cite-Sunni conflicts; for example, by having the propaganda give prominence to Khomeini's conciliatory steps toward the Sunnis (his prohibition on cursing Abu Bakr and ^cUmar, and nullification of the prohibition against Shi^cites praying behind a Sunni prayer leader and vice versa—an interdicton that had greatly insulted Sunni visitors to Iran in the first days of the revolution.[59] Furthermore, Khomeini, whose personality cult occupies a central position in publications geared for foreign as well as domestic consumption, is described in terms likely to be acceptable to Sunnis.

In this context, Ayatollah Mutahhari (died 1979), who had the strongest ecumenical leanings among Iranian leaders, set the tone in his work *The Resurrection of the Mahdi*, which was translated from Parsi into Arabic. In it the *Mahdi* is presented as a sort of messiah—a concept accepted, with slight reservations, by all schools and sects of Islam in their perceptions of the end of days and "the inevitable victory of the forces of truth, justice and peace . . . a victory that will shine the light of Islam over the entire world." Mutahhari's depiction of the end of days is bolstered by quotations from the Koran alone, the only religious source that Sunnis and Shiᶜites agree upon. Nonetheless, the *Mahdi* remains a thorny issue, and one that Shiᶜite propagandists try to avoid whenever possible. Thus, a learned commentary on the Iranian constitution published by the Arabic language organ *al-Fajr* omits any discussion of the Occultation when dealing with Article 5, which sets the historical time frame ("in the absence of the *Mahdi*") for Khomeini's rule.[60]

In a similar spirit, Ayatollah Zanjani claims actual agreement on the *usul al-fiqh* issue. He says that Sunnism and Shiᶜism both accept the Koran and the *Hadith*, and that there is unanimity today between Shiᶜite and Sunni radicals on the *ijtihad* question as well. Although this second claim is in fact correct, Zanjani does not mention that Shiᶜite and Sunni *Hadiths* differ in their sources and, to some extent, in their contents. At an Islamic convention convened in London in 1983 in a Khomeinist spirit, it was declared that "the Muslims the whole world over are all of one nation, and that all Muslim groups should return to the Koran and the *Sunna* (*Hadith*) for guidance in solving their problems."[61]

Ecumenical efforts did not bypass the "foundation myth"; they imparted to Husayn and Karbala a significance not only pan-Islamic but universal—as a manifestation of the struggle against evil, injustice, and oppression—and in a historical not eschatological framework. The struggle is not to be postponed until the end of days but is an obligation in the present, in the spirit of Gandhi's saying: "From Husayn I learned how to be downtrodden and oppressed—how to rise up and be victorious."[62] This message is disseminated in Arabic-language Iranian, Iraqi and Lebanese organs, but even more so in the popular writings of Iraqi Ayatollah Muhammad Taqi al-Mudarresi, which frequently cite the works of Shiᶜite ecumenist thinker Kashif al-Ghita', primarily on the topic of *jihad* as a struggle against injustice.[63]

With this as a basis, it was possible, for example, for a pro-Khomeini qadi from Sidon to claim that "Shiᶜites and Sunnis are both Muslims; they believe that there is no God other than Allah, and that Muhammad is his messenger." The qadi issues a call "to break loose from sectarianism and loyalty to one school (*madhhab*) versus the others," thereby rejecting the traditional distinction between Shiᶜites as true believers and Sunnis as mere Muslims. He also employs the strategy of "the five schools," with the Shiᶜites being nothing more than *madhhab Jaᶜfari*. In a similar vein, Ayatollah Mudarresi calls for greater acquaintance between Sunnis and Shiᶜites, which will lead them to understand that the differences between them are trivial relative to the common ground, and that a good portion of their differences are based upon falsehoods spread by enemies of Islam in order to foment strife and faction. The argument becomes all the more cogent considering that the common ground is the struggle of radicals "from the revolutionaries of Iran to Islambuli [Sadat's assassin] . . . from the *jihad* fighters in Afghanistan to the Lebanese combatting the American marines and Israel."[64]

The *wilayat al-faqih* issue still presents great difficulty for propagandists of the Iranian revolution. Not only is Shiᶜite radical literature in general permeated with worship of Khomeini, but even propagandistic writings, including those of Shiᶜite pan-Islamic conferences, maintain the doctrine of the special role of the ulama in leading the Muslim community and, from among the ulama, of the *marajiᶜ al-taqlid* in particular (and above them, of course, of Khomeini as the supreme leader of the Islamic revolution). This fundamental innovation in Khomeini's thought is so central to his philosophy that he and his followers do not want to (or cannot) conceal it through causistic ploys. Even so, they strive to keep the existing cognitive dissonance from grating too harshly on Sunni ears. Once again, the favorite tactic is that of the "five schools": "Khomeini is the *marjaᶜ al-taqlid*, that is the head of a specific (Jaᶜfari) legal school, within which he activates the *ijtihad* . . . the differences between his solutions and those of the other [four] schools result from normal differences of opinion among jurists exerting their juridical authority in problems of religious law."[65] Yet another tactic is to substantiate the argument for the *wilaya* as far as is possible on koranic verses rather than on Shiᶜite Hadiths and even to try and make it compatible with the principle of *shura* (consultation).[66]

It would be amazing if these and similar arguments were effective. Presenting Khomeini as merely a head of a *madhhab* is a brilliant gimmick that sweeps under the carpet the concept of *niyaba ᶜamma* (Khomeini's tie to the Hidden Imam). However, if the political dimension of the *marjaᶜiyya* is effaced, how is one to explain the central political role of the "governing *faqih*," whom the very same organs that advocate ecumenism thank and praise without any resort to the *wilayat al-faqih* doctrine? Moreover, from where does Khomeini derive the right to lead all the Muslims in the role of "the ruler of Islam," a definition used by these same organs? It is true that the specifically Shiᶜite dimension of the ulama's mission (as collective representatives of the Imam) is usually obscured, but even proponents of ecumenism slip up by quoting Shi^cite *Hadiths* in this context; for example, those originating with Imams preceding the Hidden Imam.[67]

Furthermore, can the description of Husayn as a universal hero generate any credibility as long as the ^cAshura' ceremonies continue to openly exhibit a blatantly Shi^cite character (self-flagellation, collective wailing) and occupy the same central place in the revolutionary Khomeinist catechism and ritual in Iran and Lebanon that they have been accorded since the 1960s? When Ayatollah Mutahhari "cleanses" the *Mahdi* of Shi^cism in any way, he is thereby contradicting his own Arab publisher, who says in his introduction to *Nahdat al-Mahdi* that the Hidden Imam holds supreme responsibility for materializing the revolutionary change, but that the ground for this will be prepared by his vicar — Khomeini.[68]

Thus, Shi^cite uniqueness stubbornly persists in piercing the ecumenical mantle in which they try to wrap Khomeinism. It would take a great surplus of optimism to claim — as Dr. Kalim Siddiqi, a Sunni-Pakistani admirer of Khomeini, does — that all the previously mentioned Sunni-Shi^cite disagreements are negligible, nothing more than extraneous vestiges of the past, that Khomeini is really an avowed ecumenist, and that there is no reason not to follow in his footsteps.[69]

All this is not to say that, when it erupted, the Iranian revolution did not evoke sympathy and even enthusiasm among Sunni radicals. At least temporarily, it was an example and source of inspiration. What had been considered virtually impossible had actually taken place: a modern Muslim tyrant was removed by a popular uprising. According to the Syrian Muslim Brethren, the victory of the rebels teaches "that in order to succeed, the revolution needs patience, resilience, and willingness to pay a heavy price in blood, human life, and money." The organization praised "the Iranian love of martyrdom," even though great care is taken to avoid mentioning that this inclination is founded on the Husayn myth.[70]

Apart from this didactic-moralistic lesson learned from the revolution, practical lessons on taking power also could be drawn from events in Iran during fall and winter 1978. At his trial, Lt. Col. Abbud al-Zumur, an Egyptian intelligence officer who was military commander of the Jihad radical group, admitted that these events taught him it is futile to recruit members of an underground to battle the armed forces; the strategy must rely on an uprising of the masses. (Al-Zumur did, indeed, plan such an uprising and attempted to carry it out in Asyut on October 6, 1981, immediately after Sadat was murdered and part of the political elite disposed of.) "We learned from Iran that the army and police cannot withstand a popular rebellion." He had hoped that, as in Iran, conflicts and factions would develop rapidly within the armed forces assigned to repress the masses, and that some soldiers and policemen would join the revolution (whether out of internal conviction, unwillingness to fire on their compatriots, or opportunism). Operative lessons could be learned on a tactical level as well; for example, the importance of distributing radical sermons on tape-cassettes in order to prepare the groundwork.[71]

All this notwithstanding, Khomeini's regime was never for a single moment conceived as a model to be emulated, not even during the brief honeymoon period in the beginning of 1979. Infighting within the ranks of the Iranian revolutionaries, and other vicissitudes undergone by their movement and regime (including the hostages affair, which Sunni radicals denounced as contravening the *Shariʿa*'s prohibition against harming innocent citizens) engendered growing disappointment with the enterprise among Sunni radicals, despite their basic feelings of affinity and fraternity.

The following declarations by the head of the *Jamaʿa Islamiyya* in Lebanon is characteristic:

> At the outset, the Iranian revolution demolished the division of the Islamic world into Soviet and American spheres of influence and proved that Islam can stand on its own between the two superpowers without committing itself to either of them. All Muslims admired this aspect of the revolution. The trouble is that developments in Iran during the following years benefitted only the enemies of Islam. These enemies could use the course of events in Iran as grounds to distort the true image of the Islamic regime and its mode of operation and to pervert the meaning of the establishment of a [revolutionary] Islamic regime in our day.[72]

The fact that Khomeini's government quickly entered into an alliance with the regime of Assad, the exterminator of the Muslim Brethren, naturally rendered any dialogue with Iran futile, for, even before this, Syrian radicals had constantly criticized the Khomeini regime's "blatant Shiʿite tendencies." But criticism now gave way to strong animosity ("his dictatorship is no better than the Shah's"), which reached other Sunni radical movements as well.[73] It is no wonder, then, that even though several members of the Egyptian Jihad did indeed read Khomeini's *The Islamic Government*, the ideas of the group were based on *The Absent Precept*, a work by Jihad mentor Abd al-Salam Faraj, which was inspired by Ibn Taymiyya, the avowed enemy of both Mongol and Shiᶜite apostasy. Expounding upon Faraj's doctrine during his police interrogation, one of the four assassins of Sadat accused the late Egyptian president of "spreading such lies as the one that Khomeini's revolution is an Islamic one, when this is undoubtedly false, for as a Shiᶜite Khomeini does not apply the [true] *Sharīᶜa*. And, since the Shiᶜites murder Sunnis [in the war with Iraq], to compare us to Khomeini is to try to discredit the authentic Islamic regime to which we aspire."[74]

Unity through Diversity?

Considering the remaining differences between Sunni and Shiᶜite Islam, the Sunnis may have to continue seeking a revolutionary path of their own. I say "may have to" rather than "have to" so as not to imply that what has been true in the past — and present — will necessarily remain so in the future. Muslim political theory has undergone such tremendous change at the hands of the radicals that one cannot rule out the possibility of further rapprochement between Sunnism and Shiᶜism within the fundamentalist radical movement. This would require a considerable but not inconceivable intellectual effort that could be precipitated by such real-world catalysts as Khomeini's death. Sunni and Shiᶜite radicals may consent to additional mutual concessions for the sake of unity in the ranks. After all, modernity and the military regimes are enemies common to both camps, and as such cast their heavy shadow on Sunni and Shiᶜite radicals alike.

Harbingers of rapprochement are evident in war-torn Lebanon, of all places, where Shiᶜites are usually accused of fanning sectarian hatred. The small Association of Muslim Ulama movement, led by Sheikh Mahir Hammud, systematically endeavors to bring Shiᶜite and Sunni Ulama closer together by stressing common enemies and agreed-upon ideological content, to facilitate the establishment of closer personal ties within the framework of one organization. Sunni sages active in this movement accept the Shiᶜite concept of "the *ᶜulama'* as heirs of the prophets," with all of its revolutionary ramifications including recognition of Khomeini as the "leader of religious sages in our generation," a very significant concession predicated on the notion that only the ulama can release the revolutionary potential of the traditionalist bedrock of Islam. According to this view, the ulama's virtual absence in Sunni radical movements accounts for the failure of these movements.[75] The association's periodical *al-Wahda* al-Islamiyya, contains articles by major Sunni and Shi^cite radical theorists of the 1960s and 1970s, in an effort to prove the similarity of their messages.[76] This organ runs panegyrics by Afghani and Abduh, among others, who preach Islamic unity as the sole means of confronting modern challenges.[77]

Association leader Sheikh Mahir Hammud, however, cautions that efforts at Sunni-Shi^cite rapprochement may not suffice to bring about the unification of Muslim ranks in the near future, because fourteen centuries of controversy among ulama of various tendencies cannot be wiped out at one stroke. The way to achieve this final aim passes through the crystallization of a joint stand on politics and on Holy War. In the course of this fight against the tyrants of this world, both inside and outside Lebanon, authentic Islamic fusion will come about, especially in matters of jurisprudence and *ijtihad*. Animosity toward the Lebanese state and religious establishment is no less a recurring theme than animosity toward the Israeli presence in southern Lebanon: negativism (unite against what you hate) is bound to lead to positive results in the form of sectarian rapprochement. This philosophy is only natural for a group that was born during the siege of Beirut (summer 1982) and that evolved into a combination militia-educational association. This group had come so far by June 1985 that they even declared the founding of a united Islamic Front in Lebanon, which was to be ecumenical in character, anti-SLA (South Lebanon Army) in program, and emulative of the Iranian model in strategy.

Similar trends seem to have developed in Lebanon's Hizballah ranks, inspired by Fadlallah and catalyzed by the necessities of fighting against U.S. Marines, the SLA, the secularist Amal, and sundry other local militias. The bimonthly *al-Muntalaq*, published by the Lebanese Union of Muslim Students, became Fadlallah's prime vehicle for propagating his radical-ecumenical approach. Here, again, the stress is placed on common enemies, above all Arab (and Lebanese) nationalism and the modern military regimes that render past sectarian divergencies completely irrelevant. *Al-Muntalaq*'s writers, mostly Shi^cites, use Sunni radical terminology (modernity is *jahiliyya*), but infuse it with Shi^cite *Hadiths*. Sunnis and Shi ^cites, they argue, may continue to retain their distinct characteristics for the present, much as boundaries between Muslim states cannot be obliterated overnight. But a unified-front approach is still feasible.[78] If, however, Iran is to serve as the pivot for such an all-Islamic front, might there not be a danger that the front will be stamped with an indelible Shi^cite mark? "No," answers a Sunni activist, Sheikh Dan, writing in *al-*

Muntalaq. For divergencies between schools and tendencies are legitimate and may even be [as the famous *Hadith* has it] "a blessing Allah the Compassionate has bestowed upon his community," as they enrich thought, legislation, and action. What one should reject is "blind obedience to one's sect," which ends up in people declaring their fellow Muslims to be renegades.[79]

In much the same vein that made him launch a recruitment drive among Sunni youth, Muhammad Fadlallah offered an olive branch to the Sunnis by trying to prohibit the self-mutilation so repugnant to Sunnis during the 1985 ᶜAshura' celebration in Beirut. But young Hizballah zealots disregarded Fadlallah's prohibition with an outburst of frenzy, a telling indication of the difficulties any effort at rapprochement may face at the popular affective religious level.[80]

From summer 1984 on, there have been some signs of improvement in Tripoli, in the relations between Shaᶜban's besieged movement and the Iranian regime. This may perhaps be related to the souring of the Iranian-Syrian alliance. The Tawhid (Unification) movement, which as its name denotes had always been ecumenically oriented, could now give full vent to its ecumenistic preference. It collaborated openly with Mussawi's al-Amal al-Islami movement, declaring that Sunnis and Shiᶜites, neither of whom constitutes a majority in Lebanon, should unite in order to guarantee the Islamic character of the state.[81]

All these are small and fragile attempts. Although efforts in the same direction can be dimly perceived elsewhere (in Algeria, Morocco, Egypt, Saudi Arabia, and Gaza),[82] they remain even more isolated. Thus, the great Sunni-Shiᶜite divide still holds sway over Islamic radicalism. It looks as if the Shiᶜite and Sunni radical movements will each have to pursue its own revolutionary path.

Chapter Three

The Jewish Religion and
Contemporary Israeli Nationalism

Charles S. Liebman

Observers of Israeli society are impressed by the growing attraction of ultra-nationalist policies for a significant segment of the population; a great deal of attention has been devoted to it among the religious segment of the population. Rabbi Abraham Isaac Kook (1865–1935), and especially his son Rav Zvi Yehudah Kook (1865–1935), have been identified as the major ideologues and spiritual heroes of ultra-nationalism. Gush Emunim, a predominantly religious movement, has been identified as the major extraparliamentary force espousing ultra-nationalist policies. But the ultra-nationalism of Gush Emunim and the disciples of Rav Zvi Yehudah pales in comparison to that of Rabbi Meir Kahane, whose party, Kach, finally succeeded in winning a Knesset seat in Israel's 1984 elections. Many Gush Emunim leaders condemn Kahane. But, what is relevant for our purposes is that, like Gush Emunim, Kach also describes itself as a religious party.

This chapter is an effort to explore the importance of religion as a component of Israeli ultra-nationalism in both religious and nonreligious circles. After all, the fact that some or even most Israelis who define themselves as religious espouse ultra-nationalist policies does not necessarily mean that religious belief is the necessary and sufficient condition to account for their ultra-nationalism. And, the fact that some, even many Israelis who do not define themselves as religious also espouse ultra-nationalist policies does not necessarily preclude the possibility that they are influenced by religious formulations.

Because I am convinced that the exploration of the relationship between religion and Israeli ultra-nationalism requires more knowledge than we have at the present, I want to dispel any illusions that I can measure the role of religion with any degree of precision. My purpose is to offer a research agenda that I hope others will examine, for I also believe that such research will illuminate Israel's culture and political system.

There are three foci of Israeli ultra-nationalism: territorial, ethnic, and cultural. As cultural ultra-nationalism does not command broad allegiance in Israeli society, it will not concern me here. The Territorial ultra-nationalism refers to the continued decline in the number of Israelis who are willing to surrender most of the as-yet unannexed territory captured in the Six Day War, even in return for a peace agreement with Jordan and security arrangments acceptable to Israel. According to public opinion polls conducted by Mina Zemach of the Dahaf Research Institute among random samples of Israeli Jews, the percentage of the population expressing such a willingness declined from 40 percent in March 1983 to 31.4 percent in June 1984.[1] The more religiously traditional the respondent, the less likely he or she was to favor the return of territory.

Ethnic ultra-nationalism refers to policies that would discriminate against Arabs in Israel or to attitudes reflecting prejudice and antagonism toward them. In the June 1984 Dahaf sample, 66 percent of the respondents reported they either justified or related with understanding to the group of Jews accused of conducting terrorist activities, including murder, against Arabs. Once again, the more religious the respondent, the more likely he or she was to justify or relate with understanding to the accused terrorists. A random sample of Jewish youth aged 15 to 18 were questioned in August 1984. Over half (55.1 percent) felt that Arabs in Israel should not be permitted to criticize the government, and almost half (47.6 percent) felt that Arabs should be prohibited from holding important public office. Again, the more religious the respondent, the more likely he or she was to favor denying rights to Arabs. How are we to account for this?

One possible answer is that the Israeli public is in the process of becoming increasingly religious and therefore is adopting the political or ultra-nationalistic posture of religious Jewry prior to adopting the observance of specific religious practices. This answer has the virtue of simplicity; unfortunately, it is wrong. Israeli Jews are not becoming more religious.

One way of measuring religion is to ask respondents how they define themselves. Approximately 15 percent of the Jewish population of Israel define themselves as religious (as distinct from traditional or secular), a proportion that has remained fairly constant for the last fifteen years. Another measure of the population's religiosity is to ask whether respondents observe the Jewish tradition. Based on a random sample conducted in July 1984, 28 percent of Israel's adult Jewish population reported that they observe the Jewish tradition in its entirety or to a large extent.This figure is not very different from that reported ten or fifteen years ago in somewhat comparable surveys. But surveys may be inadequate instruments to ascertain the proportion of religious Jews or the real distribution of attitudes about religion within the population.

A measure of shifts in the proportion of religiously observant Jews in the population is a shift in the proportion of school-age Jewish children in religious schools; and that proportion has declined in the last fifteen years. It even continued to decline between 1977 and 1984, when a representative of the National Religious Party served as Minister of Education and religious schools benefited from particularly favorable conditions. For example, the percentage of children in religious schools in grades 1 to 6 fell from 27.6 in 1977 to 25.0 in 1983. Although this drop may reflect changes in fertility rates among Oriental Jews, who provide most of the religious elementary school population, they certainly fail to support the thesis of increasing religiosity among Israelis.

A second difficulty in any simple identification of religion and ultra-nationalism is that it does not explain why the religious nationalist public should have suddenly become so extreme. Until 1967, "activist" elements within the Labor Party, not to mention within Herut, the dominant partner within the Likud, advocated a more aggressive nationalist policy than did the National Religious Party, the party of the religious Zionists. If religious commitment accounts for Israeli ultra-nationalism, then religious Jews always should have been the most nationalistic segment of the population.

Third, the ultra-pious, or *haredi* sector, those Jews who are presumably most religious or more committed to religious observance, apparently are less ultra-nationalist than the more modern, better secularly educated, less devout religious Zionists. Although survey research data has not tapped opinions within the *haredi* community, we can assume that the positions adopted by their representatives, in the Knesset, and in the Agudat Israel and (since 1984) Shas parties, roughly reflect the opinions of their constituents. The Knesset representatives of these two parties are more reserved on issues of territorial nationalism than the representatives of religious Zionism. Furthermore, the most religiously extreme or pietistic Jews within the *haredi* sector do not even participate in Israeli elections. They are probably indifferent to nationalist issues. Hence, the conclusion that ultra-nationalism is related to religion requires some modification.

An alternative view is that the correlation between religiosity and ultra-nationalism is spurious. According to opinion polls, Jews of Oriental (Asian or African) origin and young people also favor ultra-nationalistic policies. When ethnic and age-group status are combined, they result in especially extreme attitudes. For example, the *Jerusalem Post* (January 25, 1985) reported that, at a high school composed almost exclusively of Oriental Jews, 23 percent of the students said they supported Meir Kahane's party, Kach, and 39 percent said they agreed with Kach's views (which include expelling all Arabs), although they had reservations about its methods. It is possible, therefore, that religion does not account for ultra-nationalism or perhaps one set of factors accounts for ultra-nationalism among religious Zionists and another set of factors for ultra-nationalism among nonreligious segments of the population. But, aside from a researcher's affinity for a single set of explanatory factors, we do have to contend with the differences in attitude between Israelis who define themselves as traditionalists and those who define themselves as secularists, or between those who report that they observe some religious traditions and those who report that they observe none or almost none of them. A greater proportion of Israelis who define themselves as traditionalists espouse ultra-nationalist policies than do Israelis who define themselves as secularists, and more ultra-natonalists are found among those who observe some of the religious tradition than among those who observe none. This seems to suggest that religion does have something to do with ultra-nationalism.

To summarize (1) ultra-nationalism among Israeli Jews is related to religious commitment, at least up to a point, although very religious (*haredi*) Jews may be less extreme in their nationalist views than religious Zionists; (2) religious Jews are not always ultra-nationalists, nor were they the most nationalist segment in the population prior to 1967; (3) other population groups who favor ultra-nationalist policies are Oriental Jews and young people. Ideally, any exploration of the relationship between religion and ultra-nationalism ought to account for all these observations. I shall begin by trying to understand what distinguishes *haredi* Jews from religious Zionists.

We know a great deal about the differences between the religious Zionist (nationalist) and *haredi* movements and communities. The historical differences stem from the late-nineteenth and early-twentieth centuries, when religious Ashkenazic Jewry (Jews of European origin) was divided between those who favored and those who opposed modern Zionism. Of the two distinguishing characteristics most relevant for our purposes, the one connected to the significance of the present and this-worldly activity has received the least attention, the other being the attitude toward the State of Israel and Israeli society.

Aryeh Fishman has pointed out that religious Zionists not only affirm the modern world but, more significantly, view the present (i.e., the modern world) as a distant stage in the fulfillment of the divine promise of messianic redemption. The present, therefore, has special meaning in Jewish, indeed, in world history;[2] it is not simply a seamless web of continuity with the past. The conception confers special meaning on the social, political, and economic activity that bore no special significance in the past. Such this-worldly activity is more than an instrument in defense of group interests. Jewish groups have always legitimated it in defense of their interests, but religious Zionists view such activity as one of the mechanisms through which redemption can be attained. In the past, religious Zionist settlers emphasized physical labor, which redeemed the individual; social justice, which redeemed society; and the creation of a Jewish state and "ingathering of the exiles," which created the only basis for an authentic Jewish religious life. Emphases changed over time, so that the importance of physical labor and social justice declined in importance, and settlement of the land in Judea and Samaria (the West Bank) became a major value. But the principle that this-worldly activity was endowed with intrinsic religious meaning has remained constant.

Contrary to religious Zionists, the *haredi* community believes that Torah study alone is endowed with intrinsic religious meaning. Although I do not believe that religious nationalist and *haredi* Jews differ on the ideal of Jewish sovereignty over the entire Land of Israel, including the state of Jordan as well as the West Bank, I suspect that the *haredi* community is even less happy than is the religious nationalist community in according political rights to non-Jews.[3] However, their own religious conceptions render them suspicious of efforts to realize these values. Further, they suspect the religious integrity of religious Zionists and those who devote themselves to this-worldly activity rather than study of sacred text. The Haredim adopt an instrumental and pragmatic attitude toward politics, which is conditioned by a tradition of caution and suspicion precisely because for them politics has no intrinsic meaning and because past and present are the same.

The second and related difference between religious Zionist and *haredi* Jews lies in their conception of the State of Israel. Attitudes range from hostility to enthusiastic support among Haredim. But, unlike religious Zionists, they refuse to attribute special sanctity to the state. Hence Israeli sovereignty over the West Bank, or the rights of Arabs in Israel, do not have quite the same meaning for the two groups. These differences help us to understand why *haredi* attitudes are less extreme on issues of territorial and ethnic nationalism, but they do not explain the shift in attitude exhibited among religious Zionists since 1967. To explain this phenomenon it is necessary but not sufficient to note the emergence of new theological formulations within religious Zionist circles.

Jewish ethnocentrism and Jewish claims to sovereignty over the Land of Israel are deeply rooted in the religious tradition. Efforts have been made, however, and with justice, to trace the emphasis on these values in recent years to doctrines formulated by Rabbi Abraham Isaac Kook and applied by his son Rav Zvi Yehudah Kook. In one of his memorable lectures, delivered on the eve of Israel Independence Day in 1967 and published under the title "The Sanctity of the Holy People in the Holy Land,"[4] Rav Zvi Yehudah noted that when the U.N. agreed to the establishment of the state, he did not share the great joy that swept the country because he could not resign himself to the "evil tiding" that the Land of Israel had been divided. "Where is our Hebron? And where is our Shechem? And our Jericho where is it? Will we forget it? And all of the other side of Jordan—it is ours, every clump of dirt . . . which belongs to the land of God—is it our right to concede even one millimeter of it?"[5] He finally consoled himself, he continued, with the thought that this was God's wish.

The establishment of the state, therefore, is not in the first instance an occasion of joy. The state is not an end but an instrument whose purpose, Rav Kook suggests in the same essay, is the conquest of the land. This, in turn, sanctifies the state, the army—and even its armaments. At a later point, however, Rav Kook returns to the significance of the state, suggesting that even the rule of Jews over part of the land, coupled with the end of the exile, represents the fulfillment of an important commandment.

The Jews and the Land of Israel both possess spiritual sanctity. And, according to Rav Kook, sanctity does not derive from what a human being does or does not do. It is a physical quality, created by God, that inheres in both the Jewish people and the Land of Israel because that is the will of God.[6]

> God has determined, once and forever, that we are a holy people, a reality of holy souls, holy bodies, part of the souls of the entirety of Israel which is entirely holy. There is a reality of a holy land,

a strip of land which God chose — "because God chose Zion." This is a land "whose fruit is holy" and the working of the land is equivalent to the command of putting on phylacteries. . . . Thus have things been determined: This is a holy land and this is a holy people.[7]

Rav Kook goes on to cite texts to demonstrate that even though the State of Israel is not perfect it is the state envisioned by the prophets. Israel's two most serious shortcomings are its system of law, which is not authentically Jewish but based on foreign codes, and its reluctance to prohibit missionary activity.

The ambiguity about the state, which is sanctified yet imperfect, was particularly troubling to many religious Zionists following the revelation of a Jewish terrorist underground in April 1984. There is no ambiguity, however, about the sanctity of the land or the sanctity of the people. The first provides the basis for territorial ultra-nationalism and the second for ethnic ultra-nationalism. In the relatively moderate formulation of the present leader of Gush Emunim, the two aspects of nationalism are expressed in the statement that the *"shlemut* [perfection, wholeness, totality] of the Jewish people cannot be secured without the *shlemut* of the Land of Israel."[8] In its more extreme formulation, territorial nationalism strives to turn "the Land of Israel into the sole content of Judaism and Judaism into the sole content of the Land of Israel."[9] The more extreme formulation of ethnic nationalism not only denies that Arabs have any group rights in the land of Israel but also stresses the religious obligation of Jews to expel them:

> Doesn't granting of "autonomy" . . . to the Arabs of Judea and Samaria contravene a Torah commandment? Is the prohibition "they shall not dwell in your land" no longer a prohibition? Is the Gentile suddenly permitted to reside in Jerusalem? And has the ban already been lifted on Gentiles entering a place whereof it is said: "And the stranger who approaches shall be put to death"? And is control of the Temple Mount no longer a duty and an imperative?[10]

Noting the emergence of extremist formulations, however, does not explain their warm reception in religious Zionist circles, particularly when such views are not unchallenged within these circles. It has been pointed out that the dramatic victory in the Six Day War, which resulted in sovereignty over the Old City of Jerusalem and the West Bank virtually being imposed upon Israel, seemed to promise a new political era confirming messianic expectations. There also was a new generation of *yeshivah* high school graduates who were influenced by Rav Kook's doctrines and in rebellion against the older generation of religious Zionist leaders.[11] To these, I would like to add a third factor that, to the best of my knowledge, has not received attention, although Menachem Friedman alluded to it.[12] I refer to the religious Zionists' frustration with their mode of participation in Israeli society.

Eliezer Don-Yehiya has described the nature of religious Jewry's participation in Israeli society in the first decades of statehood as a form of segmented pluralism.[13] In those days, religious and nonreligious Jews lived out their lives in separate spheres. One's identity as a religious Jew determined one's school, one's friends, and one's cultural and leisure time pursuits. But from the 1920s until 1977, Israeli society was dominated by a secular labor Zionist elite, and religious Jews were conscious of their status as outsiders. However, they were represented in decision-making forums, on occasion even overrepresented. But they sat in such forums because the nature of the political arrangements in Israeli society dictated their presence, not because Israel's real leaders or Israeli insiders had any regard for their opinions.

The relative status of religious Jews can be gauged from Ben-Gurion's 1949 invitation to Israeli cultural and intellectual leaders, in which he asked these leaders to meet with him to plan "the shape of the spiritual image of the nation."[14] Since the meetings were informal, Ben-Gurion saw no need to invite any religious intellectuals. For, although it was evident to those present that religious tradition was an important component in "shaping the spiritual image of the nation," it was also clear that religious Jews would have nothing to contribute to such a discussion. The interchange between government leaders and the nation's cultural elite was formalized in 1952, through the creation of a Supreme Council on Culture under the direction of the minister of education and culture. But, here, too, although religious Jews were invited to participate in the council and in the deliberations of its subcommissions, as Dvora Hacohen, who reviewed the minutes of these meetings observed in private conversation, the religious representatives sat on the council and its various subcommissions by virtue of their governmental or nongovernmental positions. Unlike many other members, they were not invited because of the high regard or esteem in which they were held. And when they spoke, little notice was taken of what they said.

This condition was and still is quite tolerable to Haredim but a source of frustration to religious Zionists — the young in particular —

for two reasons. First, the latter admired and were even envious of the Zionist labor movement pioneers. They would have liked to share more fully, albeit on special terms, in their achievements, for they wanted to be integrated into the society and feel part of the establishment, not be allocated token representation and consigned to the status of outsiders. Second, precisely because they attributed a special sanctity to the State of Israel and even to Israeli Jewish society, it seemed quite inappropriate to them that secularists should dominate the society. Their frustration helps account for both an element of hostility to Israeli society and the readiness to seize upon issues on which religious Zionists could demonstrate their leadership.

Those for whom hostility was the dominant motif joined the ranks of the *haredi* community, and those in whom the desire to participate and lead was dominant had an elective affinity for ultra-nationalist pronouncements phrased in religious terminology. This affinity reflects both an identification with the normal values of Israeli society and a critique of Israeli society for inadequate commitment to the very values it ostensibly affirms. It constitutes, therefore, a claim to national leadership based upon their greater loyalty to these values.

Yoel Bin-Nun, a founder of Gush Emunim and now a moderate voice among the West Bank settlers, tells how he felt growing up in the 1950s under "the oligarchic and aristocratic rule" of the Labour party (then called *Mapai*).[15] "I absorbed a sizable portion of antireligious hatred in my youth," he writes. But by the 1970s, Bin-Nun believed, he and his religious peers had risen from the status of a humiliated and outcast minority to a central position in the nation, "exactly as it later happened to the youth from North African and Oriental origins when the Likud came to power." He thought "that the idea of the Land of Israel would unite everybody . . . and also permit a better understanding of the Torah of Israel." He believed, mistakenly, he confesses, that Gush Emunim's success in its political and settlement activity provided a historical victory. Using the metaphor of a train to describe Israeli society, Bin-Nun says that the senior religious politicians fought to control "the dining car" and the "ticket sales" on the train, but that his generation, contemptuous of that variety of religious politics, pushed forward to the "engine."

I suggest that religious ultra-nationalism speaks to an ambivalence that religious Zionists feel toward the Israeli state and society, an ambivalence reflected in the speech of Rav Zvi Yehudah Kook, discussed earlier. It is not an ambivalence based on lukewarm sentiments but rather a simultaneous affirmation of two strongly held beliefs and sentiments: (1) that Israel is an expression of divine favor and the promise of messianic redemption, a belief that leads to the celebration of both state and society as holy objects, but also (2) the sense that both state and society are unfaithful to their mandate and must be transformed before they can command total allegiance.

This analysis fails to explain why values of ethnocentrism and territorialism have been emphasized instead, for example, of values of social justice, redistribution of income, or equality for Oriental and Ashkenazic Jews. These values, to which Israeli society is ostensibly committed, are also embedded in both Jewish and Zionist traditions; as such, they might have also served as the platform from which religious Zionists might criticize Israeli society.

I am not suggesting that anyone deliberately chose ultranationalist values rather than values of welfare or social justice. That would oversimplify a process in which religious beliefs, psychological predispositions, economic interests, and political pragmatism combine to yield policy preferences. But, given the presence of social welfare—social justice values in the religious tradition, and the enormous weight given to them by early religious Zionist settlers, I wonder why they generally awaken only muted echoes among the young generation of religious Zionists who seek national leadership? Albert Hourani's observation with respect to Islam is no less true of Judaism: "Islam does not provide the exclusive language of politics. To be effective, it needs to be combined with two other languages: that of nationalism, with its appeal to the unity, strength and honour of the nation, however defined, and that of social justice, and specifically an equitable distribution of wealth."[16] Unless religious-nationalists can produce "a convincing blend" of all three languages, not just of religion and nationalism, they are unlikely to mobilize enough support to make effective claims to power.

Although this question cannot be answered conclusively, speculation does suggest areas of research. Part of the answer may rest in the association between conceptions of social welfare and social justice and notions of religious adaptionism or religious reformism in the minds of earlier religious Zionists. Tending to be conciliatory rather than rigorous in its halakhic (legalistic) orientations, this older generation accommodated rather than rejected the modern world. This is not entirely the case with the next generation, who having rejected the older generation's religious ideology may be reluctant to affirm its social ideology. Further, stressing social justice values would align religious Zionists with the extreme left, the most antireligious segment of the population; whereas espousing ultra-nationalist values aligns them with the political right, which was far more sympathetic to the religious tradition and hierarchy and to the incorporation of religion in the public sphere.

Let us turn now to the two other groups among whom ultra-nationalist attitudes are most common, Oriental Jews (those who came or whose parents came from Asian or African countries) and the young, to see what influence, if any, religion plays in their policy preferences. There is no question about the ultra-nationalism of Oriental Jews. Shamir and Arian[17] conclude that the single most important reason for their overwhelming support of parties on the right is their hawkish (i.e., ultra-nationalist) attitudes. The reasons behind this orientation, which have been summarized by Peres and Shemer,[18] include the suffering Oriental Jews underwent in Arab countries and their desire to distinguish themselves from Israeli Arabs. On this basis, one might argue that traditional Jews are more ultra-nationalistic than secular Jews because the category of traditional Jews is composed primarily of Orientals; in other words, the quality of being an Oriental (an ethnic characteristic) rather than the quality of being traditional or moderately religious accounts for the ultra-Nationalism of Oriental Jews.

If this were true, however, we would expect Oriental Jews born abroad to be more ultra-nationalist than their children born in Israel. After all, the fathers should be more ethnically Oriental, have experienced Arab hostility more directly, and are less distinguishable in speech and style of life from Israeli Arabs. But, as Arian and Shamir show in an unpublished study, Israeli-born children of Oriental fathers are more ethnically nationalistic and almost as territorially nationalist as foreign-born Oriental Jews.

An alternate argument might be that Oriental Jews are ultra-nationalist because they are traditionalists; in other words, that the distinguishing feature is the degree of religiosity rather than of ethnicity. If this argument is correct, Oriental Jews who also are secular should be no more ultra-nationalist than secular Ashkenazim. According to this argument, Oriental Jews appear to be more ultra-nationlist than non-Orientals only because most of them are traditionalists and most non-Oriental Jews secularists. This argument is supported by an examination of attitudes toward returning unannexed territories, in which it turned out that secular Oriental Jews in fact are more dovish than secular Ashkenazim.[19]

There is no doubt that religion is an important factor accounting for the ultra-nationalism of Oriental Jews, but its pattern of influence should not be oversimplified. I believe that what we observe is the impact of a culture that, in turn, reflects many religious formulations. In other words, ethnocentrism, hostility to Arabs, and rejection of territorial compromise feed directly off both Oriental and Israeli conceptions of Jew and Arab, off beliefs about the enmity of "goyim" and permanent threats to Jewish survival. Although these beliefs and conceptions are then nourished by religious formulations,[20] they are only indirectly attributable to them. Once they penetrate the political culture, however, their influence may extend far beyond the circle of those who define themselves as religious, in particular to Israeli youth. I suspect that secular Oriental Jews are influenced least by these beliefs and conceptions because, almost by definition, they reject a good part of their culture in their rebellion against the old ways.

It should be stressed that the ultra-nationalism of Oriental Jews is not entirely due to the Oriental-Jewish aspect of culture; Israeli culture also has a unique impact on most of them. My argument is that, like religious Zionists, Oriental Jews also have mixed feelings about Israeli society and respond accordingly. The political awakening of Oriental Jews in the last two decades has been characterized by the conviction that they are victims of Ashkenazi prejudice and discrimination. Like religious Zionists, they, too, were offered token representation. And they, too, resented this tokenism, not only because they were consistently underrepresented but also because, by definition, tokenism implies less than complete integration and acceptance.

The bitterness and frustration of a few Oriental Jews has found some expression in their support for the ethnic lists that have contested every Knesset election. But the vast majority of Oriental Jews have never voted for these lists. As Herzog points out, they have rejected appeals to separatist ethnic interests, seeking instead to affirm the collective values of Israeli society.[21] I feel that they have over-identified with and misinterpreted these values, in part because their subordinate and outsider status kept them from participating in their formulation and in part because they did not understand some of the hidden assumptions that rested behind their articulation. In addition, as is true of religious Zionists, affirming Israeli nationalism in an extremist formulation is the most legitimate way of criticizing the political elite and claiming acceptance, if not leadership, by virtue of greater loyalty to the nominal values of the society.

An elaboration of what I mean by the nominal values of Israeli society requires a brief description of Israel's civil religion. Civil religion is a system of symbols (a set of myths, ceremonials, sacred places) and values that legitimates the social order, integrates the population, and mobilizes its energies toward collective goals. Since the 1950s, and particularly after 1967, Israeli civil religion has pointed to the centrality of the Jewish people and the Jewish tradition. Thus, religious symbols increasingly have penetrated the political culture, in which the State of Israel is seen as representing the Jewish people and its tradition. The Holocaust, the central myth of Israeli society, conveys the message that without a state Jews are victims of non-Jews, who are perpetually hostile to them. The tradition, in turn, legitimates Jewish rights to the Land of Israel, the only territory upon which a Jewish state can be built and the only land where Jews can realize their national destiny and assure their security. As such, the civil religion has divorced conceptions of the Jewish people and the Holy Land, the foundation stones of ethnic and territorial nationalism, from their religious-metaphysical context. And, as Don-Yehiya and I have sought to demonstrate, the Jewish tradition itself has thereby been transformed and transvalued.[22] But, as the civil religion draws upon many religious constructs and legitimates its claims to Jewish authenticity by pointing to the religious tradition, the image of religion is a very positive one. Hence, it is not surprising that the closer one feels toward the religious tradition, the greater is the resonance evoked by the civil religion; but the more antagonistic one feels toward the religious tradition, the more alienated one is from the civil religion and the less likely one is to internalize ultra-nationalist attitudes. On the other hand, although religious Zionists undertook their own transformation and transvaluation of the tradition — Rav Zvi Yehudah Kook is a prime example — and arrived at their ultra-nationalist conceptions independent of the civil religion, they utilized the civil religion to suit their own purposes.

At the heart of these conceptions, whether of the religious Zionists or of the civil religion, lie the seeds of an ethnocentric and chauvinist view of Judaism and the Jewish people. Neither the founders of Israel nor the early religious Zionists shared this view. But Israeli leaders inculcated this view through the mass media, school curricula, army educational programs, and elitist rhetoric. The reasons why Israel's cultural and political elite pay lip service to conceptions and beliefs that are really not their own deserves separate treatment, and I will attempt only a brief answer here. A partial answer stems from fears that first arose in the 1950s, that the alternative would be a loss of Jewish identity, an absence of national consensus, a weakening of collectivist values among the population, and a consequent weakening of resistance to perceived Arab threats. The rest of the answer, as I already suggested, lies in the misunderstanding and misinterpretation of elitist values by population groups such as the Oriental Jews and the young.

Israeli youth are among the most extreme in their espousal of territorial and ethnic nationalism. This is true not only of 15–18 year olds, but of younger voters as well. Now, the young are predominantly secular, with the majority of young people not even defining themselves as traditional, much less religious. What possible connection, then, can exist between their ultra-nationalism and religion? Although I do not argue for a direct causal relationship, I find it highly significant that, despite their secular beliefs and behavior, Israeli youth have a very positive image of religion.

In a random sample of 15–18 year olds, only 12.3 percent of the respondents defined themselves as religious, whereas 27.3 percent defined themselves as traditional and 59.5 percent as secular. Many Israelis believe that there has been a significant shift to religion among young Israelis in the last few years, but there is no evidence to support this assumption. Whereas 23.9 percent reported that they became "closer to the tradition or the Jewish religion in the last few years," 55.5 percent said no change had occurred, and 19.6 percent said they had become more distant from religion.

One of the major issues in relations between religion and state in 1984 was the opening of movie theaters on the Sabbath. The vast majority of 15–18 year olds (71.3 percent) favored their operation; 26.8 percent opposed it. In other words, the overwhelming majority of the respondents appeared to be secular rather than religious in their behavior and attitudes. But, when these same respondents were asked about their attitudes toward a variety of types of behavior, the percentage reporting favorable attitudes was as follows: "joining sectarian groups such as Hare Krishna, etc.": 11.0 percent; "taking drugs": 2.7 percent; "sex among nonmarried couples": 50.9 percent; "consuming alcoholic beverages": 17.8 percent; and, finally, "returning to religion": 61.5 percent. Among the youth who defined themselves as traditional 75.8 percent held favorable attitudes toward the return to religion, and among those who defined themselves as secular, the figure was 47.8 percent. This phenomenon of a return to religion, which compares to the phenomenon of becoming a born-again Christian in the United States, received a great deal of publicity during 1984, when the Israeli media pointed out that "born-again Jews" are isolated from their old friends and very often from their families as well, that they do not serve in the army and sometimes adopt neutral and even hostile attitudes towards the State of Israel. But such is the status of religion in Israeli society that the return to religion was still viewed with favor. Perhaps Israeli youth have not been influenced by religious-nationalist conceptions. But it does seem reasonable to suggest that if they have been successfully socialized to a value that contradicts their own style of life and belief, they will readily adopt what they perceive as the regnant nationalist values of the civil religion.

Basing himself on historical data, Shapiro[23] has demonstrated the remarkable acquiescence of the younger generation of Israelis to the political values of their elders. There are few societies where young people in general and second- and third-generation political activists in particular have waited as patiently and obediently for their seniors to vacate the center of political power. This acquiescence, obedience, and deference stem from the successful socialization of the young to the nominal political values of their elders. Whereas ethnocentrism and territorial nationalism have always been components of the elitist value system, they only began receiving special emphasis after 1967.

Describing the process of political socialization in the period of modern Jewish settlement, Shapiro makes an observation that is no less true today: ideology and political values may be formulated by people whose own commitment to them is ambivalent. He points out, for example, that modern Zionism was formulated by an intellectual stratum "that arrived at a consciousness that they belonged to a separate nation and a different civilization but couldn't sever their ties to the European civilization they so admired."[24] Most of these intellectuals never even came to Palestine, though they devoted a good part of their intellectual efforts to emphasizing the necessity of Jewish settlement in the Land of Israel for the future of the Jewish people. This does not mean they were hypocrites or liars. The public articulation of one's values does not reflect the internal conflict, the reservations, and the doubts that may precede its formulation. Furthermore, the emphasis and stress given to some values may be an effort to compensate for private doubts and reservations. But only those who are part of the ethnic, social, generational or ideological group that articulates these values would know this. Finally, to use an example from the 1930s and 1940s, when the Israeli political elite articulated a set of public values (e.g., the necessity to create a new Jew freed from the bonds of the passive tradition), they took for granted other values or sentiments (e.g., a warm nostalgic feeling toward religious ceremony and a feeling of responsibility toward all Jews). They never considered the likelihood that a new generation would internalize the articulated values rather than the unstated assumptions, thereby misinterpreting the value system of their elders.

This helps explain both the Jewish indifference of Israeli youth in the 1930s and 1940s, as well as the reversal of these feelings, and also the ethnocentrism and chauvinism of today. Ever since the 1950s, and with growing intensity since 1967, Israeli youth has heard—at home, in school, and in the army—the message that the whole world is against us, that our enemies will destroy us if we are not strong, that the world owes us a moral debt, that no one has a moral right to criticize Israel, that the Land of Israel belongs to the Jewish people, that racism is a crime against Jews; not a crime Jews are capable of inflicting upon others. World indifference during the Holocaust is something that Jews experienced, not a lesson to Jews about the immorality of indifference. The political and cultural elite who created these formulas as early as the 1950s also believed in a universalistic ethic, in the necessity for Israel to live among the family of nations, in justice and mercy as equally important values, and in the possibility of peace in the Middle East; but these values, too, were assumed rather than articulated. No less important, Israeli leaders preached Jewish indifference to world opinion although they behaved otherwise. The fact that those who created the ethnic and territorial conceptions of the civil religion may have done so with some ambivalence, or that these conceptions were formulated in extreme terms to counter an atmosphere of indifference to Judaism by Diaspora Jewry, is not understood. Nor has the fact ever been conveyed that the Israeli construction of the meaning of the Holocaust may have been formulated in response to guilt feelings.

This argument can be reformulated in simpler terms. Zionists have always spoken about a Jewish state. Israel represents itself both at home and abroad as a Jewish state. There is probably no notion that generates greater support in Israeli society than the one that Israel is and must remain a Jewish state. But what does a Jewish state mean? The simplest and most obvious interpretation is a society ruled by Jews, on behalf of Jews, in Eretz Israel, which the Jews believe is their land. By definition, non-Jews are a tolerated minority with only those rights the Jews see fit to confer upon them. Of course, this is not the way Israel's founders envisioned their state. Their baggage of values included assumptions about civil equality, the kinship of all peoples, and a host of liberal-humanist-universalist commitments. What they failed to do—perhaps because they thought it unnecessary, perhaps because they found it impossible—was to elaborate their liberal-humanist-universalist values and explain how they were reconcilable with a Jewish state. As the Jewish content of the civil religion resonated in louder terms after 1967, these liberal-humanist-universalist values have receded among the young.

Added to this are the propensity of young people for unambiguous resolutions and a willingness to adopt extreme solutions, both of which lead to an ethnic and territorial ultra-nationalism that youth view as entirely consistent with the notion of a Jewish state. The survey of 15-18-year-old Israeli youth demonstrates that the most nationalistic of them are neither rebellious nor view themselves as part of a counterculture; they are the ones who report their willingness to serve their country, the ones least likely to report a willingness to leave the country.

Misunderstanding and selective absorption may also have been at work among religious Zionists, for the Jewish tradition as understood through the formulations of Rabbi Abraham Isaac Kook and his son Rav Zvi Yehudah seems to provide proof for ultra-nationalist formulations, and notions of the inherent sanctity of Jews provide a basis for racist doctrines. And the attribution of sanctity to a land, together with the suggestion of a mystical tie between a particular group of people and a particular land, provides a foundation for the grossest form of chauvinism. Yet, Rabbi Abraham Isaac Kook believed that, "the fear of God must never overwhelm the natural morality of man," and that love of all people and all nations, "from the depths of one's heart and soul," prepares the spirit of the Messiah to descend upon Israel.[25] And Rabbi Abraham Isaac's son wrote a letter of protest to a school principal when he saw students bullying Arabs.[26] I prefer to believe that neither the father nor the son foresaw the interpretation many of their admirers would later give to their message.

To summarize, although religion certainly plays an important role in accounting for Israeli ultra-nationalism, by itself, it is not enough to explain the phenomenon. That a moderate nationalist interpretation of Judaism is possible has been shown by the existence of such dovish religious groups as Oz veShalom and Netivot Shalom. Furthermore, even when religious conceptions and values appear to support ultra-nationalist orientations, they can be moderated by pragmatic considerations or values of compassion and natural morality.

I explain the affinity that religious Zionists and Oriental Jews have for ultra-nationalist policies as in line with their desire to legitimate themselves, enhance their integration into Israeli society, and even claim leadership by over-identifying with the nominal values of the civil religion. I argue, as well, that these values were not the real or exclusive values of the political and cultural elite who generated them. Not only were the implicit values of the elite misunderstood but, and related to this, they were formulated with a particular set of assumptions in mind and to meet a specific set of conditions. The problem arose when the same values continued to be applied when the original assumptions and conditions no longer held. This second factor also helps account for the ultra-nationalism of Israeli youth, whose attitudes are presumably unrelated to religious convictions, but are best understood by the impact of socialization processes in a culture that bears the influence of religious conceptions.

Chapter Four

The Radical Shi^{c}ite Opposition Movements in Iraq

Amatzia Baram

This chapter attempts to analyze the political ideology of the main radical Iraqi Shi^{c}ite opposition organizations since the late 1970s, in particular the most veteran and important among them, the Islamic Da^{c}wa party. While their own pamphlets, newsletters and magazines served as the primary sources, where there is clear and unequivocal evidence of convergence of opinions between the movements and their mentor, these sources are supplemented by essays written by Ayatollah Muhammad Baqir al-Sadr, who is recognized by all organizations as the main inspiration in their formative years.[1]

To place the political thought of the radical Shi^{c}ite organizations of Iraq in a wider context, it is compared here with that of the most important radical Sunni movement in the Arab world, the Muslim Brethren. The Syrian Brethren in particular were chosen for the intrinsic similarity between the two groups: both oppose the secular regimes in their countries, both represent a majority sect ruled by a minority sect and both have been operating in a society where Sunni-Shi^{c}ite and Sunni-^{c}Alawite strife are dominant features in political life.

The following pages demonstrate that, although these movements reject any political claims based on Arabism, and see Islam as the first and main basis for their political identification, they steer clear of committing themselves to any amalgamative pan-Islam, instead claiming allegiance to an Iraqi entity. By claiming such an allegiance, however, the Shi^{c}i organizations are faced with the problem of the Shi^{c}ite-Sunni rift that splits Iraqi society down the middle. On the face of it, their solution to the problem is clearcut: the various movements have issued a call for Shi^{c}ite-Sunni cooperation based on a universalist-Islamic credo. A closer look at the movements involved, however, reveals deep contradictions between them that make such cooperation much harder to attain than it seems on the surface.

Throughout his intellectual career Baqir al-Sadr (1935–1980) oscillated between ecumenical Islamic universalism and barely disguised

95

Shi^cite particularist zeal. After the downfall of the Shah in Iran, this tension increased, as mentor and disciples alike were caught between their wish to follow Khomeini's triumphant example, which was distinctly Shi^cite in some of its major aspects, and their realization that, unlike the Iranian case, in Iraq Sunni support was essential to the success of an Islamic revolution.

This dilemma was resolved after al-Sadr's death at the hands of the Ba^cth regime, when the organizations tilted decisively towards the particularist-Shi^cite pole, thereby eliminating any chance to turn the Islamic movement into a truly all-Iraqi one and, consequently, reducing their chances of success substantially.

Shi^cite Opposition Organizations

The main Shi^cite opposition group in Iraq, Hizb al-Da^cwa al-Islamiyya, was established in Najf in 1959 by the sons and agents of the chief *mujtahid* of Najf, Grand Ayatollah Muhsin al-Hakim. According to their own account, this organization was a response to the rise of communism and atheism in Iraq under the republican rule of ^cAbd al-Karim Qasim (1958–1963). This account, which stresses the weak and defensive nature of their reaction, sounds credible because there is much evidence of a fast-growing communist influence during that period, including in the Shi^cite areas. There is also evidence, however, that the Shi^cite religious establishment did its best to combat communist influence in those years. In fact, much later, between the late 1970s and the late 1980s, when both movements were being severely persecuted by the Ba^cth regime, the Shi^cite opposition still flatly refused to coordinate its activities with the Iraqi Communist party, even though it was cooperating with other groups. Until the early 1970s the Da^cwa operated chiefly as a religious and educational movement, trying first to limit "atheistic" influences and then to turn the tide and regain control over the Shi^cite (or, as they put it, "Muslim") masses of Iraq. Since then the Da^cwa party has become more involved in political and military activity. As it was the most easily identifiable Shi^cite radical organization of any significance throughout the 1970s and early 1980s, official Iraqi sources name "the Da^cwa party and those who toe its line" whenever they wish to refer to Shi^cite radical opposition.

There are some indications that Ayatollah Hakim himself was connected with the party before he died in 1970, but, if this were the case, the connection was an indirect and tenuous one. Three young sons of al-Hakim's were, however, connected with al-Daᶜwa and probably led it until the late 1970s: Mahdi al-Hakim, who lived in London, retained his connection with the party until his assassination in the Sudan in 1987; Muhammad Baqir al-Hakim became the spokesman of an umbrella organization that includes al-Daᶜwa in the early 1980s; and the youngest of the three, ᶜAbd al-ᶜAziz al-Hakim, became one of the Mujahidun's leaders in 1980. Sheikh Muhammad Mahdi al-Asifi, who was also based in Najf (where he was born in 1938) is another leader of the party. The leading religious figure in al-Daᶜwa is Sheikh Muhammad Baqir al-Nasiri, who also originates from Najf.

Al-Daᶜwa has branches with a few hundred supporters in Britain. There it publishes several magazines, the most important of which is *The Daᶜwa Chronicle*; others are *Jamiᶜat al-Rafidayn* and *Sawt al-ᶜIraq*. The party also has a large number of members in Iran, who have been trained in camps, one of which is in a part of Iraqi Kurdistan that has been conquered by the Iranian army. Al-Daᶜwa has published two newspapers in Iran since 1980: *al-Jihad* and *al-Kashif*. Although its allegiance to Khomeini's Iran is paramount and clearcut, there is some evidence that the party has maintained an open dialogue with Damascus as well since 1982.

The Shiᶜite opposition in Iraq is also represented by al-Mujahidun, which was established in 1980 and whose first military operation was to blow up the Iraqi News Agency building in Baghdad in December 1981. Al-Mujahidun's leader, ᶜAbd al-ᶜAziz al-Hakim, and his chief aides, chief of operations Ahmad al-Haydari and ideologist Jalal al-Din al-Saghir, have close ties with Shiᶜite opposition movements in the Persian Gulf. The U.S. branch issues the magazine *al-Muqatilun*, which reproduces the movement's documents.

Another Shiᶜite opposition party, Munazzamat al-ᶜAmal al-Islami, was established in the mid-1960s by Ayatollah Hasan al-Shirazi, who came from Karbala, as did the rest of the party's initial cadre. Since al-Shirazi and his elder brother fled to Kuwait and Beirut (where they lived from 1969 or 1970 until 1980, when al-Shirazi was assassinated by Baᶜth agents there), this movement has drawn some of its membership from the Gulf and, to a lesser extent, from Lebanon. In both places, and especially in Kuwait, the Shirazi brothers and their nephews, the Mudarrisis (discussed later), have established several religious institutions and acquired a significant following. In fact, al-ᶜAmal al-Islami is the most multi-national of all Iraqi Shiᶜite movements, including Iranians, Afghans, North Africans, and Africans. Its leader, at least until 1987, was Muhammad Taqi al-Mudarrisi, who, like his uncles the Shirazis, was based in Karbala for many years (and probably was born there). Al-Mudarrisi and his brother Hadi fled to Kuwait in 1968 and since have been very active there; their activities also have spread to Bahrain. The chief spokesman and organizer of this group in the mid-1980s was al-Hajj Husayn Kamil. The group publishes the weekly *al-ᶜAmal al-Islami* and the biweekly *al-Shahid*. Harakat al-Jamahir al-Muslima fi al-ᶜIraq seems to be tied to Hasan al-Shirazi, and like the other opposition movements, its main base of operations is Iran. The group's main publication is the monthly *Tariq al-Thawra*; it also issues a similar publication, *Rahe enqelab*, in Persian.

Other, smaller, much more obscure groups, whose thought will not be discussed here include, for example, the Islamic Bloc (al-Tajammuᶜ) for the Liberation of Iraq, the Imam's Army (Jund al-Imam), the Islamic Front for the Liberation of Bahrain, under Hadi al-Mudarrisi, and others. The umbrella organization under which most groups operate is al-Majlis al-aᶜla lil-Thawra al-Islamiyya fi al-ᶜIraq (The Supreme Council of the Islamic Revolution in Iraq). It was formed in late 1982, and in 1986–1987 its chairman was Hujjat al-Islam Muhammad Baqir al-Hakim. Other central figures are Sheikh Mahmud al-Hashimi, spokesman and alternate chairman, who heads a small movement of his own, and Dr. Abu Ahmad al-Jaᶜfari, the Council's secretary. The Council has a military arm called the Iraqi Revolutionary Guard, which has fought alongside the Iranians on the Iraqi border several times since 1985. In November 1986 this guard reportedly numbered 10,000 soldiers, many of them ex-POWS. The Majlis also publishes a daily paper, *al-Shahada*. In December 1986, it convened a major congress that was attended not only by Shiᶜite activists but also by Kurds, chiefly members of the Kurdish Democratic Party (KDP) under Masᶜud al-Barazani, as well as a faction led by Jalal Talabani. Present for the first time were some members of the Damascus-based Iraqi secular pan-Arab opposition to Saddam Husayn. (Interestingly enough, al-Daᶜwa and al-ᶜAmal al-Islami kept very low profiles in that congress, probably due to political disagreements with al-Hakim). The Congress published a seventeen-point platform calling for the establishment of a coordinating military committee and increased military activities against the Baᶜth regime, which was published by the Iranian News Agency on December 28, 1986. Apparently, there were also some secret resolutions.

As our analysis of the political thought of the Shiᶜite opposition in Iraq is based, for the most part, on the wealth of sources originating from the Daᶜwa, our presentation may gloss over some of the differences between it and other opposition groups. This cannot be avoided until we are able to obtain more material from the latter.

Arabism and Islam

Islam did not exclude Arabism in the political thought of Hasan al-Banna and other intellectuals associated with the Muslim Brethren in Egypt in the 1930s and 1940s. On the contrary, many of these intellectuals viewed Arabism as the active core of Islam, and the Arab nation was seen as the vital inner circle within the Muslim nation that would activate the process of Islamic resurgence.[2] These same ideas had been propagated earlier by Salafiyya thinkers such as Rashid Rida and ᶜAbd al-Rahman al-Kawakibi.[3]

This synthesis between Arab and Islamic nationalism, however, is alien to the Daᶜwa, even insofar as the Shiᶜite community in Iraq is concerned. Al-Daᶜwa members feel compelled to disassociate completely from Arabism in their attempt to distance themselves from anything reminiscent of Baᶜth thought. The break in part is due also to the close ties between the Daᶜwa and Khomeini's Iran. For it may be assumed that any hint at Arab superiority or emphasis on the past role Arabs played in Islam — not to speak of their future leadership of the Muslim nation — would not have been well received in Tehran. But, most of all, the rejection (or more often, omission) of the Arab component seems to stem from the fact that some leaders of the Shiᶜite opposition are themselves of Iranian origin,[4] and that many members are Iraqis of Iranian stock who were exiled by the Baᶜth regime in 1979–1980.[5] This is why any attempt to assign the Arabs a special role in contemporary Islam, let alone to put forward Arabism as an alternative to Islam, is regarded by al-Daᶜwa as "idolatry" and why it viciously attacks even a friendly regime like that of Hafiz al-Assad in Damascus:

> The Baᶜthis are similar to the Zionists in their belief in their racial superiority. They believe that Arab blood is superior to that of any other race.[6]

> Syria is ruled by a branch . . . of the Baᶜth party which shows all of the attributes of its twin in Iraq. The Baᶜth, based on Arab nationalism . . . which stems from Christian and secular ideologies, is bent on the destruction of Islam as a political force.[7]

And, later, in a similar vein,

> The Ba^cth as such is unacceptable to the Muslim people of Iraq . . .
> the *jahili* concept of Arabism has no place in their hearts.

> The Muslims do not believe in national or cultural differences.[8]

The Da^cwa's reservations regarding Arabism can also be seen in the way in which it portrays the Gulf war. While Ba^cth propaganda portrays this war as a battle between Arabs and Persians (and often, between Arab Muslims and Persian Zoroastrians), al-Da^cwa portrays it as a battle between honest Muslims of all races and an atheistic, anti-Muslim regime. The fact that Iranian soldiers are fighting Arabs is irrelevant, or so the Da^cwa would have it appear. Thus, for example, the men of the Iranian army are more often than not labeled "the conquering heroes of Islam," "the Islamic forces," or "the troops of Allah," whereas the Iraqi Arab army are very often called a group of "Ba^cthi mercenaries" or "Ba^cth Crusaders."[9]

An important element in the attack on Ba^cth pan-Arabism is the stress laid on the Christian origin of some party founders, especially that of Michel ^cAflaq and Iraqi deputy prime minister and minister of foreign affairs Tariq ^cAziz. (The Da^cwa party always adds the Christian name Hanna to ^cAziz's name, and at least once the name Tubia as well, thereby hinting that ^cAziz may, in fact, be Jewish.)[10] This is to imply that political Arabism and Christian missionary activity are intertwined. Thus, for example, "the souls of the pioneers of Arabism, Michel ^cAflaq and Tariq Hanna ^cAziz . . . [are full of] hatred toward Islam, and they panic when they hear the slogan 'God is Great' (*Alluha akbar*) [shouted by the masses]."[11] And, "Michel ^cAflaq is a Crusader bent on uprooting Islam from the lives of the people in the Arab world."[12]

The attack on the Ba^cth is inseparably intertwined with strong reservations toward Arabism. Thus, almost every time *Arabism* or *Arab* is mentioned, the connotation is negative or sarcastic. This is particularly true when al-Da^cwa refers to Arab rulers and Arab regimes, for none, including Libya and Syria, are regarded as righteous. Indeed, the impression conveyed by al-Da^cwa is that Arab regimes as such are totally unacceptable.[13] Even when the word *Arab* is used in other contexts, it is intended to be derogatory.

For example, when Sudan offered personnel to Iraq at the beginning of the Gulf war, the Da^cwa turned not only on the Sudanese regime but also on Arabism in general: "[These draftees] will only expand the list of those who died in defense of Arabism."[14] Similarly, Iraqi pleas for Arab help were met with the sarcastic headline: "Saddam Husayn turned again to his Arab 'brothers' for aid."[15] And, according to al-Da^cwa, the Iraqi president hoped to become "the champion of the Arab cause" by winning the war against Iran. For, even without a victory, Husayn presented himself as the "champion of progress and the resurrection of the dear Arab nation." In fact, all Arab rulers were now turning to America, asking her to "save the Arab nation from Islam."[16] And Mubarak was "being pushed by his 'Arab Honor' to supply the Iraqi tyrant [with arms]."[17]

The Da^cwa party viewed the Arab-Israeli conflict in a similar light, so that the Arab defeat in the Six-Day War is termed "a demonstration of Arab impotence"[18] (rather than the failure of deviationist Arab regimes). Further, "the Arabs," not only the Arab regimes, "will bury the Palestinian cause in [the Fez] conference," and whatever happened in Beirut in summer 1982 was "the defeat of the Arabs" as a whole, and not the defeat of one Arab regime.[19] When discussing Egypt's return to the Arab fold, *al-Jihad* could not even bring itself to mention the word *Arab* without quotation marks: "The truth is that Egypt did not turn toward 'the Arabs' as much as 'the Arabs' turned towards her."[20]

Cases in which Arabism appears in a neutral or even positive light do occur, but they are very much the exception. And this explicitly negative presentation of Arabism is coupled with a tendency to avoid mentioning it in any positive context. This is particularly evident when the Shi^cite opposition calls for the Iraqi people to unite against the Ba^cth regime or when it mourns the sufferings of the Iraqi people. Citizens of the Iraqi state are usually called "Iraqi Muslims," "the Muslim nation (or people) of Iraq," or similar names, but their identity as Arabs is never mentioned.[21]

Despite some criticism regarding the depth of its religious piety, al-Da^cwa regards the Ottoman Empire as a legitimate political body and mourns its disintegration, because the empire's downfall gave rise to Arabism, which is based on race and culture rather than on Islam.[22] Finally, the reservations of the radical Shi^cite opposition vis-à-vis Arabism are not merely ideological: on the purely operational level, although cooperation with Mustafa al-Barazani's secular socialist and largely Sunni Kurdish Democratic Party has flourished since 1980, cooperation with the secular, largely Sunni pan-Arab opposition groups did not materialize until 1986, and even then it was extremely tenuous.

To place the Da^cwa within the context of contemporary Islamic thinking in regard to Arabism, one can compare them with the Muslim Brethren of Syria, another radical Islamic movement representing a majority sect fighting against a much-hated Ba^cthi (and minority) rule. The attitude of the Muslim Brethren in Syria toward the relation between Arabism, pan-Arabism, and Islam emerges fairly clearly despite the lack of systematic and explicit treatment of the subject. The expressions "Arab nationalism" (*al-qawmiyya al-^carabiyya*) and "the unity of the Arab nation" do not appear in their party organ or pamphlets. This is to avoid any ideological affinity with the Ba^cth and its secular, nationalist creed. Nevertheless, one frequently finds phrases such as "the leadership of the Islamic front in Syria calls upon you in the name of Islamic fraternity and Arab honor (*al-shahama al-^carabiyya*)"[23]; "O brotherly citizens, O Arabs and Muslims"; and "[Arise,] Syria of glory, Syria of the Umayyads and the Ayyubis, Syria, the throbbing heart of Arabism and Islam."[24] It is clear that Arabism is a legitimate basis of identification to the Syrian Muslim Brethren as long as that Arabism is Islamic and as long as it does not separate itself from the rest of the Muslim *umma* (nation).

A similar but more explicit approach to Arabism is expressed in the writings of a prominent intellectual connected to the Muslim Brethren in Syria, Sa^cid Hawwa. As long as Arabism remains thoroughly Islamic, Hawwa accepts it without any reservations. In fact, he has even viewed the unity of Arab countries as a possible nucleus around which total Islamic unity will be forged.[25]

Thus, the Da^cwa party may be said to differ substantially from the Muslim Brethren in their total rejection of Arabism as a basis for political identification. Although its stance may have been influenced by real or presumed Iranian sensitivities, this stance must have been formulated independently, at least in the sense that there was no ready-made ideological tract to copy. In the only book of his that was translated into Arabic by 1980, *al-Hukuma al-Islamiyya*, Khomeini does not mention this issue at all.

Local Iraqi Identification and Internal Unity

Iraqi Patriotism

For al-Da^cwa, Iraqi patriotism has always been inseparably intertwined with Islam. Whereas the identification between Islam and Iraq is usually made by indirect reference, there also have been some explicit and detailed treatments of the subject. For instance, the Shiʿite opposition speaks of the Muslim nature of Iraq, or about the Iraqi people and their Muslim belief as the alternative to Baʿth rule and ideology, which are regarded as alien and hostile to the people and their sentiments. The most important aspect of the Daʿwa's criticism of the Baʿth is that the latter wishes to "Shake off the Islamic identity from the sons of our [Muslim] nation (*umma*) in Iraq . . . and to wipe out the Islamic Iraqi personality by diluting its characteristics . . . and implanting instead of them *jahili* concepts [of secular Arab nationalism]."[26]

When the Shiʿite radicals turn to their followers, they very often use expressions that imply the legitimacy of a political Iraqi entity, for example, "the oppressed, noble Iraqi people," (*al-Shaʿb al-iraqi . . .*), "the Islamic Iraqi people," "our people in Iraq," or "the great Iraqi people." There is much mention of the beloved Iraqi homeland that suffers under the boot of the alien Baʿth regime. They pray for "the victory of the revolution throughout our beloved Iraq." And, after the victory, their newspapers proclaim, "Godly justice will be established throughout our wounded Iraq," and "the oppressed people of Iraq" will be liberated.[27]

One is left with the impression that the Iraqi national entity will not disappear after the success of the Islamic revolution, at least not in the foreseeable future. Thus, for example, following Khomeini's ascendancy in Tehran, one opposition pamphlet noted—when describing the great enthusiasm in al-Thawra, the Shiʿite quarter of Baghdad— that the people there were hopefully discussing the emergence of an "Iraqi Khomeini."[28] This indicates that, despite their great admiration for the Iranian Ayatollah, the Iraqi public did not see Khomeini as a possible ruler of Iraq. In a similar vein, when Shaykh Muhammad Baqir al-Nasiri, the leading scholar of the Daʿwa, was speaking to volunteers at a training camp in al-Ahwaz, he concentrated on the vision of "the future Islamic republic in Iraq," in which, he declared, "the Iraqi people will be free to determine its own future."[29] Although Nasiri's explicit intention was to convey that the Iraqi people would define itself as Muslim, by its own free will, the connotation of the term *self-determination* (*taqrir al-masir*) goes further than that, and the sheikh must have been aware of this.

In many places, one can discern local Iraqi pride and even a certain competitive feeling toward Iran. Thus, in describing the events of February 1977, when thousands of Shiʿite participants in processions mourning the death of Husayn clashed with Baʿthi security forces, the

Da^cwa party organ claimed that, "The Muslims of the world do not know this well . . . [yet] the meaning of the uprising in Iraq in February 1977 lies in the fact that it happened before there was any sign of revolution in Iran . . . the struggle in Iraq preceded the Iranian revolution by far."[30]

When discussing what Iraqi-Iranian relations would be like after the Islamic revolution's success in Iraq, the Shi^cite leaders make it clear that, although relations would be very close due to ideological affinity, the two countries would not merge and would continue to move along separate paths. In this regard, when Muhammad Baqir al-Hakim gave an interview to the organ of the Iranian embassy in London, he confided that

> The ideological, strategic and geographical links make it imperative that relations between the two revolutions would be close. [However,] the details of the system . . . and its form are left to the decision of the [Iraqi] public . . . which make the revolution. . . . The post-revolutionary process in Iraq will not be identical to that in Iran.[31]

Another indication that the Shi^cite opposition in Iraq does not regard the Iraqi geopolitical entity as short-lived may be found in its vehement defense of Iraqi territorial integrity against the Ba^cthi inclination to concede territory to Saudi Arabia and Jordan, whose help is badly needed in the Gulf war. Since this opposition makes no secret of its intentions to spread the Islamic revolution to other Arab countries, one would not think that such minor border adjustments in favor of other Islamic peoples would be regarded as a betrayal of Muslim interests, unless one regards the Iraqi entity as a separate and long-lived nation.[32] Iraq's continued existence as a nation-state, even after the downfall of the Ba^cth regime, also emerges from a discussion of Iraq's development strategy, in which her future arms-purchasing policy is discussed in such detail that we know of the plan to diversify armament sources by relying less on the Soviet Union and more on the West, until "a modern arms industry is established to safeguard Iraq's independence."[33] Similarly, there is no mention of the possibility of unifying the Iraqi and Iranian armies, and one receives the impression that Iraq will have to shoulder the full responsibility for its own defense in the foreseeable future.

This kind of Iraqi-Islamic patriotism does not indicate any estrangement from Khomeini and his revolution in Iran, for the Shi^cite opposition in Iraq gave complete allegiance to the revolution across the border as an Islamic one. To the Da^cwa, Iraqi patriotism equals adherence to Islam; they say that Iraq without Islam would be like a body without a soul or, even worse, like a beloved body possessed by a demon. Thus, an Iraqi patriot must assist "the Islamic legions" to "free [Iraq] from the Ba^cthi nightmare (*kabus*) that possesses the country, and to bring about "Islamic brotherhood, justice, and enthusiasm . . . in our beloved Iraq."[34] Al-Da^cwa also assures the invading Iranian troops that "The hearts of the sons of Mesopotamia (*abna'al-Rafidayn*) are open to meet you. . . . Be welcome in our land and have no ear."[35] *The Da^cwa Chronicle* even attacks the unspecified circles in Iran who would consider ending the war before Baghdad is captured. For peace between the two states will be possible only "when Saddam Husayn is removed and the Islamic State of Iraq is established."[36]

This Iraqi-Islamic patriotism indicates that the Shi^cite opposition will not accept a subservient position for Islamic Iraq. Indeed, as the Da^cwa sees it, once Baghdad has been won, Iraq will have its own role to play in spreading Islam in the Arabic speaking territories, by demonstrating how Sunnis and Shi^cites, Arabs and non-Arabs, can cooperate under the Islamic banner.[37] In the same way, in a communique issued to "the sons of the Iraqi people," Ayatollah Muhammad Baqir al-Sadr, whose supreme authority in matters of both politics and ideology is recognized by all Shi^cite opposition movements of Iraq, called not only for the evil Ba^cth government to be toppled, but also for Iraq to be elevated so that her glory shines forth: "Oh my sons and brothers, the sons of Mosul and Basra, the sons of Baghdad and Karbala, Najf . . . Amarra, Kut, and Sulaymaniyya, the sons of Iraq wherever they are . . . you must unite your actions to save Iraq from the nightmare . . . and to build a free, glorious Iraq, illuminated by Islamic justice."[38] In his lengthy communique, Sadr does not even hint at the possibility of either a merger with Iran or the disappearance of Iraq within the wider framework of an amalgamated Muslim state. This is not to say that the issue of total Islamic unity does not come up from time to time.[39]

However, the infrequent resort to such declarations, and the almost constant and clearcut effort to differentiate between Iraq and Iran and to boost — or at least retain — Iraqi identification, leads one to conclude that the Shi^cite opposition's commitment to a pan-Muslim state is a vision for the distant future rather than a practical scheme to be implemented as soon as the revolution in Iraq is won. This conclusion is supported by evidence regarding the demand by elements within the Shi^cite opposition for Iraqi self-assertion in the face of near-total Iranian control over the Iraqi movements based in Tehran. Thus, for example, in a public communique in 1986 the Da^cwa demanded that Iraqi units be trained by Iraqis and be given "sections of the front" under their sole responsibility, where they would exercise "wide-ranging authority" and be given full media coverage.[40] A much more clear exposition of Iraqi self-assertion may be found in a letter written by an ardent fan of the marja^ciyya of Najf against that of Karbala and against the Karbala-based al-^cAmal al-Islami in particular. "Why are we running," asks the frustrated man, "after non-Iraqi pesonalities" such as Ayatollah Shirazi, who only "lived in Iraq for a while?" The writer points out that the ayatollah never gave up his Iranian citizenship or bothered to obtain an Iraqi one. "Are we short of men? Or are our mothers afflicted with infertility?" he asks with great indignation.[41]

On the issue of local patriotism, the Muslim Brethren in Syria have adopted an approach very similar to that of the Da^cwa. When Sa^cid Hawwa discussed Hasan al-Banna's views, he defined the Muslim "countries" (aqtar) as bricks from which Islamic unity will be built, the final result to be "the United Islamic States" (al-wilayat al-islamiyya al-muttahida). According to Hawwa, the Muslim Brethren

> do not imagine that these states will be a carbon-copy of each other. Rather, each state will have its own laws and institutions. . . . The school . . . that will prevail . . . will be that adopted by the majority of the inhabitants in a particular state, and the same applies to the language of that people and many . . . customs, as well as . . . to the choice of a regime suitable for it. . . . This, on the condition that all states . . . will be under the rule of a caliph (Amir al-mu'minin) in some form, and under the machinery of the central state.[42]

Despite the fact that the Muslim Brethren of Syria do not deal systematically with this question in their publications, one cannot mistake the deep attachment to the Syrian homeland that nevertheless emerges. It also becomes quite clear that the Syrian Muslim Brethren feel that the Syrian people is clearly separable from the rest of the region's peoples and that it forms one integrated unit, except for the ^cAlawites. Thus we read: "Our [Syrian] people, which is great in its faith, deep rooted in its testing agony, ancient in its civilization . . . deserves to overcome the ordeal that has befallen its homeland";[43] "the miserable Syrian people"; "the proud Syrian people";[44] and other, similar expressions. Like their counterparts in Iraq, the Muslim Brethren also speak, from time to time, about the establishment of an "Islamic Republic of Syria"[45] and the Syrian people's right to "self-determination."[46] Although Khomeini does not touch on this issue in *al-Hukuma al-islamiyya*, references in speeches made since he came to power make it safe to assume that this strange blend of Islam, modern, Western-style territorial nationalism in general, and Iraqidom in particular is acceptable, or at least not contrary, to his philosophy.[47]

Sunni-Shiᶜite Ecumenism in the Service of Internal Unity

The question of Islamic fraternity among Muslim speakers of Arabic, Persian, Kurdish, and Turkish, at least on the ideological level, is a relatively easy problem. Far more thorny and complex is the issue of relations between Iraq's various Islamic sects. Opposition writers leave no room for doubt: although it cannot be ignored, the internal schism within the Islamic camp should be muted as much as possible and the common denominators between Shiᶜite and Sunni Iraqis enhanced. It is not at all clear whether this stance stems from true ecumenical inclinations or from a tactical effort to attract Sunni support. There is some evidence, however, that Iraqi Shiᶜite ecumenism is an endogenic phenomenon rather than a mirror-image of Khomeini's ideology.

Islamic unity and united action against the Iraqi Baᶜth regime is the single most important feature of Shiᶜite propaganda in Iraq. As pointed out earlier, the Daᶜwa regards it as Iraq's duty to show other Arabic-speaking countries that Sunnis and Shiᶜites could coexist and cooperate well. A similar approach may be found in a communique issued by Muhammad Baqir al-Hakim, spokesman (and since 1986 "head") of the supreme council, the umbrella organization of the Shiᶜite opposition. In it, al-Hakim uses a well-known *Shuᶜubi Hadith* in a particularly Iraqi context:

> The Islamic revolution in Iraq belongs to the Sunni and the Shiᶜite, to the Kurd and the Arab. This is the revolution of all classes in Iraq . . . all being the [equal] sons of Iraq from the moral Islamic viewpoint. [As is said in the *Hadith*:] "The Arab has no advantage over the non-Arab (or "Persian," *aᶜjami*] but the fear of God."[48]

Although the opposition always seeks to prove that it has Sunni as well as Shiᶜite backing, this claim is not substantiated in fact — except for the one case of a Sunni ^{c}alim who was executed by the regime in the late 1960s or early 1970s. Nonetheless, the Shi^{c}ite opposition still maintains that "the [whole] Iraqi people retains its unity and aims all guns at the agent Ba^{c}thi regime."[49] Indeed, Sunni-Shi^{c}ite unity is a central component of the opposition's thought, if not of its political practice. In his last plea to the Iraqi people that was given publicity in the Da^{c}wa organ, Muhammad Baqir al-Sadr stressed the issue of Sunni-Shi^{c}ite unity above all others, and even demonstrated a readiness to speak directly and openly on the core issue of Sunni-Shi^{c}ite antagonism, ^{c}Ali's right to the caliphate:

> Oh my dear people, I turn to you all, Sunnites and Shi^{c}ites, Arabs and Kurds, in this crucial moment of crisis and *jihad* life. . . . Since the crisis is that of the whole Iraqi people, the brave response and struggle must also become the reality of the whole Iraqi people. Thus I am with you, my Sunni brother and son, just as much as I am with you, my Shi^{c}i brother and son. . . .
>
> The tyrants . . . are trying to convince our pious Sunni sons that the problem is a Sunni-Shi^{c}i one, in order to cut them off from the real struggle against the common enemy. I wish to tell you, the sons of Abu Bakr and ^{c}Umar, that the battle is not between the Shi^{c}ites and the Sunni rule. The Sunni rule as it was represented by the four righteous caliphs [sic!] brought the Imam ^{c}Ali to raise his sword in the defence of this rule in the *ridda* battles under the leadership of Abu Bakr. It is our duty to defend the Islamic flag whatever its factional color. . . . [During World War I] Shi^{c}i ulama issued *fatwas* which proclaimed that the defence of the Sunni rule which raised the flag of Islam was a *jihad*, and hundreds of thousands of Shi^{c}ites streamed to the battlefield to defend the Islamic call. The regime today is not Sunni, although the ruling clique belongs, historically speaking, to the Sunni branch of Islam. Sunni rule . . . means the rule of Abu Bakr and ^{c}Umar, against which the tyrant rulers of Iraq today are coming out . . . they are consecrating Islam . . . ^{c}Ali and ^{c}Umar alike, every day. . . . Don't you see, my brothers and sons, that they have forsaken the religious rites which Abu Bakr and ^{c}Umar defended? Don't you see that they are filling the land with drink, pig-fields, and all kinds of corruption . . . isolating themselves in their palaces surrounded by security forces . . . while ^{c}Ali and ^{c}Umar lived in the midst of the people and for them, sharing with them their hopes and agonies. . . . Oh my sons and brothers, the sons of Mosul and Basra, the sons of Baghdad, Karbala and Najf . . .

[unite in order to] build a free, glorious Iraq . . . where citizens of all nationalities and schools would feel that they are brothers *and would all contribute to the leadership of their country* (emphasis added).[50]

Two important elements can be seen here. One is the partial rehabilitation of ^cUmar and Abu Bakr (but not of ^cUthman). Although al-Sadr does not absolve them of the charge of usurpation, he does give them credit for adhering to many Islamic rules, and he regards them, unlike the present Ba^cthi regime, as Muslims. (Shi^cite literature often regards Sunnis as "Muslims," as opposed to "believers," *mu'minin*, a title reserved for Shi^cites alone; only a *mu'min* is a full-fledged Muslim.)[51] The second major element of al-Sadr's communique is practical; namely, the apparent readiness to share power with the Sunnis on an equal basis and a willingness to refrain from pressing the issue of Shi^cite rule. To what extent Sadr's example of past Shi^cite readiness to accept Sunni leadership means Shi^cite readiness for subservience in the future is not clear, but such a possibility is certainly implied.

Ecumenical inclinations, in fact, are fairly conspicuous in some of al-Sadr's earliest works, in which he presents the Islamic alternative to Western philosophies and social systems.[52] In these works he defends Islam using both Shi^cite and Sunni sources. He steers clear of all controversial issues and gives no hint that there are differences between Sunnism and Shi^cism. The same is true of another leading *mujtahid* who is closely connected with the revolutionary movement: the elderly, Karbala-based (until the late 1970s) *mujtahid* Ayatollah Muhammad al-Husayni al-Shirazi.[53] The important Kazimayn-based *mujtahid* Ayatollah Muhammad Hasan Al-Yasin[54] does not avoid the controversial issue of the caliphate. In fact, through it, he goes even further than his colleagues when he credits ^cUmar with reasonable modesty because he realized how much he needed ^cAli's knowledge in Islamic law, understanding that he, ^cUmar, "was not up to the level that was necessary in order . . . to answer the questions of the Muslims and to judge between them."[55] In fact, ^cUmar himself said once: "Without ^cAli, ^cUmar['s soul] would have perished [*lawla ^cAli lahalaka ^cUmar*]." The relationship of "mutual help and positive consultation" continued for a long time, according to Al-Yasin, "until it seemed to some people that ^cUmar probably promised the caliphate to ^cAli after him." Al-Yasin even goes so far as to call ^cUmar's murderer "a hand full of hatred and malice."[56] Despite a certain patronizing attitude toward ^cUmar, this approach does indicate a wish for Sunni-Shi^cite conciliation.

This conciliatory attitude also is evident in al-Da^cwa's demands that the Syrian Muslim Brethren should attack Assad as a Ba^cthi and an enemy of Islam instead of fighting him as an ^cAlawite. Here, too, we see the desire to distinguish the just struggle of Islam against atheism from interfactional strife.[57] In the same vein, al-Da^cwa gives unreserved support to such Muslim Brethren leaders in Egypt as Khalid al-Islambuli, who was executed for his part in the assassination of Sadat, and to Sayyid Qutb, who was executed by Nasser.[58]

The Da^cwa Chronicle states very clearly that the existence of different "schools" (*madhahib*) in Islam is perfectly legitimate, because "there are many declarations made by the Prophet in which he encourages the Muslims to use their own judgement based on the Koran and the *Sunna*." What is important, the Da^cwa organ stresses, is to follow God's words: "And hold fast altogether by the rope which God [stretches out for you] and be not divided among yourselves."[59]

Whether these ecumenical expressions are a genuine Iraqi phenomenon and to what extent they result from adherence to Ayatollah Khomeini[60] are questions that are probably impossible to answer in full. However, it seems that long before Khomeini emerged as a political-religious leader, the Iraqi Shi^cite ulama had an extensive history of Sunni-Shi^cite cooperation against non-Muslim conquerors and, to a lesser extent, against a central government that toed the line of an occupying Christian force. This was the case when *mujtahidun* from the holy cities issued *fatwa*s against the British invasion in 1914, calling upon the tribes of the south to join the Ottoman Sixth Army in defending the abode of Islam against the infidels. Although this cooperation was neither widespread nor long-lived—in 1915 and 1916 both Najf and Karbala revolted against the Ottoman government—it demonstrates that limited Sunni-Shi^cite cooperation is possible in Iraq.[61] Indeed, between 1919 and 1920 there was an impressive amount of Sunni-Shi^cte anti-British cooperation. Although this was mainly on the leadership level, it was also known to exist in some mass gatherings in Shi^cite and Sunni mosques in Baghdad and its environs.[62] The Shi^cites also showed their readiness to cooperate with their Sunni coreligionists during the 1920 revolt, when they were prepared to accept one of the sons of Sharif Husayn of Mecca as the *Amir* of Iraq.[63]

Many years later, under Qasim (1958–1963), some Sunni-Shi^cite anticommunist activity was demonstrated in the framework of the Islamic Party[64] connected with the Shi^cite chief *mujtahid*, Muhsin al-Hakim.[65] This, too, as well as some of Sadr's early writings that preceded Khomeini's arrival in Najf, are signs that Sunni-Shi^cite ecumenical tendencies and cooperation existed long before Khomeini could have any direct influence on the Iraqi *marjaᶜiyya*, either through his presence in Najf or through his ascendency to power in Iran. The appearance of endogenous ecumenical trends in Iraq (to the extent that endogenous trends are at all possible in such a closely knit body as the Iraqi-Iranian *marjaᶜiyya*) is not surprising, because the Iraqi political community has always been split between the two sects. Therefore, what Khomeini considered a supra-Iranian issue, the Iraqi *mujtahidun* view as an internal Iraqi affair. Thus, the Shiᶜites in Iraq know that, if they wish to oppose the central government or a foreign occupying force with any chance of success, they must enlist the Sunnis in their efforts. It should also be noted that, at least in his famous book *al-Hukuma al-islamiyya*, Khomeini did not go nearly as far as the Iraqi *mujtahidun* al-Sadr and Al-Yasin in his efforts to ameliorate or nullify the historical antagonism between Sunnis and Shiᶜites.[66] In fact, in the modern history of the "Twelver" Shiᶜism, the exposition of the Shiᶜite ecumenical tendencies in Iraq are outstanding.

As for the Muslim Brethren in Syria, although their approach to the Shiᶜites is conciliatory,[67] they make no effort to edit their writings to make them acceptable to Shiᶜite readers. Thus, for example, they define themselves as the descendants of "Khalid al-Walid, ᶜUmar b. al-Khattab, ᶜAli b. Abi Talib and Salah al-Din,"[68] and proudly describe the Syrian people as the offspring of the Umayyads, who are vehemently hated by the Shiᶜites.[69] Similarly, they denounce the Shiᶜite Fatimids for "not having participated in the wars against the Mongols and the Crusaders."[70] Even more interesting is their uncompromisingly negative attitude toward the ᶜAlawites, who like the Sunnis in Iraq are a ruling minority. The Brethren sometimes address the ᶜAlawites (often called *Nusairis*, to make it difficult for them to appear as Shiᶜites) in a nonhostile manner; for example, when they warn them to stop their support for Assad's regime. In most cases, however, the attitude of the Brethren toward the ᶜAlawites is one of total aversion that clearly and unequivocally negates their claim to be regarded as Muslims. Thus, for example, the Brethren's propaganda organ claims that the Nusairi religion is "a combination of Jewish, Christian, Buddhist . . . and Zoroastrian beliefs, and by this they have completely forsaken Islam."[71] The ᶜAlawites are also defined as a "prostitute" group.[72]

It would seem that when it comes to ecumenism, then, the stance of the Iraqi Shiᶜite opposition is unique, not so much in the sense that no others desire rapprochement between the two sects (such calls come from other Shi^cite sources, namely Khomeini's Iran, as well as from some leading Sunni ulama) but rather in the sense that they treat the subject more openly. At least in Sadr's communique, endorsed by al-Da^cwa, we find an expressed readiness to share the government with their Sunni counterparts.[73]

Finally, the issue of ecumenism in the writings of the Shi^cite opposition in Iraq cannot be appraised or fully understood without an attempt to look at what lies beyond the official declarations and communiques. To really understand the Shi^cite attitude towards Sunnis, one must resort to some of Muhammad Baqir al-Sadr's writings aimed at a more limited audience but not necessarily at an exclusively Shi^cite one. Since Sadr is regarded as the supreme ideological authority by all opposition groups and organizations, one may assume that his writings are read by many and that the positions and attitudes expressed therein are largely representative of the Shi^cite opposition movement as a whole.

Sunni-Shi^cite Controversy: The Other Facet of Shi^cite Radicalism

The Islamic State and the Role of the Jurist

Much like the Muslim Brethren in Egypt and other countries of the Middle East, Iraqi Shi^cite writers are quite clear as to the relationship between the future Islamic state and Islam. Their aim is "to win the pleasure of God by establishing His rule on earth, namely by establishing an Islamic government." The duty of this government will be "to return society to the living Islam . . . to remove the . . . *jahili* system in the Muslim and other communities throughout the world" and to imbue human society with "the Islamic bases of government, economy and law."[74]

However, there is a substantial difference between the Shi^cite opposition and the Muslim Brethren in their view of the establishment and future of the Muslim state. Without exception, all the Shi^cite movements stress that there is only one way to achieve the Islamic government and perpetuate it: through the "jurist's rule" (*wilayat al-faqih*).[75] In his open letter to the Iraqi Communist party, an al-Da^cwa leader in London explained that cooperation with the communists and other secular movements must be ruled out, because

> Relieving ourselves from oppression may be achieved through the annihilation of its roots, but not through removing its exposi-
> tions. The roots of oppression and exploitation are found in the

rejection of Islam and in the adoption of man-made ideologies.
. . . The criterion for adhering to the law of Allah is obedience to
those who carry this law and guard it . . . [76]

Another opposition group, the Movement of the Muslim Masses of
Iraq, asserts that "the *marja^ciyya*, which rests on its wide popular
base, is the only true force capable of totally and fundamentally
changing the reality of the Muslim nation"; this is what the Koran
means when it says "we have decided to be magnanimous toward the
weak and desired to show favor unto those on the earth who were oppressed, and to give them examples (imams), and make them the inheritors."[77]

The Shi^cite ideologues also interpret various *Hadiths* to support
the principle of the rule of the jurist. For example, the imams were
told: "You are the leaders of the faithful, and the columns [that hold]
the country (*sasat al-^cibad wa-arkan al-bilad*); "the ulama are the
heirs of the prophets"; and "The ulama of my nation are like the rest
of the prophets before me (*kasa'ir al-anbiya qabli*)."[78] The official
organ of the umbrella organization of the Shi^cite opposition groups
has expressed full support for this principle in the Iranian context and
implied its support in the all-Islamic context as well:

> The Muslim masses applied the principle of *wilayat al-faqih* which
> in our days is embodied by . . . Khomeini, removing . . . all
> the . . . leaderships in whose mind and everyday practice this
> principle did not crystalize . . . and this is why Bani Sadr and his
> like were dropped. Thus . . . the masses turned their obedience to
> their [jurist] rulers . . . into a fundamental condition for winning
> on the battlefield.[79]

The only way to read these declarations is to take them as a warning: whoever does not apply the principle of *wilayat al-faqih* in the
Muslim state should be removed from the political scene. According
to the Movement of Muslim Masses there is also a pragmatic reason
for this: the masses need a leading personality during their struggle
against the atheist regime in Iraq, and the best such personality is a
religious leader or a group of them. This, as the Movement puts it, is
because "the masses turn around the *marja^ciyya* as do electrons
around the nucleus."[80]

It is obvious that the main inspiration was Ayatollah Khomeini and
his regime in Tehran. All Iraqi sources made it clear that the *faqih*
who should lead the whole Islamic nation is Khomeini, and their

terminology, as well as some of the *Hadiths* they use appear to have come from his book.[81] There is some evidence, however, that the principle of the political rule of the imam, and the *calim* after him, in its contemporary form, may have originated in Iraq rather than in Iran. In a lecture that he gave in Najf at *Jamciyyat al-rabita al-adabiyya* in 1966; (that is, three or four years before Khomeini issued his *Islamic Government*) commemorating cAli's birthday, Muhammad Baqir al-Sadr defined the attributes that are to be found in all Imams starting from cAli. Sadr admitted that the Imams did not hold "the position of [actual] leadership" of the Islamic body politic. However, "despite the conspiracy[!] to keep them away from the realm of government," they continue to bear the responsibility of preventing "a complete deviation" from the principles of Islam in the Islamic state. Thus, even though not at the top of the pyramid of political power, the Imam represented an alternative political leadership "of the vast masses," and he never gave up the notion of achieving actual political rule. Instead, "he waited until conditions were ripe."[82] Sadr also combined the principles of the political role of the *calim* with the political nature of Islam: "Shicism (*al-tashayyuc*) was never . . . an exclusively spiritual tendency. . . . It is impossible . . . to separate the religious from the political aspects in . . . Shicism. . . . It is impossible for us to imagine the Imams giving up the political aspect without giving up Shicism altogether."[83] In February 1979, this time under the influence of Khomeini's revolution, Sadr took one more step and stated explicitly what was implied in his 1966 lecture at Najf. "After the . . . occultation," he wrote in a *fatwa* regarding the draft Iranian constitution, "the imamate was extended to the *marjaciyya*, in the same way that the imamate itself was in its own turn, an extension of the Prophecy." Thus, he concluded, "the *marjac* is the Deputy General of the Imam," which means that "the *marjac* is the supreme representative of the state and the supreme commander of the armed forces."[84] This statement was even more explicit than Khomeini's wording: in his book on the Islamic government, the Iranian ayatollah used the expression *faqih*, which also could stand for a Sunni jurist.

This concept of the political role of the religious leader reportedly has been practiced as well as preached to the extent that conditions allowed it in Iran. Ever since Khomeini came to power, Shicites from all over Iraq have been sending delegates to Sadr in Najf to ask for his advice and instructions.[85] In fact, judging by the descriptions of the many years of political activity of ayatollahs Hasan al-Shirazi [86] and Muhammad Baqir al-Sadr[87] before their deaths in 1980, it may be suggested that Iraqi Shiᶜites applied the novel principle of *ilayat al-faqih* in their own environment even before Khomeini's ascendancy to power. The leadership of men of religion is a basic aspect of the Daᶜwa's ideal picture of party organization. The party's manual states that one cannot reach the highest echelon of party leadership without being a full-fledged *mujtahid*.[88] If this represents the party's original demands of senior activists, it dates back to the early 1960s and has nothing to do with Khomeini's ascendancy in Tehran, as it predates by a decade or so his book, *al-Hukuma al-islamiyya*. It emerges, then, that the concept of political rule of the Imam, and after him the *faqih*, at least was not imported into Iraq from Khomeini's Iran. But more important to our argument, this whole issue is a specifically Shiᶜite one, with a long history in Shiᶜite doctrine and practice.[89] Khomeini's demand that government be placed entirely in the hands of the religious leaders is the culmination of a long rivalry between the religious establishment and civil government in Iran and, to a large extent, in Iraq as well. This problem, however, has had very little significance in Sunni history, for the special role of the *mujtahidun*, who regard themselves as the legitimate guardians of the faith until the hidden Imam returns, is alien to Sunni thinking. There is no better example of this than the writings of Sayyid Qutb, one of the most eminent thinkers of Egypt's Muslim Brethren:

> The kingdom of Allah on earth will not be established by some people, the people of religion, ruling over the land as was the case under the church [in Europe], nor by people who would speak in the name of the Gods as was the case in the [regime] known by the name of theocracy. . . . Rather, it will be established when the *shariᶜa* of Allah reigns.[90]

This objection to rule by religious leaders may be understood better if one bears in mind that, in the case of the radical Sunna in modern times, criticism is aimed against the religious establishment more than the iniquitous political ruler.[91] The fact that the Shiᶜite opposition places such heavy stress on this issue, and its insistence that only a Shiᶜite *marjaᶜ* may rule; that in our day only Khomeini could be regarded as the political and religious leader of the whole Muslim world, is a demonstration of an extreme Shiᶜite-centered approach.

Political Activism and Sacrifice

Although the question of political activism and the readiness to sacrifice in defense of the faith is not alien to Sunni Islam, the way this issue is treated represents another demonstration of the Shi^cite tendency to ignore Sunni sensitivities. In Sunni Islam, one who wishes to rebel against an unjust government must confront the traditional animosity to any act that might lead to anarchy through civil strife (*fitna*). There is no sign, however, that the Shi^cite opposition has ever been ready to consider the problems that confront Sunnis. Instead, their entire treatment of the subject focuses on the political passivity of many Shi^cites that stems from the traditional interpretation of the Shi^cite principle of *taqiyya* (precautionary dissimulation), the traditional way in which the political passivity of the Imams has been explained. For, with the exception of only a few cases (namely those of ^cAli and al-Husayn), the Imams did not resort to open war in their opposition to the Umayyad and later the Abbasid governments. Since their way of life is supposed to serve as a guideline for every Shi^cite, this can be interpreted as legitimizing political passivity. In addition, the traditional approach to the issue of the Expected Imam (*al-Imam al-mahdi al-muntazar*, Muhammad Abu al-Qasim, the Twelfth Imam, who according to Shi^cite tradition disappeared in 874 A.D. and is expected to come back as savior and redeemer) emphasizes patient expectation rather than revolutionary uprising.

In their efforts to convince their followers to rise against the Ba^cth regime, Shi^cite leaders have attacked this passivity. In the process, however, they express adherence to Shi^cite articles of faith that may not be acceptable to Sunnis. Thus, political activism is dealt with in the context of the birthday of the Twelfth Imam: "all the Muslims and humanity as a whole" are congratulated in honor of "the birthday of the spreader of truth . . . and refuter of lies upon whose appearance the sun of freedom and independence will shine . . . and the land will be filled with justice and equality."[92]

In the context of "expectation" or "waiting" (*al-intizar*), Sunnis are completely excluded by statements such as "We all live today in the era of the greater occultation. Many of us do not know our duty in the age of occultation and expectation of the leader Imam." One must therefore explain the meaning of these concepts to avoid catastrophic mistakes, for "Our societies are split down the middle in the way they understand the expectations."

According to one prevalent Shi^cite (literally, "Muslim") interpretation, one should do nothing about an evil regime because Allah has ordained that all will be righted by the Imam when he reappears. One should sit back and let the tyrants rule, settling for prayer and pleading to God to redeem the community. There is thus no need "to sacrifice money and soul"[93] in order to bring about an Islamic revolution in our generation, for expectation becomes "a negative tool of despair." This is why some Shi^cite youngsters detach themselves from religion, even objecting to it, because they view it as implying acceptance, passivity and stagnation.

The other approach is an active one:

> the fact that the expected Imam is on the way does not mean inaction . . . our inability to reach a total and fundamental solution [which will be reached only upon the arrival of the Imam] does not justify relinquishing all hope to right what can be righted, just as the absence of the sun for long months in the North Pole does not mean that we should refrain from any deeds, and only sleep because we know that the sun will not rise again for six months.

In his *Hadith* the prophet himself said, "the best deed of my nation is expecting delivery" (*afdal a^cmal ummati intizar al-faraj*), meaning that expectation itself is a deed, is active and not passive. *Expectation* means that we should "clear the way and create the conditions for the appearance of the *Imam al-hujja*, as an army does when expecting the arrival of its commander before . . . starting the [main] attack."[94]

A similar treatment of the same problem and the same movement, which deals with the real meaning of the Koranic verse "Do not bring destruction upon yourselves with your own hands,"[95] brings another Koranic verse as a counterweight to this one: "Do not call those who died for Allah dead because they are alive with their Lord, who looks after them."[96] Indeed, the reason for the success of the Islamic revolution in Iran and its failure thus far in Iraq is explained by Ayatollah Mahmud al-Hashimi (one of the two leading figures in the umbrella organization, SCIRI, and the head of the small group Jama^cat al-^culama' al-iraqiyyin, the Association of Iraqi Ulama), in terms of a major difference in the level of "the intervention of the Hidden (*al-ghayb*)" in the two countries. Whereas in Iran "the Muslim people and the leadership are tied in the strongest way to the Hidden World, [i.e., to] the causes of the Expected Imam . . . and the turning toward God," in Iraq "the nation did not rise to the level [of *jihad* and belief] to which it did and does here in Iran." Al-Hashimi adds that the readiness to sacrifice one's life on the altar of Islam (al-Shahada) is "one of the emanations of the Hidden." The conclusion to which he is leading his listeners is that by sharing such readiness and connecting it to the cause of the Hidden Imam, a community can bring about the "intervention of the Hidden," and thus a change in the course of history. Needless to say, this whole theological discussion is exclusively Shi^cite.[97]

In the fight against passivity, much has been said about the real meaning of *taqiyya*, another particularly Shi^cite issue. Basing itself on a Shi^cite source, *Nahj al-Balagha*, which is believed in the tradition to be a collection of sayings by ^cAli, the Shi^cite organ quotes ^cAli saying that the Koranic verse, "order [to do] good and forbid the forbidden (*al-amr bilma^cruf wal nahy^can al-munkir*)," may be practiced "in the heart," "via the tongue," or "via the hand." The Shi^cite monthly interprets ^cAli's *Hadith* very conservatively, agreeing that the choice between these three levels of struggle against deviation depends on circumstances and that, in any case, it should not lead to "bringing death closer" or to "reducing [the believer's] livelihood." All the same, however, it stresses ^cAli's view that the highest of all duties in this regard is "[to say] a just word to an unjust ruler" [literally, imam], because, if the ruler does not then correct his ways, his rule will be undermined by an open challenge. The ideologues of the modern Shi^cite movement also emphasize the active nature of all three levels, all of which are aimed at actually correcting false perceptions and changing society. To drive this idea home, it is very clearly pointed out that, while "some people believe that *taqiyya* means stagnation . . . the legal meaning of *taqiyya* is clandestine activity at the state of the oppositional struggle [to change society]."[98]

Another subject that exemplifies the Shi^cite-centered treatment of an all-Muslim subject is the readiness to sacrifice oneself at the altar of one's Islamic beliefs. Although this principle itself can be accepted by Sunnis, the Shi^cites teach about it by using historical examples that at best mean little to Sunnis and in some cases are even offensive. For example, in the story about the confrontation between Ubayd Allah n. Ziyad, the Umayyad governor of Kufa, and Abdallah n. Afif al-Azdi, the Azdi paid with his life for defending ^cAli and al-Husayn and attacking the governor, the governor's father, and Mu^cawiya and Yazid. This story also includes an implicit denouncement of ^cUthman, the third caliph.[99] Similarly, there are many stories about some of the twelve Shi^cite Imams and their heroic defense of their principles against the Umayyad and Abbasid rulers;[100] these serve as inspiring examples for Shi^cites, but may not be seen in the same light by Sunnis. Although the Umayyads are somewhat controversial in Sunni historiography, some of them, notably Umar n. ^cAbd al-Aziz, are regarded by all Sunni sources as righteous. And, although some medieval Shi^cite sources describe ^cUmar as righteous relative to the rest of his dynasty,[101] there is no trace of this in publications of the Shi^cite opposition. As for the Abbasids, at least in modern Iraq, they often serve to illuminate her past glory, and portraying them as unjust rulers is bound to arouse Sunni resentment.

Another example is the painful issue of the martrydom of al-Husayn at the hands of the Umayyad army, which serves to denounce Umayyads altogether by presenting them as deviationists and falsifiers, while al-Husayn is presented as a guardian of true Islam. Thus, it serves to exacerbate Shi^cite-Sunni differences. Shi^cites also label Saddam Husayn as *Yazid* (the Umayyad ruler whose troops killed al-Husayn), and sometimes *al-Hajjaj* (ibn Yusuf al-Thaqafi, the ruthless governor of Iraq for the Umayyads [694–714] who put down Shi^cite and other revolts). It is thus easy to see how an innocuous theme such as the need to sacrifice oneself on the altar of Islam can be turned into an anti-Sunni call.[102]

Shi^cite Legitimism

Both the Shi^cite opposition press and the writings of Muhammad Baqir al-Sadr have included expressions that range from an open challenge to the Sunni community over the question of succession in Islam to the almost explicit call for a Shi^cite takeover. The emphasis on the question of succession is not surprising, as this is the most central issue in the historical controversy between the two sects. More surprising, however, is the fact that the intensity of the debate has not diminished despite all the expositions of ecumenical intent. One example of how the succession issue is treated may be found in an issue of the organ of the Movement of the Muslim Masses, in which there is a very conspicuous greeting to the Muslim nation marking the religious festivals *^cId al-adha* and *^cId al-ghadir*.[103] Whereas the first is all-Muslim, the second is particularly Shi^cite, celebrated to commemorate the occasion on which the Prophet told ^cAli, near a stream called Ghadir Khumm, *"man kuntu mawlahu fa ^cAli mawlahu"* (which Shi^cites understand to mean: "He whose patron I am, ^cAli is his patron"). Although Sunni sources do not dispute the authenticity of this *Hadith*, they disagree with the Shi^cite interpretation that in saying those words Muhammad appointed ^cAli his heir.[104] The same festival is also hailed by Shi^cites as "one of the great Islamic festivals . . . because it is the continuation of prophecy . . . and of God's government."[105] It thus is difficult to see how a Sunni reader could identify with such a message.

This same approach to the issue of succession also appears in Muhammad Baqir al-Sadr's introduction to al-Fayyad's book on the history of *Imami* ("Twelver") Shiᶜism that was published in 1970. Although Sadr does not attack ᶜUmar directly, he quotes a *Hadith* in which ᶜUmar is shown in a very bad light. When the Prophet was dying, he asked those present to give him ink and something to write on, saying: "I will write you a letter after which you will never go astray." ᶜUmar prevented the Prophet from dictating his last message, explaining that the Prophet's agony overpowered him. Sadr thus implies that the Prophet was about to write that he was to be succeeded by ᶜAli. In the same treatise, he makes it very clear that Abu Bakr and most of the companions of the Prophet (the *muhajirun* and the *ansar*) were untrustworthy, immature, and unworthy of government, that ᶜAli was the only suitable candidate for the caliphate, and that he was designated by the Prophet to be his successor. The fact that the Muslim community did not rise to the occasion after the Prophet's death was an indication of its lack of maturity, as well as a source of tragedy and disaster for subsequent generations of Muslims.[106]

Even though Sadr refrains from the vicious condemnations of ᶜUmar, Abu Bakr, and ᶜUthman that often are accompanied in Shiᶜite sources by curses (which in itself may be seen as a contribution to Sunni-Shiᶜite rapprochement), his criticism nonetheless comes through clearly and could not be accepted with equanimity by the Sunni readers at whom the introduction is aimed. (The book was published with the assistance of Baghdad University and ostensibly was written for history students of all creeds.) Apart from Sadr's communique, I have found no mention of the aforementioned three *khulafa* in the Shiᶜite opposition's publications. Although this may be viewed as a sign of moderation, as a possible attempt to avoid unnecessary friction with Sunnis, it can also be seen as extreme reluctance to follow the lead of Sadr himself by trying to rehabiliate these three even partially.

A Shiᶜite Revolution?

In reply to an overture from the Communist party, a Daᶜwa leader in London writes:

> After the prophet-messenger, the successors carried the flame of Islamic faith and continued the struggle against every deviation . . . the forces of falsification did not manage to deal a death blow to the message when it comes to the Koran [itself]. . . . But

they managed to give it a falsified interpretation . . . and managed to attain political rule in order that they could better spread their false version and continue to exploit the nation . . . under Islamic guise. This deviationist trend was embodied in history in the Umayyad kingship and in the [Abbasid] governments that followed it. They established schools for *fiqh* and ideological trends which gave a *shar^ci* countenance to this deviation and oppression. The [true] Islamic leadership as represented by the successors continued struggle against oppression and deviation from the *shari^ca*. . . . [A true Muslim must] believe in Allah and in the next world and the complementary striving towards them under the leadership of the Prophet and the Imams[!]. . . . The Da^cwa [party] . . . [acts] for a fundamental change by calling people to Islam and rejects every partial form of Islamic faith . . . the belief in Allah is embodied in the adherence to the *shari^ca*, and the criterion for adherence to the *shari^ca* is obedience to those who carry and defend it. . . . The belief in Allah, in the day of judgement, in his Prophet Muhammad and in the *imama* of the *awsiya* after him these are the roots of [true] Islam. . . . If we do not agree on the roots, how can we agree on the branches?[107]

It is very difficult to see in this paragraph anything other than the demand that all those who wish to cooperate with the Da^cwa must first adopt the Shi^cite brand of Islam. *The Da^cwa Chronicle* makes it very clear whom it considers to be worthy of leading the Iraqi Muslims: "The *jihad* warriors have to guard against the possibility that, as the Abbasids followed the Umayyads, the Tikritis will be followed by other imposters. Only the true heirs of the thought of the Sayyid [Muhammad Baqir al-Sadr] will be allowed to flourish and to lead the believers."[108] Even with a substantial stretch of the imagination, it would be impossible to define any Sunni ^calim as "the true heir" according to this statement.

In a book published in 1975, Sadr himself treats the issue of the future of Sunni-Shi^cite relations in a way that leaves something, but not much, to the reader's imagination. It is true, he claims, that the Imams did not turn to armed activity against the central government, but there is much evidence that, in every generation, the respective imam was always ready "to conduct an armed struggle if he was convinced that he had supporters and the ability to achieve the Islamic aims that lie behind such armed action." If we observe the history of the Imams carefully, he pointed out, we will find that:

The Shi͑ite leadership as represented by the Imams of the Prophet's family believed that coming to power alone is not sufficient and cannot achieve change . . . as long as the government is not supported by a popular base that is imbued with awareness and believes in the aims of this government . . . and acts to defend it and to interpret its stances to the masses. . . . [A few generations after the Prophet] the generations that emerged were fading in the shadow of deviation. [Thus] a government takeover by the Shi͑ite movement would not achieve their large aim due to the lack of supportive popular elements. . . . [Thus] there was no alternative but to do two things. One: to build the basis . . . that will prepare the grounds for taking over the government. The other . . . to keep the conscience . . . and the will [of the Muslim nation] . . . at a level of life . . . that will keep the nation from completely relinquishing its personality and honor in favor of the deviating rulers. [The fact that] the Imams forsook . . . direct armed action against deviationist rulers does not mean that they relinquished the political side of their leadership.[109]

Sadr revealed his approach to the issue of an armed revolution in a source dating back to 1966. Before the imams can topple the regime and take over, he wrote, they must "prepare an ideological army (jaysh͑aqa'idi) that unqualifiedly believes in the Imam and his omniscience." This army will give full support to the imams' actions and "will guard the achievements that are won for the nation." To clarify the depth of commitment that the imams expect from their followers as a precondition for armed revolution, Sadr told the story of a man from Khorasan who came to al-Imam al-Sadiq [Abu ͑Abd Alla Ja͑far, the sixth Imam, d. 765], and asked him to adopt the movement that revolted against the caliph in Khorasan. In reply, the Imam pointed at the oven and asked the Khorasani to jump into the fire. When the man froze in his place, the Imam called upon his disciple, Abu Başir, to jump into the oven; the latter demonstrated his readiness to fulfill the Imam's order. The Imam then turned to the Khorasani and asked him "How many do you have like Abu Basir?"

Among his other duties, the imam was always expected "to supervise the Shi͑ite [believers] directly because they are the group connected with the Imam . . . guarding them . . . and supplying them with all that enables them to hold fast and rise to the level of Islamic need." That is, one of the imam's duties was to prepare his community to become "an ideological army and a believing avant-garde."[110] This statement is nothing short of a promise to rise up against Sunni rule as soon as the Shi^cites manage to build up a political and military organization that has a reasonable chance of taking over the government. The precondition here may be interpreted as an elegant way of postponing armed revolt on the pretext that the much sought-after "ideological army" does not yet exist. However, in view of frequent Shi^cite opposition calls for direct action in the sense of military and political activism, this does not seem to be the case. Furthermore, Sadr himself warned that using the Imams' way of life as legitimatization for passivity "holds a danger from the practical point of view, because it urges negativeness and aloofness as well as detaching oneself from the problems of the nation and the realm of its leadership (*majalat qiyadatiha*)."[111] Indeed, this is the position of the Da^cwa organ published in Tehran in Arabic, which preaches against "remaining quietly and placidly in expectation that the expected Imam will appear," and calls upon al-Da^cwa followers to actually "rise to the struggle and *jihad*" immediately.[112]

Conclusion

Iraqi Shi^cite radicals today differ from their predecessors in the early twentieth century on two major ideological issues: their attitude toward the Arab component of their identity and their attitude toward Iraq as a nation-state and the people living in it as Iraqis. Radical Shi^cite reservations regarding Arabism are relatively new in Iraq. During the last years of Ottoman rule, between 1913 and the end of World War I, expressions of Arab pride and defiance in the face of Turkish oppression were quite frequent.[113] A little later, during the 1920 anti-British revolt, "the Arab flag" was the only one to be hoisted over public buildings throughout Iraq, including Najf and Karbala.[114] In the same vein, the rebel army near Kufa branded itself "the avantgarde of the Arab Army." When they defeated the British column near Kifl, it was announced that these were "the Arabs" who defeated the British.[115] There are also many expressions of Arab pride in the poetry composed during that revolt.[116] To be sure, Shi^cite and ecumenical all-Muslim sentiments also were expressed widely in those years, but as implied by these examples, Islam and Arabism were perceived as mutually supportive.

It may be suggested that the change in attitude came with, or at least was enhanced by, the advent of secular socialist pan-Arabism, particularly following the downfall of the monarchy.[117] Alongside their unequivocal and explicit allegiance to Islam, and to Khomeini's

revolution as its actual political expression in our time, the Shi^cite opposition groups and their main Iraqi source of inspiration, Ayatollah
Muhammad Baqir al-Sadr, express their belief in the legitimacy of a
political Iraqi identity or Iraqi nationalism, albeit mostly by insinuation, but sometimes explicitly. There is absolutely no support for the
notion of immediately merging the Iraqi and Iranian peoples, or for
dismembering the Iraqi state. This means that at some point in the
course of the past sixty years of Iraq's existence as a nation-state, the
Shi^cite community changed its attitude towards the state in an important way. For during the 1920 revolt, the Shi^cite leadership exhibited
separatist inclinations[118] alongside and in apparent contradiction to
its expressions of Iraqi and Arab identification.

Recognition of the legitimacy of an Iraqi political entity necessitates a certain degree of differentiation between Iraq (or the Iraqi
people) and the rest of the Muslim nation. A common denominator
also must be found for all Muslim members of the Iraqi people. The
first task is achieved by walking a tightrope between expressions of
allegiance to the pan-Islamic cause and frequent expositions of local
Iraqi pride and identifications that sometimes even imply a competitive attitude toward Iraq's eastern neighbor. As for internal Iraqi
unity, although unity among the speakers of different languages
within the Muslim community of the Iraqi state poses no serious difficulty for Muslim thinkers, this is not the case with regard to sectarian
divisions. The Da^cwa party and Sadr show that they are ready to go a
long way in this direction, and there is no reason to doubt that they are
sincere in wishing to bring Sunnis and Shi^cites together for joint
political action, or even to share power in Iraq after the Ba^cthi regime
is defeated. The flip-side of their ideology, however, greatly under-
mines their ecumenism, if it does not actually eliminate it altogether.
In advocating Sunni-Shi^cite political power sharing and accepting
Sadr's version of this partial rehabilitation of ^cUmar and Abu Bakr,
the Da^cwa party has gone further than Khomeini himself. For,
although Khomeini mentions ^cUmar in al-Hukuma al-Islamiyya and
does not add the traditional curses, he still refrains from any expression of approval or praise. However, even if one considers Sadr's last
communiqué, and the publicity given it by the Da^cwa (among other
organizations) as a sign of a profound ideological metamorphosis,
they were not able to go far enough with their theological change to
fundamentally resolve the factional strife or even to provide a reliable
basis for practical cooperation. To do the latter they would have had
to relinquish the novel principle of the rule of the *marja^c* that al-Sadr

legitimized and the application of which he and they demanded so forcefully a year or so before his execution. Only in this way could their offer of power sharing be taken at its face value.

On the more fundamental plane, mentor and disciples would have had to distance themselves from the fierce recriminations leveled against the whole institution of the caliphate after °Ali. Since Iraqi Sunnis cherish the memory of the great Abbasid caliphs of the Golden Age, to depict them as "the enemies of Islam" and bloody oppressors of the Shi°a and their Imams[119] only serves to exacerbate Sunni-Shi°i differences. Even more important, al-Sadr did not go so far as absolving the first three caliphs of the charge of usurpation, as the *Zaydiyya* did in Shi°ite history. Not having done so, al-Sadr's communiqué could have been interpreted as a mere tactical maneuver. Judging by later publications of al-Da°wa and other radical Shi°ite organizations, this, indeed, was the way in which it was understood by his disciples. The demand that Sunnis adopt the imama as one of the tenets of their faith is so radical and uncompromising that it undercuts any attempt at serious cooperation. Despite the remarkable ecumenical innovation he introduced just before his death, then, al-Sadr left the seed of Shi°ite-Sunni strife untouched. Furthermore, by expressing so explicitly his support for the principle of the rule of the Shi°i *faqih*, he seriously undermined the chances for success of the Islamic revolution in Iraq for which he gave his life. When his disciples were faced with the need to choose between the two mutually exclusive components of their mentor's legacy, for reasons that can only be guessed, they chose the particularist-Shi°i one and drove it to its logical conclusion, thereby contributing to the isolation of their movement and its total dependence on the bayonets of the Iranian army for any chance of success in Iraq.

Chapter Five

Jewish Zealots: Conservative versus Innovative

Menachem Friedman

When zealot groups in Israel are discussed, two diametrically opposed religious-political viewpoints — Neturei Karta (NK) and Gush Emunim (GE) — are considered the two poles on Israel's religious map. In this chapter, these groups are shown to be manifestations of two types of fundamentalism: "conservative" in the case of NK, and "innovative" (or revolutionary) in the case of GE.

Because the concept of fundamentalism originally evolved within the framework of the history of Christianity,[1] the term cannot always be used in the same way with reference to non-Christian religions, such as Judaism or Islam. We use the term to define a religious outlook shared by a group of believers who base their belief on an ideal religious-political reality that has existed in the past or is expected to emerge in the future. Such realities are described in great detail in the religious literature. And the fundamentalist believer is obliged to use whatever religious and political means are necessary to actualize these realities in the here and now.

Both conservative and innovative fundamentalism refer to the traditional Jewish religious conception of Jewish history, which is said to be in a state of dialectical tension between "Exile" and "Redemption." However, although Redemption signifies an ideal religious-political reality, paradoxically, within contemporary Orthodox Jewish society, the exilic past, particularly that which evolved in Eastern Europe, is viewed nostalgically as the very model of Jewish life. Thus, conservative fundamentalism looks to the past; any deviation from the idealized Jewish society, whether on the religious-social or religious-political plane, must be fought. From this perspective conservative fundamentalists condemn as "deviant" the Jewish reality in the State of Israel today.

Radical or innovative fundamentalism, on the other hand, sees a diametrically opposite "reality," one in which the State of Israel today exists in a condition that is categorically different from the exilic state.

Although radical fundamentalists do not view the reality of the State of Israel today as a sign of complete Redemption, they do perceive it as a signal that the period of the "footsteps of the Messiah" is beginning. Thus, images and precepts that are part of the traditional messianic literature sometimes assume radical "new" significance for innovative fundamentalists.

Although Neturei Karta (trans., "Guardians of the City") cannot really be regarded as a formally organized movement,[2] more attempts than ever before are currently being made to organize those who identify with its religious-ideological views in an institutionalized framework. These attempts have been increased since the deaths of two NK founders and leaders, Amram Blau[3] and Aharon Katzenelbogen,[4] who, by virtue of their personalities and work, succeeded in spontaneously rallying many of those who had identified with the entire NK ideology and practices or had joined the group because they agreed with one or more of the issues it was fighting for. The deaths of Blau and Katzenelbogen created a vacuum that exacerbated existing differences and tensions between NK, which represents the extreme isolationist view that rejects every form of contact with the political-economic Zionist establishment, and the Edah Haredit,[5] another ultra-Orthodox group that rejects the aspirations of Zionism in Palestine by adhering to the principle of "isolationism."

The increased tensions arose because, as an organized community, the Edah has been forced to make some compromises with the political-economic reality of the State of Israel in order to ensure that its members receive the full complex of communal services. This is in contrast with NK which, despite attempts to become more structured, remains a fairly loose, mostly spontaneous association of people who define themselves as "zealots" in the terminology of traditional Judaism. Whereas the NK to a certain degree is a protest group, its zealotry goes much further than mere protest. Deeply rooted in the Jewish religion, zealotry expresses the tension between a religion based on ancient sacred writings and the reality that characterizes the Jewish religion in today's world.

Neturei Karta first appeared in the wake of the political developments of the 1930s, when the conflict between the Jewish *yishuv* and militant Arab nationalism was becoming increasingly violent and the Nazis were rising to power in Germany. These developments impelled Agudat Israel,[6] the extreme anti-Zionist Jewish religious-political movement that until then had included NK leaders, to reconcile themselves to some forms of political cooperation with the Zionist leadership in Palestine. This signified a major turning point for Agudat Israel, which had opposed Zionist *yishuv* institutions from the beginning of the British mandate, when the Agudah and the Edah were identical in Palestine. Agudah-Edah activities aimed at delegitimizing Zionist efforts to establish a new secular Jewish society in *Eretz Israel* found their most stringent expression in the "exodus" of both from the organized Zionist communities (*knesset Israel*) and in the establishment of the Edah as an anti-Zionist group on its own. But, after the riots of 1929 in Palestine and the worsening economic and political position of Jews in Poland and Germany, Agudat Israel saw no choice but to identify with the minimum demands of the Zionist *yishuv*, in order to ensure Jewish immigration, especially for their own members.

The problems of European Jewry notwithstanding, Amram Blau and Aharon Katzenelbogen, who were then the leaders of Tzeirei (The Young Guard) Agudat Israel, remonstrated against the Agudah for having betrayed its fundamental principles in abandoning isolation by cooperating with secular Zionist organizations and institutions. Originally calling themselves Ha-Chaim (Life), they adopted the Aramaic name Neturei Karta (Guardians of the City) in 1939, when Blau and his circle published a proclamation against a fundraising campaign — in actuality a tax—for defending Jews against the Arab Revolt of 1936–1939. The name derives from a passage in the Jerusalem Talmud (Hagiga 76:B) that calls religious scholars rather than armed watchmen the guardians and true defenders of the city. In their proclamation the group argued that, as religious students and scholars, they (NK), and not the defense units of the Zionists (*Haganah*), were the guardians of the city, as the latter desecrated the Sabbath in public and did not observe the dietary laws of *kashrut*, in line with the secular character of Zionism. Amram Blau and his friends raised this challenge both verbally and in writing. They even raised it physically, when they took to the streets to interfere with attempts to collect the "defense" money.

Although secular Zionists were the proclaimed enemy, Agudat Israel became the principal target of the NK protest. For, in the eyes of NK, the Agudah was unwittingly helping legitimize the Zionist organization by cooperating with this effort. When Edah Haredit elections were held in July 1945, NK, in cooperation with some Edah leaders, obtained control over its institutions and ousted the representatives of Agudat Israel from this body.

Although NK and the Edah expressed the same political-religious point of view after July 1945, they still differed in organization and function. The Edah was and still is a communal organization with its own bureaucracy, whose main function is to provide its members with communal services, in particular with regard to *kashrut* and personal status (marriage and divorce). Yet, paradoxically, the very same isolationist principle that dictates providing separate religious and communal services has forced the Edah to accommodate itself to "Zionist-atheist" institutions in order to have the wherewithal to do so.

After the State of Israel was established in 1948, political reality as well as financial need dictated some form of cooperation with the state. For example, even the most extreme and anti-Zionist elements are not prepared to relinquish government sanction of marriages, as without it the Edah could not take any binding legal measures against a member who leaves his wife and children. Although some protracted and enervating procedures for applying pressure are always available in such a community, the outcome is not at all certain. They therefore must accept formal authorization from the Ministry of Religious Affairs in order to perform legally binding marriages and to grant divorces. Further, the provision of separate Edah *kashrut* services necessitates municipal and sometimes also governmental licenses (e.g., for slaughtering houses), as well as arrangements with Zionist enterprises and corporations such as Tnuvah (a Histadrut affiliate), which supplies most of the country's dairy products, fruit, and vegetables. Moreover, having its own bureaucracy has almost inevitably led the Edah to make further concessions in its isolationist principle when it fights for its economic interests by trying to gain a greater share of the Israeli food market for ultrakosher products. As long as the standard of living in Israel remained low, these tendencies were hardly noticeable. But by the mid-1960s, as it rose and the *haredi* (ultra-Orthodox), community sought to share in it, an increasingly sharp controversy developed between NK and Edah leaders.

The controversies between NK and the Edah, between these two and Agudat Israel, and between all three and secular Jewish society provide the background and context for the activities of radical extremist elements in NK and related groups, whose acts of religious zeal often take on a verbal and physical violence. Paradoxical as it may seem, these activities are directed not only against the secular Zionist but also against recognized, accepted rabbinic authorities and distinguished leaders of the ultra-Orthodox groups. Again paradoxically, these expressions of the tension between groups are based on shared historiosophical and historiographical views as *yahadut haredit*: *haredi* Jewry. It is only with this knowledge that we can understand such acts of religious zeal and their dialectical nature, for it is my thesis that this particular social context fosters conservative fundamentalism.

Without elaborating on the development of the term *yahadut haredit*, the historiosophical and historiographical principles that determine the social confinement of this society are formulated in a brief and in a somewhat simplified manner.

1. The term *Jewish nation* is meaningful only within the context of the mystical unity of Israel, the Torah, and God. Thus, Jewish identity has meaning only when there is faith in God, as well as in the Torah (both written and oral) as the expression of his absolute will. The Torah must therefore be obeyed by observing the halakhic commandments as interpreted by the *gedolei ha-Torah* (Torah sages) of every generation.

2. The historic destiny of the Jewish people derives from the special relationship between the Jewish nation and God, as described in the biblical quote, "Not like the other nations is the house of Israel." The Jewish nation cannot escape its special historic destiny of Exile and Redemption, both of which are basic concepts of Jewish existence. And Agudat Israel, Edah Haredit, and NK all define Jewish existence in the current political reality of Zionism and the State of Israel as being in a state of Exile. Whereas the adherents of Zionism define it as "the return of the Jewish people to history," ultra-Orthodox Jews view it as a revolt against the "not [being] like other nations." The *haredi* viewpoint, perforce, leads to viewing Zionist attempts to control Jewish history as a mutiny against God. This viewpoint leads to its isolationist principle and policy toward Zionist institutions and the State of Israel. Hence, every deviation from this policy, if justified at all, is justified on pragmatic grounds alone, in other words, *a posteriori*.

3. The way of life that developed in traditional Jewish communities, especially in the Ashkenazi communities of Central and Eastern Europe before the process of modernization and secularization (*haskalah*) began, is viewed as the fullest expression of Jewish society. Thus, *haredi* ultra-Orthodoxy takes this traditional Jewish society as its standard for determining the legitimacy of Orthodox Jewish life in the modern reality. From this point of view, *haredi* ultra-Orthodox religiosity to a large extent can be defined as "neo-traditionalism," a term used here deliberately because *haredi* religiosity is certainly not consistent with traditional religiosity. Although one finds traditional

religionists, whose adherence to the traditional way of life is absolute and who make no attempt whatsoever to adjust to modern society, *haredi* Jews seem to be able to deviate from tradition when necessary. However, it should again be stressed that any changes in traditional ways of life are justified only *a posteriori*, generally as a concession to social or personal imperfection.

Haredi society therefore is viewed hierarchically, in accordance with the degree of adherence to the old way of life. Since adherence to tradition as expressed in outer appearance (traditional garments, beard, side-locks), speech (Yiddish), and the education of children (*heder*) is considered the most legitimate, Neturei Karta who follow the traditions of the old Ashkenazi *yishuv* in these respects, are not merely the best representative of the isolationist approach, but also the embodiment of extreme and uncompromising loyalty to the traditions of "Israel of old."[7]

Haredi self-identification therefore is determined not only by its special historiosophical and historiographical points of view but by the awareness of the degree to which these have been deviated from on the political, religious, and social levels. Thus, *haredi* society is characterized by continuous feelings of self-delegitimation, guilt, and weakness *a posteriori* in the face of Zionist reality. These feelings determine the strength of NK as a *radical religious group*. To a large extent they also determine its dialectical relation with all of *haredi* ultra-Orthodoxy, as well as, in a sense, with religious Jewish society in general.

But radical though they may be, these paradoxical and complicated relations place NK and similar groups in the camp of conservative fundamentalism. This is because Jewish traditional society is their context of reference and they consider themselves living in conditions of Exile, which limits their use of power to traditional "exilic" means of behavior. Religious groups such as NK express their radical viewpoints in activities that they call *zealotism*, viewing this as a legitimate religious phenomenon in the context of Judaism. The classical example of such religious zeal is that of Pinhas, son of Elazar, son of Aaron the Priest, who killed both Zimri, son of Salu, "a chief in the Simeonite family," and Cozbi the Midianite, daughter of Zur, before the entire congregation of the children of Israel.[8] The Talmudic commentary on this event provides the following sociological analysis of Pinhas' act.[9] Although God praises Pinhas in the Bible, the Talmud justifies his deed only *a posteriori*. The ambivalent attitude toward such direct, violent acts may be sensed in the discussion between the Talmud sages. The Talmud says that if Zimri had killed Pinhas, he would not have been punished, "for he [Pinhas] is a persecutor." And when a man chases his fellow with a weapon in his hand, he who takes the life of the pursuer does not have to be punished, as he has in fact saved the lives of those being pursued. However, a deed such as that of Pinhas can be justified only "if it was committed spontaneously, in a mood of uncontrollable anger."

Despite the ambivalence of the halakhic sages, they recognize that such outbursts are inevitable expressions of religious emotion. But, as it is described in the Talmud,[10] the story reflects another important aspect of the "zeal syndrome": the tension between zealots and their leaders. For, by acting in front of the entire congregation, Pinhas demonstrated the weakness of the leader Moses. Indeed, it is one of the crucial aspects of this syndrome that, whatever their intention, zealots always end up challenging the established religious leadership. Even though their anger is directed at sinners, it ultimately implies criticism of the established leaders, however respected they may otherwise be.

Numerous examples of religious zeal, manifested in acts of verbal and physical violence against "sinners," can be found in various historical contexts. However, such acts are more likely to occur during periods characterized by secularization, when religion has lost control over the behavior of the people. For example, the old Ashkenazi *yishuv* in Jewish Jerusalem at the turn of the century provided a particularly favorable climate for religious zealots. The process of change and modernization that took place in Jerusalem toward the end of the nineteenth century, triggered by the activity of Western European Jewish philanthropic organizations with reformist tendencies, made possible the development of an economically and socially strong class of intellectuals (*maskilim*). But, although this new way of life was regarded an antithetical to the tradition of the old *yishuv*, the religious leadership was too weak to take serious action against it. The difficult economic and political situation also compelled them to rely upon these deviators from tradition to maintain contact between them and the philanthropic organizations. However, precisely this weakness of the religious leadership allowed the zealots relative freedom of action.

Within the social structure of the old *yishuv*, among rabbis who possessed authority and were respected in the traditional Jewish world, the zealots were able to find religious authorities to be their patrons and to sanction their activities. From this point of view, such figures as Rabbis Y. L. Diskin and J. H. Sonnenfeld played a very important role in the phenomenon of religious zeal in Jerusalem. This patronage had economic significance, too. For the rabbinic scholars who sanctioned the activities of the zealots enabled them to assume a relatively independent position in the economic set-up and power centers of their society by supporting them while they devoted their time to religious activities. Thus, the tradition of religious zeal that developed in Jerusalem constituted a source of direct or indirect subsistence by allowing zealotism to become a "profession." And this structure has remained the same in essence down to this very day.

An analysis of zealot activities demonstrates that they are facilitated by three levels of participation on the part of their community:

1. *Active zealots.* Unlike Pinhas, who acted alone, the zealots' acts of verbal or physical violence usually are influenced by the group. In other words, those who act against either "sinners" or rabbinical authorities, by shouting, protesting, blows, or vilification usually act as a group, with mutual encouragement.

2. *Sympathizers or passive zealots.* Public sympathy for zealotry is a complex phenomenon, with sympathizers ranging from those who support activists wholeheartedly and publicly, yet do not dare to join them, to those who object to the acts themselves, yet refrain from doing anything that might lead to the identification or arrest of the perpetrators because they identify with their final aims.

3. *Rabbinical patrons.* Recognized and respected rabbinical authorities legitimize zealous acts. They are especially necessary when such acts are directed against other rabbinical authorities.

The relationships among these three groups are neither static nor fixed, but rather dynamic. Nor are they harmonious; indeed, they are subject to permanent tension stemming from the violent and unpremeditated nature of some zealous acts.

Against such a social reality, violence is inherent to acts of religious zeal. Indeed, in the case of Pinhas, the archetypical zealot, the violence led to death. This has not been the case with *haredi* zealots, whose violence is confined mostly to verbal or written harassment and the destruction of property. Although people have been hurt by stones thrown at cars traveling on the Sabbath, this has not resulted in any fatal injury. Moreover, the zealots have never taken up weapons or used any other means deliberately aimed at killing people.

The reasons for this restraint are critical to our understanding of the distinction between conservative and innovative fundamentalism, as one of the factors that lead *haredi* zealots to exhibit restraint is their awareness of mutual Jewish responsibility, which is strengthened by their very affinity to Jewish tradition. However, they express this in a very curious manner: even when they are explicitly stating their hope that the mutinous and atheistic State of Israel will vanish, they add

> This Lord of the Universe . . . knows how to lead His world in mercy and benevolence and to remove the obstacles and delays of the coming of the Messiah [an allusion to the State of Israel] without, Heaven Forbid, hurting anyone in Israel. . . . He who passed over the houses of Israel in Egypt and saved those who waited for redemption shall also show us wondrous things at the time of future redemption.[11]

This quote, by one of the main supporters of the zealots in Jerusalem, is evidence that, despite all their differences with other Jews, there is a clear sense of a common Jewish fate in a hostile world.

The affinity of extremist zealots for the complex social structure that constitutes Orthodox society in its entirety, and their dependence on it as well as on recognized religious authorities, inevitably keeps their activities within tolerable confines. And, because they do not serve in the army, extremist *haredi* zealots usually are not familiar with the use of fire arms. In fact, as a very small and visible minority, they can be easily harmed themselves.

Finally, the extremists have no political ambitions in terms of reaching positoins of power within Israeli society. On the contrary, they want to continue to live in Exile as a minority protected by the powers that be. The central religious import of the concept of Exile in traditional Jewish society is not as a mere political-geographical one delineating relations between Jews and the society and sovereign political framework that surround them. It is essentially religious in that it determines the historical framework of Jewish existence as the basis of the unique relationship between the Jewish people and God. According to kabbalistic tradition, notably that of the Lurianic Kabbalah, the reality of Exile encompasses the Divine system itself, which has been "damaged," as it were, and requires "restoration."

To define the historical reality as one of Exile is to evoke much of halakhic significance that does not admit of elaboration within the present framework. Fundamentally, however, defining the political reality as one of Exile serves as a mechanism of adaptation to the unique conditions of Jewish existence on both the political and religious-halakhic planes. Therefore, not only are Torah laws relating to or bound up with Temple rites sequestered from day-to-day Jewish life in Exile, but the entire network of precepts dealing with relations between

Jews and gentiles is perceived as not binding in accordance with the
Jew's political experience as a persecuted minority.[12]

Two levels of simultaneously existing religious rulings are dis-
cernible within this framework. One bears an affinity to the political
reality of Exile, and the second relates to a utopian "reality" that either
existed in the past or is destined to emerge in the future, when "Israel's
hand shall be high." The reality of Exile enables political-social ideas
from the non-Jewish world to be absorbed and adopted while preserving a binding and fundamental affinity to religious-political precepts
that are completely opposed to such ideas. Indeed, ever since the
emergence of the modern era, Jewish society has been characterized
by the existence of two different worlds, which demand contradictory
systems of social-cultural norms.

Without going too deeply into the different interpretations given
to exile by various groups of *Halakhah*-bound Orthodox Jewry, some
remarks are called for on the Jewish society in *Eretz Israel* as it evolved through the agency of the Zionist movement. Secular in nature, the
Zionist movement sought to establish a sovereign Jewish society that
would be "modern" not only on the technological plane but also, and
perhaps chiefly, on the culture-value plane. In such a democratic
society, it was envisioned, non-Jews would enjoy full personal and
religious equality, in contrast to the discrimination and persecution
that Jews and Jewish culture had suffered in non-Jewish societies.
These basic concepts were first put to the test in *Eretz Israel* in the formative stage of Zionism, when the religious-political question of
women's right to vote for institutions of self-government arose after
Britain took over Palestine.[13] The two positions of principle adduced
on this issue were the modern-secular view, which could not accept
discrimination against women as it conflicted with the political-social
values of modern society, and the religious outlook, grounded in
Halakhah and in the values of the traditional religious society. This
question was not resolved in the religious community as a whole, as it
split along the lines of Zionist and anti-Zionist identification. The
anti-Zionists, who rejected Zionism as an attempt to annul the state of
Exile by the secular-political-material means, viewed the enfranchisement of women as a substantive expression of secular Zionism. As
such, they refused to take part in the Jewish institutions established at
the outset of British mandatory rule in Palestine.

Notwithstanding halakhic pronouncements by rabbinical authorities whom it also accepted, the religious Zionism that found expression in the stand of the Mizrachi movement[14] relied upon halakhic rulings

of other authorities, who acquiesced in the secular Zionists' stand on this question. Although the Mizrachi movement's "decision" on the issue of women's enfranchisement did not follow from its obligation to *Halakhah*, it viewed itself as true to its commitment to both the Jewish people, the Torah, and God, on the one hand, and to the national goals of the Zionist movement, on the other. This is what led to their imbuing the Zionist enterprise in *Eretz Israel* with a "positive" religious definition in terms of the traditional concepts of Exile and Redemption, and of what underlies the fundamentalist religious innovation of religious Zionism. This principle of religious Zionism vis-à-vis Exile and Redemption, which was concealed and downplayed in the past, is highly visible in the radical religiosity of Gush Emunim's Zionism.

Paradoxically enough, within the framework of the dialectic between Exile and Redemption, the ability of religious Zionism to cope with the secularization process undergone by Jewish Palestine was almost inevitably grounded in the religious conception of the uniqueness of Jewish history, of being "not like all the other nations." In other words, it was based on a principled religious outlook holding that the historical process, as it evolved in Palestine, implied a change in the state of Exile or the transition to the state of Redemption. Hence, the "secularization" of the Jewish community in Palestine, as part of a reconstructed sovereign Jewish society, could be perceived and explicated both in terms of the sanctification of the entire historical process and as an essential part of a Divine plan for the redemption of Jewish people by extricating them from the state of Exile.

These concepts were given their full expression in the writings of Rabbi Abraham Isaac ha-Cohen Kook.[15] Though religious Zionists did not necessarily accept all or even part of Rabbi Kook's religious philosophy, such realities of Jewish existence as World War II and the establishment of the State of Israel as a sovereign political entity were perceived as an inherent part of the process of Redemption. In other words, the fact that the State of Israel offered Jews a place for ingathering from Exile was enough to accord religious legitimization to it and even to the secular Jewish society existing there. These same basic principles, however, also became the rationale for another kind of political radicalism and fundamentalist religious positions derived from Jewish "writings" relating to Redemption.

The Six-Day War was a turning point in the political expression of religious radicalism. If Israel's 1948 War of Independence is viewed as a Zionist war for the establishment of an emergent secular Jewish state, the Six-Day War can be defined as a Jewish war that reflected a substantive historical change in dialectic between Exile and Redemption. For, whereas the Six-Day War did not necessarily constitute total and absolute transition from Exile to Redemption, it marked the point at which a substantially different religious reality came into existence.

The background to this development stems from social changes in the Israeli polity, as well as from such historical circumstances as Israel's rapid and astonishing victory over Egypt, Jordan, and Syria, which brought all of *Eretz Israel* under Jewish rule. Now that places denoting the Jewish people's essential affinity to *Eretz Israel*, such as Jerusalem with the Temple Mount at its center and Hebron with its Tomb of the Patriarchs, had come under Jewish rule, a new geopolitical reality was created. And the young religious-Zionist elite that encountered this new reality was ready to accord the war and the situation it generated an existential-religious meaning through which the State of Israel became the Land of Israel and the Zionist state the Jewish state. This concatenation of events led to the emergence of Gush Emunim, a movement that regards itself as religious-Zionist in its fulfillment and within whose framework expression has been given to fundamentalist concepts that represent what I term *innovative fundamentalism*.

Religious Zionism represents an attempt to combine a modern way of life with observance of *Halakhah* as it traditionally has been interpreted. The consolidation of modern religiosity inevitably entailed selecting the traditions and practices that conformed to this new way of life. Thus, some traditional elements were excluded and observance of such central Jewish commandments as prayer, Torah study, and premarital chastity became less stringent. The pattern of life that emerged from this basically spontaneous and socially activated process might be termed one of diminished religiosity.[16] Although this religiosity allowed religious Zionist Jews to play a role in the developing society and its economy without affecting their self-identification as Orthodox Jews, there was no ideological development in this atmosphere. Once the intensive pioneering activity of prestate Eretz Israel leveled off, and the rise in living standards facilitated the establishment of high-school *yeshivot*, religious Zionist youth became aware of the painful contradiction between their parents' way of life and what they felt was prescribed in the halakhic literature they studied. The helplessness of parents in face of this direct and indirect criticism from their children began a delegitimation of parents that has had social and political repercussions. Whereas some of the national religious youngsters who graduated from high school *yeshivot* were absorbed by ultra-Orthodox "great" *yeshivot*, others went on to those that were more in line with the principles of religious Zionism. The oldest and most important of these latter *yeshivot* was the Mercaz ha-Rav Yeshivah of Rabbi A. I. Kook. Under the direction of his son Zvi Yehudah Kook, Mercaz ha-Rav presented young people with a world view that offered a meaningful religious existence in the State of Israel in accordance with Zvi Yehudah's interpretation of his father's teachings.

Rabbi Kook's historiographic views are directly opposed to those of *haredi* ultra-Orthodoxy. His doctrine perceives the historical reality of his generation as more complex and essentially dialectical. In this view the reality defined as "the footsteps of the Messiah" is considered part of the historical development toward future Redemption, because it views secular-Zionist society as playing a positive and crucial role in the Messianic process, which is also essentially dialectical in nature.

Although Rabbi Kook's use of the concept "the footsteps of the Messiah" was not intended to express an innovation in religious Zionist policy, it constituted a turning point in Jewish religious thought. Indeed, extremist zealot fears regarding the potential for innovation and change are not without basis, since the concept was meant to help religious Zionism integrate into Zionist society and politics in Eretz Israel as a "junior partner." Thus, as a religious-political manifestation, Gush Emunim reflects changes in the religious-Zionist community in Eretz Israel on two levels:

1. On the plane of historical consciousness within the framework of the dialectic between Exile and Redemption, GE reflects an awareness and inner sense of confidence that the "history" of the Jewish people has already passed the incipient stage of the "footsteps of the Messiah"—although it is still not clear exactly how far Jewish history has advanced in the stage of Redemption.

2. In the normative-halakhic sphere, GE essentially signifies the criticism and rejection of "light" religiosity and a concomitant commitment to the strict and stringent religiosity demonstrated, paradoxically enough, by the ultra-Orthodox standardbearers of "anti-Zionist" religiosity: the Haredim.

A comparison of the conservative religious radicalism of *haredi* Neturei Karta and the innovative radicalism manifested by various circles within Gush Emunim reveals many structural similarities. Fundamentally, both forms base themselves on the same "writings" and see themselves as committed to the same halakhic-midrashic-kabbalistic literature. However, as NK unequivocally defines the historical reality as a state of Exile, it regards any deviation from the "traditional" way of life as constituting a "revolt" against Divine Providence. In contrast, by designating the current historical situation a state of Redemption, GE broadens the historical frame of reference to encompass the "utopian realities" in traditional religious literature, which lay down different norms, especially in the political-religious sphere.

Indeed, the religious radicalism of Gush Emunim encompasses features that were of only theoretical import in the stage of Exile but that suddenly became "compatible" with the new political situation as interpreted by GE's religious leaders. However, in areas relating to "normal," day-to-day life, GE manifests a clear tendency to reject "diminished religiosit" in favor of the "strict religiosity," characteristic of today's Haredim, of which NK is an integral part. However, the "innovative" religious radicalism of Gush Emunim sometimes finds itself in polar conflict with conservative fundamentalism, the differences between them relating to elements central to the Jewish faith; for example, to the question of a Jewish religious presence on the Temple Mount. Moreover, as we have seen, the relations between groups such as Neturei Karta and religious authorities accepted by ultra-Orthodox Jewry places restrictions on their freedom of action as well. For the dialectic that characterizes these relations is an integral part of the self-identity of members of these groups as traditional Jews committed to heeding the instructions of "Torah sages."

The radical-religious groups who feel that the fundamental change after the Six-Day War denotes a new religious-historical experience are bound along a new track from the outset. Their certainty that there is a reality that differs substantively from the traditional one, one that is as experiential as it is imbued in consciousness, must encompass elements of a religious-political activism that will find little if any legitimation in religious authorities outside their own frameworks. Moreover, this certainty, which derives its sanction from the political reality of Jewish control over all of *Eretz Israel*, requires the legitimation of religious authorities who are even more of an anathema to Orthodox Jewry. Yet, it is precisely the gap that inevitably exists within a political reality that is both the very actualization and symbol of extrication from the states of Exile and Redemption which is expressed in Israel's democratic character. This tension will no doubt become increasingly intolerable as time passes. "Painful" contradictory realities, such as Muslim worship on the Temple Mount, are liable to push groups of individuals into seeking renewed sanction for what they feel is the character and essence of current Jewish history. And the need for repeated sanction of the inner reality of Redemption in the face of the more complex and less unequivocal political reality bears within it the possibility of a religious innovation that has the potential of thrusting radical religious groups into confrontation with the Jewish religious establishment.

Chapter Six

Pro-Iranian Fundamentalism in Gaza

Thomas Mayer

Following the Islamic revolution in Iran, a group of Palestinian Muslims have become ardent supporters of the Iranian call for the reunification of the Shi^cite and Sunni communities and the recreation of a united Islamic nation. The person most responsible for the organization of this group, its goals, its relations with similar groups in Arab countries and Europe, and its structure and size is a young Palestinian physician, Fathi ^cAbd al-^cAziz Shqaqi. Therefore a close look at the career of this group leader would seem appropriate to any examination of this phenomenon and its effects on Palestinian society.

Fathi Ibrahim ^cAbd al-^cAziz Shqaqi was born in Gaza in January 1951 and moved with his family a year later to Rafah, in the southern part of the Gaza Strip, where his father developed a small business. When Fathi's mother died of cancer in 1966, he decided to become a doctor. In 1974 he was accepted to the faculty of medicine at the University of Zaqaziq in Egypt.[1]

At the time Fathi Shqaqi arrived in Zaqaziq, campus life was bustling. Egypt's university campuses, no longer controlled by pro-Nasserist student organizations, were experiencing a return to old influences, notably that of the Muslim Brethren. The growing criticism of Nasser's political system, sanctioned and encouraged by his successor and amplified in the media, severely damaged the popularity of all the student unions associated with it, including the Left and the Arab Socialist Union. President Sadat's support for the rehabilitation of the Muslim Brethren encouraged the creation of Islamic groups on campus. And, in the absence of an alternative vanguard ideology, these groups attracted a growing following. One by one student federations in all of Egypt's universities fell into the hands of Muslim groups, usually called *al-jama^cat al-islamiyya* (the Islamic groupings), and campuses were flooded with religious literature and bustling with religious activity.

This activity, which intensified during most of Shqaqi's seven years of study in Egypt (1974–1981), considerably influenced the Palestinian student. Thus, Shqaqi came to believe that the ills of his society were not merely physical but to a great extent spiritual. He joined Ikhwan (Muslim Brethren) circles on campus, adopting their view that Islamic society had become weak and vulnerable because, directly or indirectly, external imperialist powers had succeeded in propagating such foreign ideologies and doctrines as liberal Westernization, military or scientific socialism, and communism. The advent of the Islamic revolution in Iran in 1978, and the worried reaction of the West, seems to have greatly impressed young Shqaqi, as well as many other Muslim students. Like some writers in the West, he and his friends regarded the Iranian revolution as the only possible response to foreign domination, viewing it as an omen as well as a model to be adopted in the Arab East.

Shqaqi put his thoughts into writing, and early in 1979 the publishing house al-Mukhtar al-Islami published his pamphlet, *Khomeini, the Islamic Solution and the Alternative* (*Khumayni, al-hall al-islami wal-badil*). Shqaqi dedicated it to "the martyred leader (imam)" Hasan al-Banna, general guide of the Muslim Brethren, and "the revolutionary imam" Ayatollah Khomeini, both of whom he regarded as advocates and strugglers for "the Islamic solution." According to Shqaqi, the solution to Islam's problems was embodied in the demand to liberate Islamic society from external, imperialistic doctrines and to apply Muslim jurisdiction and a Muslim way of life to society. Like Hasan al-Banna and Ayatollah Khomeini, Shqaqi made no distinction between Western and Eastern imperialism: both were evil powers that ceaselessly conspired to control Muslims by confusing them with their ideologies. Shqaqi reminded his readers that the Jews, enemies of Islam and agents of imperialism, had contacts with both the Soviet Union and the United States, and that the Muslim world therefore should be prepared for the possibility of a Soviet-Israeli alliance side by side with the American-Israeli partnership.[2]

Imperialism then, especially in its ideological manifestations, was the principal enemy of Muslim society. The modern history of both Egypt and the Arab East had witnessed numerous imperialist attempts to invalidate the religious laws of Islamic society. First Napoleon, then Muhammad cAli and his successors, who sent student missions to Europe, sought to replace Islam with liberal Westernization as a ruling ideology. But the Muslim masses (*jamahir*), under the leadership of ulama and military officers such as cUrabi rose and revolted. Then imperialists chose Arabism as an alternative to the unity of the Islamic nation under the Ottomans. Thus, the English assisted Sharif Husayn in the Great Arab Revolt because they conspired to take over the Arab territories after the Ottoman Empire was dissolved. Once they realized this aim, the imperialists used agents such as cAli cAbd al-Raziq and Ahmad Lutfi al-Sayyid to enforce liberal ideology on Arab society while suppressing such Muslim causes as Shaykh cIzz al-Din al-Qassam's Palestinian movement, the Egyptian Muslim Brethren, and the Libyan Sanussis.

The humiliating defeat of 1948 demonstrated to Shqaqi liberalism's ultimate failure to serve Arab and Muslim society. Yet, this collapse of liberalism did not frustrate "the secularist current of Westernization" in the Arab East, which now attempted to prevent a return to Islam by means of CIA-sponsored military coups. Moreover, a new alternative, in the form of revolutionary socialism (*ishtirakiyya thawriyya*) or anarchic socialism (*ishtirakiyya fawdawiyya*) had begun to gather strength while the physical elimination of those who advocated the Islamic movement continued. The 1967 military defeat, like that of 1948, however, demonstrated that "the tenth crusader invasion" was still on, and therefore, the Islamic movement could be the only response to imperialism. The history of the Muslim Brethren revealed that the Islamic movement, as the sole group that enjoyed genuine popular support, alone was capable of resisting imperialism.[3]

So far, Shqaqi's views were not particuarly innovative. He appears to have leaned heavily on a series of books by a former Ikhwan member, Yusuf al-Qardawi, on the "Islamic Solution"[4] a title borrowed by Shqaqi. Nonetheless, Shqaqi, in the second and third chapters of his book devoted to the rise of Khomeini and Shicism, deviates from Qardawi's teaching. Thus, in writing about Khomeini, "the teacher and the struggler (*mujtahid*)," Shqaqi praises both the theories and the practices of the Iranian leader, particularly with regard to the Palestinian question. Shqaqi argues that, like Hasan al-Banna, Khomeini grasps that Palestine has become the axis of imperialist encroachment and that the State of Israel has been the incarnation of imperialist struggle against Islam. The Palestine question therefore has become the core issue for the Islamic movement, and hence, Khomeini's strong support for Yasir cArafat, chairman of the Palestine Liberation Organization.[5]

In an apparent effort to recruit the support of his readers for the Islamic revolution in Iran, Shqaqi contends that Shicites are not as averse to or different from Sunnis as has been alleged. Shqaqi draws attention to substantive similarities between Sunni and Shi^cite normative laws, and uses Sheikh Shaltut's 1959 *fatwa* (legal opinion) to describe Shi^cites as followers of the fifth "*Ja^cfari*" school (*madhhab*), reducing the role of the *Mahdi* to a mere symbol of justice.[6]

Theology, then (in which young Shqaqi evidently did not excel), did not tip the scales against support for the revolutionary Shi^cites in Iran. On the contrary, Shqaqi seems to have been fascinated by the Islamic revolution there. The major part of his book is devoted to a detailed description and analysis of the historical development and imlications of the Iranian revolution. Shqaqi argued that the revolution's success emanated essentially from the positive response of the Muslim masses to the Islamic movement. This support turned the movement into a people's revolution and enabled the victory over imperialism and its local agents in Iran. The benefits of the revolution, however, have not been confined to Iran. The Arab and Muslim worlds at large could enjoy the fruits of the Iranian revolution, for Shi^cite enmity to imperialism of all kinds, and to Israel, added a powerful new friend to the Arab cause, particularly the cause of the Palestinian Arabs. It is strange, concluded Shqaqi, that a number of Arab countries have adopted a negative attitude toward the Iranian revolution. The only explanation he offered is that the Arab rulers fear lest the Islamic revolution reach their own states.[7]

Shqaqi does not mention the names of these rulers, although he does survey the opposition to the revolution by Saudi Arabia, Kuwait, and Iraq. Nor does he elaborate on the impact of the Iranian revolution among his fellow students. Clearly, however, Shqaqi was not the only Muslim student who was impressed by the Iranian revolution and its leader and looked to it for material and spiritual support. At the time that Shqaqi wrote his book, other members of Islamic groups at Egyptian universities staged demonstrations and rallies in solidarity with the Iranian revolution and against giving the Shah asylum in Egypt.[8] Elsewhere, in Jordan, Muslim students at the local universities reportedly circulated a clandestine publication, *Sawt al-islam* (*The Voice of Islam*), which applauded Iran's Islamic revolution and its leadership.[9]

Support for the Muslim revolutionaries in Iran was not confined to Muslim youth circles. Even prominent Sunni leaders of the Muslim Brethren movement, such as ^cUmar al-Tilmisani of Egypt and ^cAbd al-Rahman Khalifa of Jordan, at different points, expressed satisfaction with the triumph of an Islamic revolution in Iran.[10] In Jordan, sympathy with Khomeini's Iran was reported to have surpassed the bounds of fundamental Muslim Brethren circles; whether for reasons of religious sentiment or because of Iran's political support of the PLO, wider sections of the population were believed to be sympathetic to the Iranian revolution. By late 1980, public support grew to such an extent that the Jordanian government had to use repressive measures to curb the propaganda of pro-Iranian advocates. Thus, a number of Muslim preachers who championed Khomeini during Friday sermons in various mosques were arrested.[11]

Yet, despite official opposition to the Iranian revolution, there remained Sunni politicians, who at some point in their political careers still regarded Khomeini as a model for personal emulation. Among them was Ahmad al-Sabahi, head of the newly created Nation Party (*Hizb al-umma*) in Egypt. In July 1983, Sabahi chose to sign his first party communiqué with the name "Ahmad al-Khomeini," explaining that "Khomeini has stimulated an Iranian revolution without spilling a drop of blood."[12] This amazing statement reveals much of Sabahi's own ambition, as well as his one-time admiration for the leader of the Iranian revolution.

As late as 1985, when the extent of Khomeini's oppression had become well known, many radical Muslims still refused to publicly condemn the Iranian revolution. In an interview for a leading Egyptian journal, Sheikh Hafiz Salamah, leader of the Society of Islamic Guidance (*jamᶜiyat al-hidaya al-islamiyya*) blamed the Western or Westernized anti-Islamic media for disseminating false reports about Iran and refused to criticize developments there.[13] Although Salamah may lack the zealous admiration for Khomeini that characterizes Shqaqi, Shqaqi is not alone among Sunni believers in retaining his regard for Khomeini. Other Muslim and non-Muslim fundamentalists also have taken Khomeini and his political theory as a model to emulate.[14] It is clear that Shqaqi's work could not have been published had he not found some support for his views on the part of his Muslim publishers.

It is nevertheless equally clear that not all fundamentalists viewed favorably the Shiᶜite triumph in Iran. Many Sunni educators, particularly those living near Iran, in Saudi Arabia and Pakistan, watched Khomeini's rise with great concern and warned their fellow believers of the Shiᶜite danger. Thus, in 1979, the same year that Shqaqi's favorable account of the Islamic revolution in Iran was published, another fundamentalist publishing house in Cairo reprinted an essay on *The Shiᶜa and the Sunna*, by a Pakistani ᶜalim, Ihsan al-Hay Zahir, apparently as a response to it. The essay, first published in Lahor,

Pakistan in 1973, was reintroduced by the Egyptian Asᶜad Sayyid Ahmad and the Cairo publishing house *Dar al-Ansar* as a major study unmasking the false Shiᶜite propaganda about the Sunni community. The nation, warned the publishers, was facing a new cultural and spiritual invasion. Ostensibly advocating rapprochement with the Sunnis, it in fact was promoting their "Shiᶜitization" or their "de-Islamization." The publishers and the author argued that Shiᶜism in fact was the foster daughter (*rabiba*) of the Jews and Shiᶜite calls for the unification of the Islamic nation therefore were a mere cover for a vicious plot to infect the Sunnis with poisonous Jewish and pagan beliefs.[15] The republication of such a polemic during the heyday of the Shiᶜite revolution in Iran reflects the substantial differences of opinion on this issue among Muslim Arab fundamentalists. Thus, the publication of Shqaqi's essay triggered some sharp reactions. Indeed, Shqaqi's adversaries claimed that it led to his explusion from Ikhwan circles.[16]

Criticism of Shqaqi's composition and opposition to it was not confined to Muslim radicals in Egypt, however; the Egyptian government also intervened. President Sadat's own political orientation and his personal friendship with the Shah, who eventually found refuge in Cairo, determined the Egyptian regime's opposition to the Muslim revolutionaries in Iran. In Egypt, as in other Arab states, any support voiced for the Iranian revolution was immediately silenced. Thus, Shqaqi was jailed and his book confiscated. After three months in jail, Shqaqi apparently satisfied his Egyptian interrogators that no external force had financed his book and that he himself posed no danger to the regime; and he was released without trial or bail. However, this rather quick exoneration by no means implied that Shqaqi had renounced his support for Khomeini or the Muslim revolutionaries in Iran. The security forces in Egypt, convinced that Shqaqi still clung strongly to his ideas, left his file open. After Sadat's assassination, in an attempt to round up all radical activists, the police again sought out Shqaqi. But the Palestinian student had already returned home.[17]

Shqaqi obtained a position as a physician at an East Jerusalem hospital, but did not give up his religious activities. He made frequent visits to mosques, especially those in the Gaza Strip where he still lived, in an attempt to seek followers for his views. He developed particularly good relations with a Rafah-born student he knew from Egypt, Bashir Nafiᶜ. Shqaqi found in Nafiᶜ, who in Egypt had given refuge to a suspect in Sadat's assassination,[18] an ideological friend.

In 1982, Nafi[c] departed for London for doctoral studies and there became involved in the publication of the Muslim Students Federation's periodical in Britain, *Majallat al-ghuraba*. Thus he became acquainted with the various Islamic publications in Arabic issued by the Iranian-run Islamic Center for Studies and Publishing (al-Markaz al-islami lil-dirasat wal-nashar). Occasionally, he sent copies of their literature to Shqaqi, who, realizing that it reflected his own views, disseminated the contents among a larger audience. Thus, in 1982, Shqaqi reproduced 1000 copies of a handwritten statement on Islam and distributed them in Gaza Strip mosques via Muslim students. On another occasion he reproduced 500 copies of the text of a speech by Khomeini that he had received from Nafi[c] and distributed them in mosques under the auspices of a self-proclaimed Movement of the Children of the Koran (harakat abna' al-Qur'an).

Such occasional activities became more serious and consistent, once Shqaqi became acquainted with a new Islamic monthly in Arabic that began to appear regularly in London in early 1983. Titled *al-tali[c]a al-islamiyya* (The Islamic Avant Garde), it was one of a series of periodicals published by the Iranian-run center in London.[19] It advocated the same ideas that Shqaqi and Nafi[c] had been promoting for years: the need to create a united Islamic front (*jabha*) composed of Sunnis and Shi[c]ites alike against imperialism. Sayyid Qutb's phrase "one way, one program" (*tariq wahid minhaj wahid*) was borrowed and freely interpreted to serve an entirely different purpose.[20] Nearly every issue of the periodical recounted the massacre of Muslim believers, Sunnis and Shi[c]ites alike, in different parts of the world — the Philippines, India, Afghanistan, Iraq, Syria, and Israel and the West Bank — emphasizing the need to launch a united Sunni-Shi[c]ite *jihad* to repel imperialism from Muslim lands and restore Muslim sovereignty over them. Leaning heavily on the writings of Hasan al-Banna and Sayyid Qutb, the periodical persistently attacked Arab Marxists and the secular Arab regimes, praising actions such as Sadat's assassination and calling upon Muslim revolutionaries to emulate them in their own countries.

So important did Shqaqi deem the contents of this periodical that he took steps to distribute it in the West Bank and the Gaza Strip. To this end he organized some twenty Muslim volunteers, ranging in age from eighteen to thirty-two, who reproduced each issue and distributed it in Palestinian universities, refugee camps, and mosques. Half of this group were students, most at the Islamic University of Gaza.

Among the others were several workers and at least one mosque imam, who also taught at the Islamic University of Gaza.[21]

In order to regulate importation of the periodical, and perhaps also to obtain funds for his operation, Shqaqi flew to London in 1983. He saw Nafi[c], and together they met one of the periodical's editors, [c]Abd al-Majid Muttahasbi, who promised to help the group. Binding and distributing the issues cost several hundred Jordanian dinars, the greater part of the cost paid through financial contributions by Shqaqi and other group members and through the sale of issues to the public (at the equivalent of one dollar per copy).

Altogether the group reprinted 7000–7500 copies each of the first eight issues of *al-Tali[c]a al-islamiyya*, many bound together in volumes. Despite the short duration of their operation, Shqaqi and his assistants apparently succeeded at least in spreading the call for unity of action by the Sunni and Shi[c]ite communities among a large audience. Although *alJ-Tali[c]a al-islamiyya* is outlawed in the administered territories, copies continued to circulate through mosque libraries, Palestinian universities and private libraries of Palestinians. Beyond this distribution success, however, it is not clear how successful Shqaqi and others like him in other Arab and Muslim states were in their call for the reunification of the Sunni and Shi[c]ite communities.

Clearly, it is still early to assess the overall impact of the Shi[c]ite revolution in Iran on the Sunni world. To this day, Iranian revolutionaries seem determined to export their model of revolution to other Muslim states. Shi[c]ite revolutionaries in Iran are said to have indoctrinated cadres of Sunni students from Saudi Arabia, Egypt, Morocco, and Afghanistan, teaching them "revolutionary Muslim ideals" in order to stimulate Islamic revolutions in their respective countries when they return home. In addition, the Iranian regime reportedly has assisted Muslim revolutionary undergrounds in Malaya, Turkey, Yugoslavia, and even Trinidad.[22]

Iranian revolutionary influences seem to be particularly effective in Lebanon, where a limited measure of cooperation has been established between several Sunni and Shi[c]ite militias against either the Christian or Syrian forces.[23] Yet, sympathy with the Shi[c]ite revolution in Iran can also be detected in the more homogeneous Sunni communities of Egypt and even Jordan. In May 1984, former Jordanian prime minister Ahmad [c]Ubaydat, in a speech at the House of Representatives, recounted some of the unfortunate outcomes of radical Sunni cooperation with Shi[c]ite Iran. "Hardly a week passes," he complained, "without the authorities impounding explosives or weapons transferred here to be used in this country." Among those he charged with responsibility for subversive actions were several groups connected to Iran. The first was the Jihad organization, active in Egypt, which recruited both civilian and military Jordanians to form a branch in Jordan. The members of this branch were few, admitted cUbaydat, but they contacted Iran with the aim of coordinating actions. "Weapons were seized, and it was revealed that they received training in Lebanon and in other places." cUbaydat went on:

> There was also another religious organization owing allegiance to Iran, under the patronage of the Iranian Embassy in Jordan. Jordanian citizens were involved. They exploited the mosques to begin their campaign. They did not name their organization, in order to avoid being pursued. Those responsible for this organization visited Iran twice, contacted the Iranian charge d'affaires in Amman, and contracted other sides.[24]

cUbaydat did not disclose specific details on the structure or composition of these secret revolutionary organizations: they remained classified. Given the structure of Jordanian society, however, these groups likely included a number of Palestinian Arabs. This also is probable because the Palestinian Arab leaders have shown the greatest support for the Iranian revolution. Until recently, PLO leaders expressed unequivocal support for the revolutionary regime in Iran. Palestinian leaders proudly boasted of the material assistance they had given Khomeini and the Iranian revolutionaries before their advent to power. After Khomeini's return to Tehran, PLO leaders made frequent visits to Iran, lavishing praise on the revolution and its positive implications for the Arab struggle for Palestine.

PLO relations with Iran have soured following its mediatory efforts in the Iraqi-Iranian war, and Chairman cArafat's renewed honeymoon with Iraqi leader Saddam Husayn, Khomeini's avowed enemy. These high politics, however, did not prevent other educated elements in the Palestinian community from expressing admiration and support for the Iranian model of revolution. Shqaqi was neither the only Palestinian intellectual who advocated adopting this model nor the only one who, in an obvious attempt to elicit Arab sympathy for the Iranian revolution, minimized the theological controversy between Sunnis and Shicites. In 1979, the year Shqaqi's book was published in Egypt, another Palestinian academic, cAbd al-Sattar Qasim, attempted unsuccessfully to gain official Jordanian approval for his own favorable account of the Iranian revolution. In this study (which

Qasim finally succeeded in having published without alteration in the West Bank in 1981), Khomeini emerges as a liberal who represents his people's conscience (damir al-sha^{c}b). Like Shqaqi, Qasim ridiculed the Sunni-Shi^{c}ite theological rift as essentially political rather than ideological. He admitted that there may be minor theological disagreement between Sunni believers and Shi^{c}ite advocates over the function of the imam.[25] But both Sunni and Shi^{c}ite believers abide by the same Book and divine laws. Qasim blamed the Arab regimes for emphasizing Sunni-Shi^{c}ite legal differences in order to retain their hold over the Arab masses and evade participation in the sacred duty of a holy war to liberate Palestine. Khomeini, he claimed, has developed and presented to the Arab masses a model for fighting tyranny and oppression. Yet no Arab regime, other than the more progressive Syria and the PLO, was prepared to support the Islamic revolution in Iran, for emulation of the Iranian model required first the downfall of the regimes and second the liberation of the Arab personality as a step toward the liberation of Palestine by jihad.[26]

Both Shqaqi and Qasim clearly saw and interpreted Sunni-Shi^{c}ite reunification in political rather than theological terms. For both, the desired Muslim unity of action is intended to serve specific political goals, particularly solution of the Palestine problem. In this they do not differ from many other Muslim believers who expect to find in and through Islam a remedy to their political as well as religious predicaments. Like the former Palestinian leader Hajj Amin al-Husayni, who invited Shi^{c}ite representatives to his 1931 General Islamic Conference in Jerusalem, they also expected to realize their desire for a Palestinian state in Israel's stead by eliciting the cooperation of the Shi^{c}ite and Sunni communities. Pan-Islamic solidarity thus was recruited once again to promote, indeed to realize, particularistic Palestinian nationalism. In their attempt to realize this solidarity, both Shqaqi and Qasim ignored, or were inclined to dismiss as negligible, the various theological problems posed by the expected reunification of the Islamic nation. Similarly, the required jihad that both advocate was not so much a spiritual struggle for the liberation of the self as a militant holy war to free a Muslim land.

For this last interpretation, Shqaqi found support mainly among Palestinian youth. And among the youth, the main pool of supporters is to be found with the more religious students. For some, such as those who in July 1983 issued a pamphlet signed by the Islamic Struggling Movement (Harakat al-kifah [H.K.] al-islami), jihad could be the only response to the killing of Palestinians by Jews, commonly depicted as "the descendants of the monkeys and the pigs."[27] For others, such as the members of the Islamic Student Movement (al-Haraka al-tulabiyya al-islamiyya), who have been publishing an illegal periodical, *al-Bayan* (the Statement, or Koran) since early 1985, *jihad* is the only option left for the Muslim masses—particularly the Palestinian Arabs—against imperialism and its agents in the Arab East. (Its agents include all the Arab leaders.) There is a great similarity of views between the writers of *al-Bayan* and the writers of *al-Tali^ca al-islamiyya*. Like Shqaqi, they also revered the teachings of Hasan al-Banna and Sayyid Qutb, citing the latter particularly frequently. They agreed that Islamic society had been under constant threat from imperialism, Western and Eastern alike, and was in urgent need of salvation. And they concurred that the road to spiritual and political salvation is through the unification of the Muslim masses, regardless of affiliation, into a single strong entity capable of carrying out the required *jihad*.

Jihad, then, emerges as the outcome of Muslim unification. But, since the agents of imperialism, the secular Arab regimes, have opposed this unification, the Muslim masses must first overthrow them. Hence, the editors of *al-Bayan* sharply denounced the February 1985 agreement between the PLO and King Husayn of Jordan. The Palestinian experience with Arab leaders, the writers warned Yasir ^cArafat in an open letter, was very bitter. History had taught the Palestinians to trust none of them; only Holy War could initiate the final solution. ^cArafat should therefore count on the Muslim masses, and put his trust in them alone.[28]

Like Shqaqi and the team of *al-Tali^ca al-islamiyya*, the editors of *al-Bayan* have advocated Sunni-Shi^cite cooperation and unity of action. In the Sunni-Shi^cite alliance that they perceive in Lebanon, they have found in the mid-1980s an omen for a larger alliance, and a model for the future. They praise statements advocating greater cooperation by both Sheikh Muhammad Husayn Fadalallah, Lebanese leader of the Shi^cite *mujtahidin*, and Sheikh Sa^cid Sha^cban, leader of the Muslim militia in Tripoli, and accuse the Syrian regime of conspiring to frustrate the Sunni-Shi^cite-Palestinian alliance. They express their confidence that the Syrian conspiracy will fail. For them, the unity of the Islamic movement, a term frequently used by both Shqaqi and *al-Tali^ca al-islamiyya*, is "a religious duty (*wajib shar^ci*)" and "a basic demand" that emanates from the dangers facing the Islamic nation. Therefore, a major need exists to draft a program (*barnamaj*) for "joint action," starting with the lowest common denominators between Sunnis and Shi^cites, and developing by means of continuous debate on the issues that still remain disputed.[29]

It is difficult to establish the extent of *al-Bayan*'s distribution and readership. The periodical is printed secretly and distributed through volunteers, mainly at the Islamic University in Gaza, where its editors presumably study. Copies of new issues of *al-Bayan* are sent to Palestinian newspapers, which inform the public of their appearance.[30] But this moderate publicity cannot indicate the volume of support for the ideas *al-Bayan* puts forth. And since no Islamic student movement has ever run for election in any Palestinian university, the dimensions and influence of the organization responsible for this publication remain a mystery.

The obstacles that both *al-Bayan* and Shqaqi's group confront are difficult to surmount. To begin with, these movements have had to operate under the watchful eye of the Israeli authorities. These authorities, quite naturally, have been unwilling to sanction the development of a movement that calls for a militant *jihad* to liquidate the State of Israel and advocates emulation of the suicide attacks launched in southern Lebanon against Israeli or pro-Israeli targets. Therefore, Shqaqi and his followers were arrested shortly after they expanded their operations. They were charged with membership in an illegal organization and with agitation. They pleaded innocent and, after arguing in court against a militant solution to the Palestine question, received relatively light prison sentences. Once freed from jail,[31] they refrained from publicly advocating the adoption of a militant *jihad* against Israel. They resumed such slogans only with the outbreak of the *intifada* in December 1987. Some, including Shqaqi himself, continued all through the mid-1980s to preach a Sunni-Shi^cite alliance, a view also advocated by *al-Bayan*. But this approach appears to have made very little headway among Palestinian Arabs — or among other Arab and Muslim societies. One major obstacle is the opposition of the religious establishment; the Sunni *qadis* and *muftis*, to the advocacy of reunified Islam. This body of religious dignitaries — including Sheikh Muhammad Hasan ^cAwad, president of the Supreme Shar^ci Court of Appeals in Gaza; Sheikh Tawfiq ^cAsliyya, his counterpart in Israel; and Sheikh Sa^cd al-Din ^cAlami, president of the Supreme Islamic Council in East Jerusalem — still retains great influence over a large following of Muslim believers. Most of the clergy are well versed in Islamic law and jurisdiction and emphasize the great theological differences separating Shi^cites from Sunni orthodoxy. More important, they all dissociate themselves from the militant turn taken by the Shi^{c}ite revolution in Iran, denouncing, for example, the regime's tyrannical nature and Iran's long refusal to end the war with Iraq. Moreover, since all these clergy receive their salaries from the Israeli or Jordanian governments, it is understandable that revolutionary calls to overthrow all Arab regimes and reform their institutions have failed to attract their sympathy. But, even among the silent majority of the Palestinian Arabs living in the administered territories and Israel, an Islamic solution for their national problem is not favored.

Shqaqi's ideas are disputed even among the more radical Islamic movements. As in Egypt, the reaction of these movements is all the more critical because Shqaqi threatens to recruit support from among their own pool of followers. Thus, the leaders of the largest and most influential Islamic society in the Gaza Strip, al-Majma^c al-islami (better known in the colloquial as al-Mujamma' al-islami, the Islamic Congregation), may sympathize with the radical solution of *jihad*, but their teaching accepts no compromise with Shi^{c}ites (or Sufi Muslims). In fact, they condemn as infidels all Muslims who do not abide by strict interpretation of the Koran. Ibn Taymiyya, who branded the Shi^{c}ites infidels, is their source of inspiration and emulation, rather than Khomeini.

The leaders of the revivalist movement of Israeli Muslims, the so-called Muslim Youth Movement (Harakat al-shabab al-muslim) are no less critical of Shqaqi's view. Shqaqi, they declare, aroused discord and disunity (*shqaq*), as his name implies, rather than agreement and support. They not only criticize the militant nature of the Shi^{c}ite revolution in Iran but also emphasize the inapplicability of this solution to their own needs. The course they seem to follow resembles that suggested by Qardawi in the 1970s, concentrating on social activities for the community as a means of recruiting public support for Islam.

The strong opposition evinced by Palestinian Arabs in Israel and the West Bank to the Islamic solution proposed by Shqaqi and other Muslim radicals suggests that local proponents of Sunni-Shi^{c}ite reunification still have a great deal of work to do in the field to succeed in turning their movement into a major ideological and political force. Indeed, whereas Islamic radicals play an important role in the ongoing *intifada* in Gaza, their impact on the West Bank is minor. Even in Gaza, Sunni groups, led by Sheikh Amhad Yasin, control the movement. Pro-Khomeini ecumenists such as Shqaqi are still a negligible force. Shqaqi himself was deported in September 1988 by the Israeli military authorities.

Chapter Seven

Redemption as a Catastrophe:
The Gospel of Gush Emunim

Gideon Aran

Gush Emunim (Bloc of the Faithful, henceforth GE) which came to public attention only fifteen years ago has by now become an integral, even central, part of Israel's sociopolitical scene. This chapter reports in brief on some findings and conclusions resulting from a comprehensive study of this salient and significant social movement and its culture.[1] No attempt will be made here to describe or evaluate GE, or to present its program and its doctrine, all of which have been dealt with elsewhere.[2] Instead I shall concern myself with only one theme of the rich spiritual complex that has materialized, a specific motif in the theology of GE, which is permeated by ideological elements that render it a basis for social action.

To be sure, the belief system I discuss does not in itself account for the phenomenon of GE. This awaits a full description and analysis, including the relevant social conditions, political interests, and psychological motives. For only this full complex, together with the GE symbolic system, can suffice to explain the appearance of the movement, how its behavior has been molded, and what its implications are.

During the course of my anthropological research, I have closely followed the evolution of the religion of GE, by means of intensive participant observation, for over two years. This, plus many in-depth interviews and content analysis of original GE documents, are the basis for my study of how this symbolic system has crystalized out of mutual relations with its social environment.

Before proceeding to my thesis, a few introductory remarks on the nature and background of the movement are in order. From its beginning in 1974 and throughout its various incarnations, GE has not only succeeded in finding an ongoing place in the headlines, but its influence has also been felt in some major Israeli institutional areas. What first appeared to be a marginal and ephemeral group of eccentrics crystalized around an esoteric doctrine has become a factor to be dealt with, one that no longer can be ridiculed or dismissed.

GE's influence on Israeli political culture and public morale is expressed in new norms regarding law and order, in reinforcing rightist tendencies and tendencies toward maximalism and activism in foreign and security policy, and in the challenge it presents to Israel's democratic regime. But this influence and even the creation of a new geopolitical reality in the region—crucial as these are to the future of Israel and other nations in the Middle East—in my opinion are not the most important implications of GE. Rather, the decisive and lasting impact of GE is in the context of the struggle over the very basis of legitimation of Israeli society. Although it is a minority movement—comprising a nucleus of several hundred activist true-believers, mostly yeshiva students or graduates, and a periphery of tens of thousands, mainly from the religious-Zionist camp—it gives vent to widespread moods in Israeli society and strikes sensitive chords in the Israeli collective.

The main public expression of GE is its settlements in the Israeli occupied or "liberated" areas of the West Bank (Judea and Samaria), the earlier and more important of which were formed contrary to government decision and the will of significant segments of the Israeli public. Today, thousands of Jews inhabit dozens of small settlements, surrounding and penetrating hostile Palestinian population centers. The constantly growing number of fait accompli settlements changed the West Bank landscape and atmosphere radically; they represent a planned effort to extend Israeli sovereignty over the territories and to have them included within the boundaries of effective and legitimate Israeli control. Hidden within this political struggle over territorial boundaries, however, is the struggle over the boundaries of Judaism. At issue here are not only the borders of the country and the state but the borders that distinguish between the country and the state: between traditional religion and modern national civic order. This, then, renders the problem one of Kulturkampf.

Would-be members of GE took the Israeli victory of 1967 and subsequent Israeli military administration of large territories, which they considered an integral part of the historic holy land and critical for the security of the state, as a decisive step toward the consummation of Redemption. It was only in the aftermath of the 1973 war, which brought in its wake international pressure and subsequent withdrawal from sacred and strategic areas, that GE was formally established. The anomie, deterioration in public morale, weakening authority of official leadership, and erosion of the dominant ideology provided good soil within the national religious society for the emergence of sentiments and values that heretofore had been passive. A dynamic force emerged that led the militant campaign aimed at eventual annexation of the "Whole Land of Israel" by means of settlement, both legal and illegal.

The classical phase of GE, its formative and purist period, was between 1974 and 1977, until the Labour Party was defeated electorally and the Likud, Israeli's right-wing party, came to power. The political turnabout of May 17 enabled GE to cooperate with the admiring and obliging Begin government. This resulted in significant progress toward realizing the movement's strategic objectives. Ironically, under this very supportive framework, the golden era of GE came to an end. Although the preceding four years under a Labour government did not bring everything hoped for, they represented the peak of GE glory and self-assurance. This era had been characterized by a charismatic drive, distinguished by authentic spiritual excitement and ingenious operational and political activity. It culminated in the establishment of an active organization and pioneering settlements, which — together with gifted, dedicated, experienced and confident GE cadres — provided the infrastructure for future achievements.

GE became even more powerful in Israeli public life between 1977 and 1982, when it was accorded some legitimacy and underwent partial institutionalization. But its self-conception is still that of an informal and extra-establishment movement, and its public image remains one of an extremist and bizarre sect trying to enforce its will on democratic governing institutions. This is due partly to its activities during the early days and partly to GE's consistent refusal to transform itself into a new political party or allow itself to be absorbed by an existing parliamentary bloc. In recent years, although GE is no longer the sole actor in the arena of the "Greater Israel," it has remained the dynamic force behind the continuing settlement enterprise in the West Bank, providing ideological backing and organizational support even for settlements sponsored by the government.

The Belief System

True to its self-image, though contrary to the general opinion that it is mainly a political group of extreme nationalists, GE is a religious revival movement par excellence. It represents an authentic and original attempt to revitalize traditional Judaism, which its members feel has been challenged by the reality of the secular modern Israel within which it lives and draws its resources. It is a Jewish movement that carries the flag of Zionism, its competitor. Although known mainly from its activities in the field of national politics, GE emanates from Orthodox Judaism, has never transcended the limits of traditional religion, and was from the beginning intended to reinforce a religion in crisis. The politics of GE are a religious medium used in the name and for the sake of religion.

Thus, notwithstanding the general expectation that the movement would become progressively secularized, GE manifests signs of religious radicalization. Parallel and not without connection to its increasingly extreme nationalism, GE shows a tendency to move deeper into religion in its Orthodox form, which is ultimately incompatible with Zionism. The religious conception of GE is a genuine and uniquely effective response to the existential distress of the Orthodox Jew in Israel. The problems are clearly religious, while the attempts to resolve them, though religious as well, pursue secular options of political activism. The contention that the secular appearance of GE's operations is deceptive, and that their mass demonstrations in cities west of the green line and settlements in the hills of Judea and Samaria east of the green line are ritual religious acts, is not meant to detract from GE's very real impact on the geopolitical system of Israel and possibly of the entire area. Indeed it seems plausible that the emergence of GE will have a critical effect on the future of the people of Israel and her neighbors. I nevertheless maintain that the extremist politics of GE are only an expression of intrareligious dynamics. For this reason, understanding GE as a religious phenomenon is essential to the elucidation of its public or national significance.

No less important than GE's influence on the sociopolitical scene is its impact in the area of culture. Behind the power struggles over the nature of government and strategic conceptions lies the arena of symbolic confrontation over the collective identity of contemporary Israel, which is caught between traditional religious Judaism and modern secular Zionism. The ideological-theological heritage on which GE is based represents one of the possible options for the resolutions of this dilemma. Its sources are to be found in the teachings of Rabbi A. I. Kook (d. 1935), as transmitted and interpreted by his son, Rabbi Z. Y. Kook (d. 1982) and appropriated and elaborated in the Mercaz Ha-Rav Yeshivah in Jerusalem and the Torah educational institutions it inspired.[3] These teachings, which began to be known and embraced in the early 1950s and became especially prevalent during the 1960s and 1970s, were adopted with minor adaptations and varying degrees of understanding and commitment by the bulk of the young generation of Israel's national religious camp.[4] This segment of Israeli society overlaps the periphery of GE considerably. Its essential association with the movement led Kookist teachings to become popular within it, and its position in society has changed dramatically. From an insecure, passive element of low prestige and power, national religious youth have become a central factor exhibiting pride and entrepreneurship, serving as a model for broad strata of the society and for the entire state, and making a bid for leadership in the religious camp and in the nation. This radical change has been both a product and a prerequisite of GE activism. The movement's success is an indication of this reversal in status.

The inner circles of GE, its leaders and activists in its *yeshivot* and in its settlements, are ardent believers in a crystalized if not necessarily coherent set of ideas and values, which guide the public actions. The GE doctrine propounds a mystic-messianic system that serves the hard core of GE as the base of both their religious and Zionist orientations. Its uniqueness lies in its ability to effectively link these two elements, usually considered polar, and in its capacity to contain both, though not without an inner tension. The coexistence of traditional religion and modern nationalism within a mystic-messianic system of GE (henceforth MM-GE) does not represent a synthesis. Rather religion usurps nationalism which it then presents as its function or manifestation. Thus, here is no less than an original variant of a religious phenomenon that tries to come to grips with the secularity confronting it by converting the latter into its revelation. According to this belief, the existing lay civil order in Israel (particularly its *etatist* pioneer version as reflected in hawkish policies and settlements a la Greater Land of Israel) is only a crude and provisional manifestation of the "ultimately sacred" and appears as sinful and heterodox only to those of limited faith. Such supernationalism, in fact, is an expansion and elevation of the old religion, and the completion of true Judaism to its full, original scope, which transcends Orthodoxy.

MM-GE is a "theology of secularism,"[5] a theodicy that attempts to interpret the secular by conferring on it positive religious valuation. More precisely, MM—GE is a "theology of Zionism"; that is, a theology of the secular-nationalist version of Judaism. Thus, traditional religion endorses a revolutionary force that, although particularly threatening to Orthodoxy, also arouses envy and excitement on the part of the pious. According to this initially defensive vision, Zionism is conceived as deriving from religious roots, on the one hand, and striving toward religious destination, on the other. It is a phenomenon whose episodic appearance has a religious mission that, when completed, will be easily recognized and widely praised. Hence, whether the Zionists realize it or accept it, religion is Zionistic and Zionism is religious. Quoting their spiritual fathers, MM-GE believers stress that Zionists are "saints despite themselves." This appropriation of Zionism by religion has been made possible by the "mystification" and "messianization" of the normative Jewish conception. MM-GE marks a transition from religious Zionism, in the background of the movement, to Zionist religion, to which the movement is leading.

The MM-GE might be viewed as a modern heir to the Jewish mystical heritage, the Kabbalah. More specifically, it might be looked upon as a unique offshoot of Lurianism, that most influential six-teenth-century kabbalistic trend that infuses messianism into mysticism.[6] Apart from similarities in content and structure, this chapter shall be concerned particularly with MM-GE and Lurianism from the point of view of their sociological implications as functional equivalents: although different in some respects, both are capable of affecting the social system in the same way.[7] It must be emphasized, however, that even if it is latent, marginal, or possibly even deviant, MM-GE is still a current within normative Judaism and linked organically to its mainstream. Mutual relations between MM-GE and the halakhic-rabbinical heritage contribute to the vitality of both. MM-GE has managed to express its original religious experience through the idiom of traditional Judaism; it is not by chance that kab-balistic MM-GE not only adopted the symbols of Orthodoxy but bor-rowed its language and, to some extent, has cultivated its typical life-style.

As a mystical system the GE doctrine has succeeded in combining the quest for the immediate presence of a godhead with the classical forms of religion. As a messianic one, it has succeeded in combining the aspiration for the immediate realization of a revolutionary vision with the institutional structures of religion. As a mystic-messianic system, it has managed to contain even its drawing on the myth, in-cluding its primitive psychic dimensions, within a rationally controlled framework of progressive monotheism. Thus, the Torah retains its validity even though its commandments become something of a magic act due to their kabbalization. The GE doctrine, then, constitutes an attempt at a novel interpretation of Judaism and the world in general

—a rationalization of the continued validity of the law of Moses and the sages as determining our way of life.

Indeed, there is in the MM-GE a new myth of Judaism. GE doctrine deals not with history as such, but with events hinted at and allegedly testifying to those within the godhead itself. True to the kabbalistic tradition, GE believers view manifest reality as a symbol of the hidden inner essence, which is no less real and surpasses revealed reality in importance. This raises the existential problems of humanity from the mundane to the cosmic level and confers religious meaning on the sociopolitical reality. The annexation of all profane realms to the divine sphere and the viewing of all existence through the prism of the sacred are the means through which the GE spiritual belief-system copes with distress in its believers. Where traditional religion fails to account for the actual circumstances that challenge belief, MM-GE confers acceptable and encouraging meaning on contemporary Jewish existence. In this way, MM-GE has extricated religion from the crisis posed by modernization, gaining popularity and influence in the process.

The MM-GE as an authoritative theology offers a myth that reflects the historical experience of Judaism in our time and place and, at the same time, responds to its frustrations. From now on, the Jewish national condition, subsumed under the old symbols of Exile and Redemption, becomes a hint of the heavenly condition. Thus, Exile is viewed as alienation of the sacred from itself, whereas Redemption is seen as resulting from its return to the recognition of the roots of its essence. This belief has a built-in activist potential, in that the believer is entrusted with the mission of sharing in cosmic events. There is a need for *tikkun*—the return of the sacred to its sources, and the bringing of the profane into the sacred.

As in the Lurianic Kabbalah, Exile and Redemption in MM-GE are concrete conditions in the history of Israel and offer a glimpse of cosmic revolutions. Thus, the two axes of the mythic symbol, at the same time, also are entirely realistic in nature. This concretization of the symbols of Exile and Redemption makes it possible to use them for ideological purposes. Without trying to detract from the value and importance of MM-GE as a spiritual trend, it appears to owe its wide acceptance and success as a motivator primarily to its ideological core.

It should be noted here that the system originally was not conceived for ideological purposes, but rather to express an authentic religious experience. Nevertheless, those who composed its doctrine knew how to strike the right chords in contemporary national religious existence, so that it would come to have considerable social impact.

The doctrine even affected many not normally sensitive to esotericism of any kind. Thus, what might have become an esoteric dogma tending toward exclusiveness and quietism became a major factor in mass dynamics due to its sensitivity to psychic nuances and to the primary needs of the collective. Though interpreted by many Orthodox groups as heterodoxy, this actualization of faith is really a direct heir of tenets and pattern of living commonly regarded as fully legitimate.

The MM-GE is a gospel of paradox: adopted and developed under a reality fraught with paradox, it attempted to cope with the paradox by rationalizing and legitimizing it, and in the process turning it into a key principle and value in its own right. MM-GE continued to be nurtured by the paradox, which in turn was accentuated. A circular process began, with both MM-GE and the paradox growing in strength and depth.

The paradox, from the point of view of religion, is the realization of Zionism, as Zionist actualization carries frustrating implications: the triumph of the secular, replacement of a life lived according to the rules of the Torah by growing heresy and sin, and the refutation of faith. But, at the same time, Zionist actualization also means the opposite: a religious climax, the fulfillment of central religious tenets, and the implementation of faith. In its struggle with the contradiction inherent in Zionism, MM-GE finds itself first idealizing the secular and then going on to nourish and be nourished by it. Thus, the MM-GE elaborates the paradox and uses it. Though rather apologetic about it in the beginning, with time MM-GE has tended increasingly to emphasize the paradox and present it as an a priori principle, a virtue. Parallel to this, the behavior of believers using this argument has become gradually more self-assured as well as militant.

Traditional religious Judaism is quite aware that the rise of Zionism presents a real danger to its survival. However, despite its negative implications for religion, Orthodox Jews feel admiration, sympathy, and attraction for this new Jewish power. The option of a total rejection of Zionism, which exempts traditional religion from coming to grips with the elements of nationalism and statehood in a modern secular world, has not been chosen by all sectors of Orthodoxy. Some prefer the alternative option of conferring on it a kind of religious sanction, as this seems to be the only way for them to reach a positive orientation toward Zionism. Orthodox legitimation has appeared under a number of variants, based on levels of rationalization of Zionism that parallel different degrees of active commitment to the national spirit and state organs.[8]

The religious mandate that MM-GE has given to Zionist revival and its institutions is unconditional. This extreme religious Zionism seems to be associated with two characteristics typical of MM-GE believers and reflects the tension between them: on the one hand, the believers belong to the sector of Orthodoxy that had been exposed to modern secular elements, especially those in the national and political area, and have cherished and internalized them to a considerable degree; on the other hand, the believers are also distinguished by having undergone a genuine spiritual experience, which is at the base of their religiosity. The dialectic link between these two elements leads to sacralization of the essentially secular Israeli entity. This appropriation of Zionism by religion is carried out by means of the ideal of Redemption. The State of Israel is declared to be the realization of the messianic vision—the consummation of Redemption[9]—a central religious tenet.

The conception of Zionism as the materializaton of a messianic ideal is not as farfetched as one might think. Zionism has realized the central components of the messianic vision as crystalized in the long religious tradition, in the Bible, in prayer, in the *Halakhah*, and in the *Aggadah*. "Zionistic" components have always been the axis of both the rabbinic and the kabbalistic conception of Redemption: the ingathering of exiles; the conquest and colonization of the Land of Israel; the establishment of state frameworks for creativity, security, welfare, national pride, and political independence. When something extraordinary happened and the miracle occurred, elements of a dream that had been cherished but delayed or repressed for 2000 years suddenly became a reality.

Not by chance was the national revival shaped on a model preserved throughout the ages by the guardians of tradition. Even secular Zionists were motivated by the ancient messianic drive, and their aspirations were molded on the patterns of the old messianic idea. It is not surprising, then, that once the vision became a reality, the Orthodox, who until then had reservations with regard to the Zionist enterprise, were seized by genuine messianic excitement. And, once provoked, this messianic trend has been growing in strength among the Orthodox, along with a sense of envy for and a tendency to join forces with the Zionists. Their messianism, both as experience and as point of view, has increased in direct proportion to their deepening Zionistic involvement. Since messianism has a sweeping dynamic of its own, the messianization of Israel has been progressively gathering momentum.

Imagine, then, the disappointment on the part of religious Zionists when the Zionist entity, declared to be the realization of the messianic vision, appeared to signify the triumph of secularity. Their frustration has been compounded by the fact that Israel's areligious if not anti-religious reality had their sanction. But this sanction was based on the original sincere enthusiasm of the religious Zionists as well as on the necessity to adjust to the fait accompli by justifying it retroactively. The legitimation of Zionism by religion was explicit and comprehensive. It means that, despite its blatantly devastating implications for religion, the historic reality was a redemptive reality.

In both theory and practice, Zionism implies the opposite of what would have been an acceptable way for the Orthodox to acquiesce to the new national condition. The confrontation with the Zionist challenge has been caught in a paradox that the religious Zionists who were to form GE resolved in a highly original way: they converted the paradox itself into a base of the belief and its law. Thus, the gist of the substance of MM-GE is sacralization of the totality of being, including the profane. This allegedly religious and fully redeemed reality however, has shown itself increasingly defective. If, in its early stages, MM-GE could be optimistic that religiosity would grow in Israel and in the world, it has become less and less possible to maintain this hope. And, as the paradox becomes more acute, MM-GE belief becomes more daring and increasingly popular.

The messianic experience that provoked those Orthodox who approached the Zionist enterprise in its initial stages eventually became an inner reality. Naturally, this national religious sector expected that the correlation between the inner reality of their hearts and the outer reality would continue and become complete. Yet, exposure to historical developments led this sector into a dissonance between these two realities, corresponding to the two levels of messianism. The gap deepened between their inner truth, to a large degree already redeemed, and their environment, in which the early signs of Redemption were swallowed up by a dominant reality that indicated its opposite. Moreover, as the national-political aspects of the signs of Redemption have grown stronger and clearer, so the prospects for its traditional-religious aspects have declined.

According to a basic psychosocial law, people aspire to a state of congruence between outer and inner reality, to consistency between their attitudes and their observations.[10] According to a somewhat parallel kabbalistic conception, "this-worldly" reality is seen as a symbol for a mysterious heavenly reality that, although it can only be expressed and grasped by a hint, can be experienced genuinely by believers who excel in the profundity of their faith. A Jew tends to search for almost automatic consistency between the symbol and what it stands for, in effect between historical reality and the divine state. In exile, the people of Israel found a parallel for this in the exile of the *Shechinah*, one of the manifestations of the Divine Presence, while the nation's Redemption was experienced as a cosmic cure or restoration of heavenly realities, a *tikkun*. The initial congruence between the two messianic levels both confirmed and stimulated messianic belief, but the days of this spontaneous awakening did not last long. The chasm between experienced truth and historic truth grew too wide. But the salvation offered by MM-GE bridged the gap between heaven and earth, solved the contradiction between inner — redeemed — and outer — unredeemed — truth.

When a symbol no longer effectively symbolizes what it is supposed to, it is usually abandoned. And when a historic condition ceases to be a reflection of and platform for a spiritual existence viewed as of superior reality and value, there is a temptation to give less weight to the former for the sake of the latter. The center of gravity then tends to shift from the externally observable to the hidden, believed reality. This shift exempts the messianic conception from the empirical test of history and thereby saves the "truth" of the faithful from the danger of refutation. Such a religious orientation no longer reflects the world as it is but rather interprets it freely. When believers inhabit an interpreted world and their imagination is not subject to conventional constraints, they are able to cope with the contradictions inherent in reality. The function that mitigates the dissonance between the two contradictory levels of Redemption resides in the exegetic sphere. And since the principle of interpretation is the paradox itself, it becomes central. Once it is no longer possible to ignore the fact that the messianic perspective has been refuted at least partly by the test of history, explication and justification of what might have been inferred naturally as the belief's failure is sought in terms of the belief itself. The refutation then becomes glorified and is held to possess special virtue.

MM-GE is the very ideology that explains away this inner contradiction, enabling believers to live with and even be inspired by it; the paradox thus becomes the axis of religious revival. As in the cases of Christianity and Sabbatianism,[11] historic developments that entail refutation of a belief engender a new religious drive and conception. In the case of MM-GE, the system is built on the experience of believers who refuse to accept the verdict of history proclaiming their faith as false. The more severe the test of reality and the more blatant the refutation of the claim, the greater is the weight they attach to the "inner" essence of things. By the same token, the exegetive tendency increases and the weight given to things as they appear and are self-defined decreases. With the increasing gravity of the paradox, its religious value increases—and so MM-GE is strengthened and flourishes.

Somewhat like Lurianism, MM-GE has broadened Redemption from an occurrence in the sociopolitical realm into a cosmic event as well. The change in Lurianism has been assumed to result from the protracted suffering of exile, aggravated to an unprecedented level of national agony that called for an ideological account as well as a practical solution. In MM-GE, however, the same change comes about as a result of the successful realization of Redemption, the transformation occurring in the wake of a national revival that involves a religious climax. With MM-GE, the shift in focus of belief from the historical world to the deep strata of the believer's soul or to the lofty places of the cosmos seems to come about as a reaction not to aggravated suffering but rather to the triumphant termination of that suffering. The wished-for state not only improves the existential condition of the people, but simultaneously accomplishes its religious mission.

This kabbalization of the faith of the national religious Jews in contemporary Israel is taking place just when they have finally fulfilled their age-old duty and dream, only to find that this religious climax has turned out to be a threat to religion. Religious crisis, which accompanied national disaster in ancient times, is now a function of national success. Today the kabbalistic system of GE is to Zionism—and especially to the establishment of the independent State of Israel—what the sixteenth-century kabbalistic system of Rabbi Luria, according to the prevalent view, was to the Crusades, the Inquisition, and especially the expulsion from Spain: a theology that absorbs historic events threatening traditional religion and legitimizes them in terms of novel interpretations that seek to preserve the traditional frameworks intact.

Studies of Jewish mysticism and messianism show a positive correlation and causal relationship between deterioration in the actual condition of exilic Jewry and increased awareness of the mystery and superworldliness of Redemption.[12] Though the messianic vision has preserved the hope to return to the glorious sociopolitical reality of the past—namely, the biblical kingdom of David—it has tended to transcend this vision outward, toward supernatural worlds. Thus, the creation of the Lurianic Kabbalah followed the lowest ebb of the Jewish condition. But MM-GE, the modern version of the mystic-messianic system, has been created precisely at what most would term the summit of Jewish history. This is because the realization of Redemption, as revealed in contemporary Zionist Israel, is viewed as a calamity to the traditional religion. In his sermon on the state, an eminent GE leader said: "The third destruction of the people of Israel is the destruction of the Exile, i.e. the Emancipation of European Jewry, which led to Zionism."[13]

The tragic nature of the present Redemption revolves around the realization that the national revival and the establishment of a sovereign state have, rather, increased and emphasized the impossibility for Orthodox Israelis of realizing their Judaism in full. Redemption in our time and place therefore is a catastrophic event from the standpoint of traditional religion. This problematic truth has been partially acknowledged in an essay by one of the prominent ideologists of settlement in Judea and Samaria. Writing about "The struggle for survival from the Holocaust" brought upon Orthodoxy by the Western secularity that characterizes modern Israel, he said: "We are now confronting a national disaster of gigantic proportions. . . . It is not Hitler setting Jewish communities ablaze, but part of a paradise of messianic realization—an 'apocalypse now'—that makes Judaism redundant."[14]

With the help of a belief system that depends on some form of kabbalization, the GE Orthodox are attempting to extricate themselves from the Zionist catch into which they were propelled by their great messianic momentum. It is well known that important elements of religious Jewry a priori rejected the possibility of legitimizing Zionism, because of necessity this would entail messianic value being attributed to it. Another part of the traditional camp joined forces with the Zionists, but did so with reserve and conditionally, careful to avoid outspoken recognition of its messianic aspects. It seems that at the base of the reluctance of authoritative figures and considerable segments of Orthodoxy to wholeheartedly accept Zionism is more than just the fear that the national enterprise might fail after having been religiously sanctioned and thereby expose Zionism as a false messianism espoused by the Orthodox. More likely, they sensed the more plausible though more dangerous possibility that the Zionist enterprise legitimized by them might indeed succeed. In this case, it would be difficult to avoid admitting that Redemption indeed had been fulfilled. However, to do this would call for great courage, because messianic realization involves extraordinarily far-reaching implications: it entails an acceptance of reality that, according to rabbinic Judaism, is totally negative or, rather, acceptance of the fact that the Torah and its commandments are no longer valid in the redeemed reality.

The messianism of Zionism is threatening even to those of relatively conservative and moderate religious orientation, because it necessitates acceptance of full halakhic responsibility. It opens old and new vistas calling for the application of traditional norms to the entirety of Jewish life, which now includes the public spheres of society and state. Messianic realization therefore would necessitate the kind of fundamentalism that expresses itself in claims for compliance with holy texts suddenly made relevant or for radical changes in the authoritative old codes to adapt them to modern circumstances. In either case, the conception of national fulfillment as religious fulfillment must confront religious Jewry with a severe crisis. The longed-for consummation of the vision is pregnant with disaster. That GE believers are sensitive to this irony is manifest not only in their acknowledgement of the problems inherent in the implementation of messianism through a secular outlet but also in their admission that "destroying the dams that have contained it so far will cost Judaism the loss of the very values of redemption."[15]

Having shown that the source of the MM-GE is a paradox, I shall now try to show that this paradox has become the movement's central value. GE believers cultivate a system whose rationale is paradoxical. They have done so by decreeing that, despite its appearing religiously neutral or even antireligious, the national reality is one of Redemption, that behind the Zionist revival lies the revival of the holy, and that the highest degree of sacredness resides in the innermost part of the profane. The paradox also is applied to the opposite and complementary side of messianism; namely, that Exile is a mode of being in which only the sacred obtains, without anything profane to bear upon. The exilic entity is exhausted by its total immersion in the traditional boundaries of religion, which is self-sufficient to the point where the profane is rendered superfluous.

One expression par excellence of this paradoxical system is found in the MM-GE version of the idea of *segulah* in Judaism; that is, the indelible and undeniable property characterizing the people of Israel, who are unconditionally holy and in whose hearts hides a sacred spark. This principle makes possible post-factum accounts that allow phenomena whose conventional implication would negate religion to be accepted as sacred in their essence. This is achieved through ascribing to them a particular quality, alleged to have been their original characteristic, which qualifies them for fulfilling a mysterious holy mission. Thus, manifestations of transgressing religious boundaries and of deliberately and blatantly rejecting religion are testimony to a supreme religious worthiness in the eyes of the believers. The following is what one eminent GE leader has to say about the national enterprise in Israel considering itself in revolt against traditional belief and involved in renouncing the *Halakhah*:

> Paradoxically enough it contains a great message. . . . The element of *segulah* is far above whatever the patterns of manifest halakhic education can possibly educate for. . . . The belief of Jews who meticulously observe all Torah commandments is grossly defective as long as they do not accept the element of *segulah* through which God spoke to the human soul, bypassing the prism of manifest tradition. . . . This is why we strongly condemn both the ultraorthodox and the liberal-orthodox. . . . Since I believe in *segulah*, I consider that a man who has undergone the test of fire on the Golan Heights or in the Sinai is a Jew in the full sense of the word, even if he has never been exposed to formal Torah education. . . . This is an innovation that is not grasped even by the Zionists of the national religious camp.[16]

The emphasis shifts here from the conventional appearances of worldly phenomena to the mysterious qualities ascribed to them. And this is so not only with regard to the Torah, which is interpreted as having many hidden meanings, but especially with regard to the other two elements of the "holy trinity" — the Land and the Nation — which thereby acquire mystic significance. They, too, are to be seen as essentially religious entities, even though they may appear or pretend to be secular in nature. The key to the MM-GE paradox rationality is *pnimiyyut*, "the inner" or "the inner essence."

The concept of inherent virtue is a means toward easing tensions and solving contradictions. But it, too, contains a grave contradiction, which is injected into the traditional religion and threatens to explode it from within: from the moment the profane, which had threatened religion from the outside, is declared the realization of the sacred, the theology becomes exposed to an inner tension that it may not be able to contain. There have been some equivalents to this paradoxical "theology of the profane" in other religions, with different historical settings. And they, too, have represented a kind of defense of traditional religion as challenged by risking secularity; they, too, have appropriated the secular and presented it as a unique realization of those religions' essence. Thus, after World War II, certain Protestant church circles interpreted progressive secularization as an essentially positive development that manifests pure Christian potential.[17] There also exists an obscure Pravoslav trend that, in its desperate struggle against the revolutionary Russian state, found a secret holy nucleus hidden in Marxism-Leninism.[18]

Returning to MM-GE, it induces specific practical attitudes toward the various areas of life—and these, too, are marked by a paradox. The following two typical examples are relevant to the political and operational implications of GE. First is the believer's tendency to regard remote barren hillocks somewhere in the Greater Land of Israel as holier than sites generally considered holy on the basis of their biblical or mishnaic connotations. In some instances, the measure of geographic-religious importance stands in obverse relation to its traditional importance. Second is the argument that colonization of the entire Land of Israel, by the Nation of Israel, in the final analysis is a blessing for all humanity, in particular for the Palestinians! Jewish settlements in the very midst of Arab population centers, this argument continues, are motivated by feelings of responsibility for the Arabs' future. Thus, meeting Arab demands for withdrawal would only encourage their degeneration and moral decline. But, enforcing the "Jewish national will" upon the Arabs will bring about a religious revival among them that will find final expression in their spontaneous desire to support the reconstruction of the Temple for the Redemption of Israel, because they will understand that this will also bring about their salvation and that of the whole world.

A peculiar, paradox-oriented mentality has made an appearance among the believers, one that has a fondness for a "paradox perspective," the expressions of which sometimes border on the ostentatious and seem to be deliberate attempts to shock the general public. Revealing examples of this tendency are found in the believers' language and peculiarities in personal style. For instance, their dress usually includes dissonant combinations that look odd to the conventional person. Men wear blue jeans, flight jackets, and commando boots in combination with skullcaps, beards, dark jackets, and extravagantly long fringed garments. They have also forged phrases that reverse conventional associations, mainly by coupling polarities or pairing terms alien to each other: "a K-47 assault rifle and hammer make a perfect match with a book of Talmud and tefillin" and so on.

More jarring linguistic innovations include juxtapositions of expressions of holiness, normally enunciated with awe and reverence, with secular words denoting everyday routine, materialism, and even coarseness: "the accounting of the Almighty," "divine cramming," and so forth. These expressions, although repeated endlessly and with apparent nonchalance, are intentional and meant to shock listeners. The believers enjoy watching others recoil from such seeming profaning of the sacred, for they know that what they are "really" doing is sacralizing the profane. In fact, those who make use of such paradoxical expressions are considered spiritually superior.

These illustrations are only partial testimony to the birth of a novel religious terminology that reveals an original religious code. The rhetorics of paradox hint at the tensions experienced by the believers and at the contradictions inherent in the actualization of Redemption itself. The believers' passion for the paradox is linked with a compulsive attraction to those phenomena in the Israeli environment whose manifest, popular, and formal appearance can be seen as contrary to their hidden nature, which is alleged to be their real and true nature. They search systematically for cases that lend themselves to such paradoxical interpretation and will support their doctrine. Thus, the dominant reality of heresy and sin has only an apparitional existence, whereas the reality hidden behind it is one of deep and compelling faith. This attitude is sometimes carried, ad absurdum, to the point where this inner religiosity, which appears antireligious, is seen as a religiosity of a higher order. From here it is only a short step to the somewhat heterodox assumption that the religiosity of those whose appearance is true to their innermost character may be suspect. It follows that those who observe the halakhic laws punctiliously may not be among the highest rank of the believers.

Such "social psychology of paradox" brings to mind the Conversos or Marranos at the time of the Spanish Inquisition. A revealing precedent to our case can be found in the intriguing association between the phenomena of the Conversos and Sabbatianism.[19] In Sabbatianism the forced converts, struggling with the problems of their mixed identity, were conferred legitimacy. Sabbatianism also supplied a theology that turned the gap and contradiction between a formal definition and appearance, on the one hand, and the essence covered by them, on the other, into a religious model. Thus, the Marranos were regarded as secret saints, and their problematic status was glorified. The Secret and the Mission resided within their Christianity; there was Jewishness behind their conversion, and the conversion was for the sake of their

Jewishness. And MM-GE believers say that this is precisely the case with secular Zionism; it is possible to find extra- or super-religiosity in the apparent apostasy of the national revival. To detract from the value of the external realities that menace religion, the believers resort to overvaluation of inner reality. MM-GE allows them to view the whole world as Marrano. I have shown elsewhere that the believers have been obsessed by the idea of the Marranos, whose image plays an important role in their perception of their secular surroundings.

A theodicy based on paradoxical laws has given the adherent of MM-GE self-confidence; the attraction for the paradox and the ability to come to terms with it has given them a feeling of uniqueness and superiority vis-à-vis their environment. Their successful struggle with the paradox has been a liberating experience, and the absolute freedom thus tasted is intoxicating. The options now open to them to contain tensions, to bridge gaps, and to solve contradictions are exhilarating. Breaking down logical and empirical iron laws and transcending the limits of conventional consciousness has produced in them an illusion of omnipotence that makes them feel entitled and able to burst all bounds and throw off all yokes. They may even view the shattering of normative frameworks as a kind of mission. This has created an anarchic potential that can materialize in either the religious or the civil sphere.

The believers might be defined as "spiritualists" whose emphasis on pure faith, nourishment by the mysterious, and contempt for the manifest and the conventional render them above this-worldly laws. For they are already in the sphere of a secret and redeemed new world. It should be stressed that this inner freedom, which is of a messianic nature, does not result from specific revelations or exceptional peak experiences; it is a permanent state. Their elevated position allows them to treat the standards of the here and now with contempt and to behave with arrogance toward the rest of humanity, which has not yet been illuminated. The category of "believers" thereby is automatically differentiated from that of the uninitiated, as is their distinct "holy belief" from the common variety of imperfect Judaism and Zionism.

In conclusion, the Redemption itself, in its Zionist version, has caused the Israeli Orthodox to lose their liberty as Jews. What had been refuted and renounced on the level of actuality sought and found expression on the theological level, as MM-GE ideologized the defeat of religion by history and thereby enabled the believers to attain the freedom to consummate their Jewishness. Thus, they accomplished in the religious sphere what they failed to attain in the sociopolitical realm. They use the frustrations brought about by their circumstances to fill their hearts with certainty of faith, the exclusive property of the enlightened. It is natural that the mystical and messianic rationalization endeavors to shift the center of gravity away from history as such. Yet, ironically enough, the believers confer increased value on history. For, after all, the holy was found to reside deep within society and politics. The law of paradox, intended to neutralize tension in the belief system, in fact charges it with tensions of a higher order. GE's unique belief system remains within the traditional boundaries, which employ the old concepts of religious Judaism, and yet implants a dialectic explosion within them.

The explosive potential of this mystical-messianic system was not actualized until several years after its inception and crystalization. The revolutionary drive of the movement cannot be ascribed solely to the theological elements just discussed or rather to their ideological nucleus. These elements must be complemented by psychosocial factors not described here, for example, the unexpected encounter of young Israelis with the biblical sites of a fatherland longed for but never actually seen until after the Six-Day War and the euphoric times that followed; or the strategic withdrawal, depression, and ideological vacuum that befell Israeli society in the aftermath of the Yom Kippur War. The emergence of these factors, and their encounter with the symbolic system analyzed in this chapter, has caused the eruption of GE.

It was precisely the true believers' inability to live up to the religious demands of MM-GE that was responsible for the movement's transition from quietism to activism. Only then, as GE resorted to extremism, did the center of gravity move back from heaven to earth and an esoteric spirituality turn into sophisticated but brutal politics.

Chapter Eight

Khomeini's Messengers:
The Disputed Pilgrimage of Islam

Martin Kramer

According to the tradition of Islam, Mecca during the annual Muslim pilgrimage is a city open to all Muslims, in which all forms of strife and bloodshed are forbidden. The peace of Mecca is a concept so rooted in Arabia that it even predates Islam and was observed by sojourners in Mecca before the Arabian shrine became the center of Muslim faith. But in 1987 Mecca became a site of unprecedented carnage when demonstrating Iranian pilgrims clashed with Saudi security forces in a bloody confrontation that claimed over 400 lives. The Saudis and their supporters called the event a premeditated riot: violent Iranian demonstrators crushed themselves to death in a stampede of their own making. The Iranians and their sympathizers call it a premeditated massacre: the Saudis conspired to provoke and shoot Iranian pilgrims. The following year, 1988, Mecca was transformed into an armed camp as tense Saudi security forces patrolled a pilgrimage from which Iranian pilgrims were excluded. The pilgrimage to Mecca, far from providing a respite from the conflicts that beset Islam, itself became a point of confrontation between rival visions of Islam. The pilgrimage peace has been shattered by the brickbats and bullets of Muslims.

The disruption of the pilgrimage peace admits multiple interpretations. It occurred at a moment of escalating tensions in the Iranian-Iraqi war, following the reflagging of Kuwaiti tankers and the introduction of foreign escorts in the Persian Gulf. This foreign intervention, favored by Saudi Arabia and opposed by Iran, created an atmosphere of crisis between the two states. Yet, the deterioration of the pilgrimage also expressed tensions dating back to Iran's revolution, an event that kindled a broader rivalry between Saudi Arabia and Iran over primacy in the Persian Gulf and in Islam. That conflict has its remoter origins in the great historical animosity of Wahhabism, the fount of Saudi Islam, to Shiʿism itself. Nor can the most recent pilgrimage strife be divorced from the history of mistrust between Shi^cite pilgrims and their Sunni hosts, a history that stretches back as far as the sixteenth century. At a still deeper level, the event echoed Sunni-Shi^cite animosities that have their origins in the seventh century, at the very dawn of Islam.

Even if it is allowed that the Persian Gulf crisis triggered the violence of 1987 and the coercive measures of 1988, both have been understood by Muslims in a larger historical context. Much of that understanding is implicit and unspoken, because it is essentially sectarian. Sectarian bigotry dares not speak its name openly: like racial and ethnic prejudice in other societies, sectarian prejudice is not professed openly in the Muslim world. "They are now propagandizing and claiming that this incident was a war between Shi^cis and Sunnis," charged Iranian president Ali Khamene'i after the 1987 violence. "This is a lie! Of course there is a war; but a war between the American perception of Islam and true revolutionary Islam."[1]

The pilgrimage controversy is not merely one between Shi^cites and Sunnis, nor is it simply between Khomeini's truth and America's falsehood. It is a conflict that is simultaneously political and sectarian, that combines a present-day clash of interests with the historic clash of sects in Islam. Some of these sectarian differences touch upon the Muslim pilgrimage itself and involve conflicting notions of sanctity and asylum. The aim of this chapter is to understand the interaction of present politics with the enduring prejudices that Saudis and Iranians bring to Mecca.

Between Sunnis and Shi^cis

The pilgrimage ritual itself is not an issue about which Sunnis and Shi^cites have conducted an elaborate polemic. The bedrock of sectarian conflict has always been the matter of the imamate; the question of legitimate authority in Islam, which is a matter of theological controversy outside the ritual sphere. Yet over time, theological differences were transformed into political, social, and cultural differences, and these infected both sects with bigoted lore about Shi^cite pilgrims and Sunni hosts. This was particularly evident after Sunni-Shi^cite differences took the form of Ottoman-Safavid armed conflict, beginning in the sixteenth century. That was perhaps the most divided century in Islamic history, marked by great wars of religion between Sunnis and Shi^cites. When the holy cities were under Sunni Ottoman rule, Shi^cites from Safavid domains were banned from pilgrimage for years. The Safavids reacted by trying to discourage the pilgrimage to Mecca and emphasizing the importance of Shi^cite shrines in their own domains.[2]

The Sunni corpus of libel perhaps is more readily documented, if only because it sometimes led to violent acts against Shi^cite pilgrims. At the root of the Sunni lore is the belief that Shi^cites feel themselves compelled to pollute the holy premises. Much evidence for Sunni belief in this libel can be found in both Islamic textual sources and European travel literature. This pollution was said to take a particularly repelling form: Burckhardt and Burton, the great nineteenth-century explorers of Arabia, both heard about attacks on Shi^cite pilgrims, prompted by the suspicion that they had polluted the Great Mosque in Mecca with excrement. According to Burton, "their ill-fame has spread far; at Alexandria they were described to me as a people who defile the Ka^cbah."[3]

The Shi^cite libel was just as farfetched. It held that Sunnis did not respect Mecca as a sanctuary, and that the lives of Shi^cite pilgrims were forfeit even in these sacred precincts, where the shedding of blood is forbidden. Shi^cite pilgrims were indeed liable to humiliation at any time; as Burton wrote of Shi^cites on pilgrimage, "that man is happy who gets over it without a beating, [for] in no part of Al-Hijaz are they for a moment safe from abuse and blows."[4] Yet it would seem that, for the most part, Shi^cite pilgrims were as secure as other pilgrims, provided they exercised the discretion (*taqiyya*) permitted them by Shi^cite doctrine and conformed with the customs of their Sunni hosts. During the Ottoman period, the Iranian pilgrims' caravan also bought its security through a special tribute, paid both to desert tribes en route and to the guardians of the sanctuaries.[5] Since toleration could be had at a price which Shi^cite pilgrims were prepared to pay, their lives were rarely as threatened as their dignity. The open manner in which Shi^cites observed Muharram in Jidda epitomized the tolerance of the later Ottoman years. When the Dutch Orientalist Hurgronje witnessed these ceremonies in 1884, he found the Ottoman governor in attendance. Hurgronje reported that the governor "not only drank sherbet but also wept piously."[6]

But sectarian antagonisms were exacerbated following the advent of Saudi rule over Mecca in 1924. The doctrinal divide that separated Ottoman Sunnism from Shi^cism seemed narrow in comparison to the chasm that separated Saudi Wahhabism and Shi^cism. Wahhabi doctrine regarded Shi^cite veneration of the Imams and their tombs as blasphemous idolatry. The Wahhabi iconoclasts had earned lasting notoriety in Shi^cite eyes when they emerged from the Arabian desert in

1802 and sacked Karbala, the Shi^cite shrine city in Iraq. They slew several thousand Shi^cites on that occasion, and desecrated the revered tomb of the Imam Husayn, whose martyrdom in the seventh century is the pivotal event in Shi^cite religious history. Those Shi^cites who perished became martyrs in the eyes of their coreligionists, sacrificed on the very site of Husayn's martyrdom.[7]

When a revived Wahhabi movement swept through Arabia during the first quarter of this century, it appeared as hostile as ever to Shi^cism's most fundamental assumptions. The leader of the movement, ^cAbd al-^cAziz Ibn Sa^cud, when asked in 1918 about the Shi^cite shrines in Iraq, could still declare that "I would raise no objection if you demolished the whole lot of them, and I would demolish them myself if I had the chance."[8] He never had that chance, but he did besiege and occupy Medina, and his bombardment of the city produced a general strike in Iran and an uproar throughout the Shi^cite world. For whereas the pilgrimage (*hajj*) to Mecca holds the same significance for Sunnis and Shi^cites, the visitation (*ziyara*) to nearby Medina is of special significance for Shi^cites. The cemetery of al-Baqi^c, near the city, is the reputed resting place of the Prophet Muhammad's daughter Fatima and four of the Twelve Imams. It was the Shi^cite practice at this cemetery to pray for their intercession with God.[9] The Wahhabis, for whom prayer through these intercessors represented a form of idolatry, had leveled much of this cemetery in 1806, during an earlier occupation of Medina, but its domed tombs had been rebuilt by the end of the century. Now the Saudis, in their purifying zeal, again demolished al-Baqi^c, a move regarded by Shi^cites as desecration of their hallowed shrines.[10]

The demolition created such profound sentiment in Iran, especially in religious circles, that the Iranian government refused to recognize Ibn Sa^cud's rule.[11] Instead, Iran demanded that a general assembly of Muslims be created to regulate the holy cities, while a Shi^cite conference convened in Lucknow, India, called upon all Muslims to use every possible means to expel Ibn Sa^cud from the Hijaz.[12] Denial of recognition was combined, in 1927, with a decision by Iran to forbid the pilgrimage to its nationals, as an act of protest against the alleged intolerance of the Wahhabis and their destruction of tombs.[13] Still, the ban failed to discourage the most determined pilgrims from Iran, who continued to arrive via Iraq and Syria. And in a pragmatic step, Ibn Sa^cud moved to defuse the extensive Shi^cite agitation against him by a show of tolerance designed to win official Iranian recognition. Shi^cite pilgrims from Arab lands met with exemplary treatment during the year in which Iran imposed the ban, and Iran's ulama soon were demanding the restored right to perform the pilgrimage.

In 1928, Iran lifted the pilgrimage ban, and in 1929 Iran and Ibn Sa^cud's kingdom concluded a treaty of friendship. Article Three of the treaty guaranteed that Iran's pilgrims would enjoy treatment identical to that of pilgrims from other countries, and that they would not be prevented from observing their own religious rites.[14] Iran's pilgrims came to enjoy a measure of toleration that reflected the pragmatism of Ibn Sa^cud on Shi^cite matters, an approach that also guided his policy toward his own Shi^cite minority in the east of his kingdom. Ibn Sa^cud, in both hosting and ruling over Shi^cites, now asked only that they avoid public enactment of distinctly Shi^cite rituals. In less than a decade, a pattern of tolerance seemed to have been firmly established.[15]

All the more striking, then, was a serious recurrence of the Sunni libel of Shi^cite defilement. In 1943, a Saudi religious judge ordered an Iranian pilgrim beheaded for allegedly defiling the Great Mosque with excrement supposedly carried into the mosque in his pilgrim's garment. Ibn Sa^cud remarked to some Americans that "this was the kind of offense which might be expected of Iranians." The verdict in local coffee houses held that "the Iranians always act that way."[16] The incident, which infuriated religious opinion in Iran, culminated in an official Iranian protest and a demand for payment of an indemnity. Iran even severed diplomatic relations. The Iranian press indulged in a campaign of anti-Wahhabi polemic shriller than anything published since Ibn Sa^cud's conquest of Mecca. Once again, tales of Wahhabi barbarism were retold, and the story of the sacking of Karbala was recounted with anguish and embellishment. The government of Iran imposed another pilgrimage ban, which it lifted only in 1948, after the dust of controversy had settled.

The pilgrimage controversy became dormant again following the political rapprochement between Saudi Arabia and Iran during the 1960s, which was the outcome of shared apprehension over Egyptian-sponsored subversion. Theologians on both sides of the divide continued to publish intolerant polemical attacks and legal opinions directed against the rival variety of Islam. Yet, the doctrinal disagreement was accompanied by a steady increase in the number of Iranian pilgrims, thanks to the introduction of a direct air service for pilgrims. The number of Iranian pilgrims rose steadily from 12,000 in 1961 to 57,000 in 1972.

The Pilgrimage Reinterpreted

This influx coincided with the appearance of an introspective and overtly political genre of Iranian writing on the pilgrimage. The radical Iranian publicist Ali Shariati, in his book *Hajj*, sought deeper meaning in the Meccan pilgrimage in his quest for a solution to contemporary Islam's broader philosophical and political dilemmas. Shariati urged the pilgrims "to study the dangers and consequences of the superpowers and their agents who have infiltrated Muslim nations. They should resolve to fight against brainwashing, propaganda, disunity, heresy, and false religions."[17]

In 1971, several Iranians were arrested in Mecca for distributing a message to Muslim pilgrims from one Ayatollah Ruhollah Khomeini in Najf, the Shi^cite shrine city in Iraq:

> At this sacred pilgrimage gathering, the Muslims must exchange their views concerning the basic problems of Islam and the special problems of each Muslim country. The people of each country should, in effect, present a report concerning their own state to the Muslims of the world, and thus all will come to know what their Muslim brothers are suffering at the hands of imperialism and its agents.

Khomeini then presented his own scathing "report" on Iran, describing it as "a military base for Israel, which means, by extension, for America."[18]

After 1971, hardly a year passed during which some Iranians did not distribute a similar message from Khomeini to Muslim pilgrims. The effort usually met with Saudi apathy, for the Saudis did not regard this preaching as directed against themselves. Khomeini worded his annual pilgrimage message in such a way as to appeal to Iranian pilgrims and to alert other pilgrims to the "shameful, bloody, so-called White Revolution" of the Shah. Such propaganda was liable to complicate Saudi relations with the Shah's Iran, so Saudi authorities took measures against the more brazen distributors of Khomeini's messages. But the Saudis did not regard these few troublesome Iranians as a serious threat to their own standing as rulers of Islam's holiest sanctuaries. Khomeini himself performed the pilgrimage in 1973, without incident.

But the truly radical feature of Shi^cite doctrine as expounded both by Khomeini and Shariati was their abrogation of the Shi^cite principle of discretion (*taqiyya*) during the pilgrimage, a discretion that generally had been reciprocated by Saudi tolerance. By urging their followers to view the pilgrimage as a political rite, they set Shiᶜites apart from other pilgrims, with serious consequences for the fragile tolerance that the Saudis had displayed. The new preaching upset the delicate balance that preserved the pilgrimage peace, by urging a line of action that implicitly underlined differences between Shiᶜite pilgrims and Sunni hosts.

Following the Iranian revolution, Iran sought to act on the principles elaborated by Khomeini, by appealing directly to the Muslim pilgrims of other lands through political activity during the pilgrimage.[19] The process of politicization was gradual. In 1979, Iran's pilgrims engaged in no more than light propagandizing, and in 1980 Iran organized a much reduced pilgrimage, due to the outbreak of war with Iraq. But large demonstrations, resulting in violent clashes with Saudi police, first took place in 1981, when Iranian pilgrims began to chant political slogans in the Prophet's Mosque in Medina and the Great Mosque in Mecca. Saudi security forces acted against the Iranians in both mosques, and a subsequent clash in the Prophet's Mosque resulted in the death of an Iranian pilgrim. In 1982, the Iranian pilgrimage took an even more radical turn, when Khomeini appointed Hujjat al-Islam Musavi-Khoiniha as his pilgrimage representative. Khoiniha was the mentor of the students who had seized the United States Embassy in Tehran. Saudi police clashed with demonstrators whom he addressed in both Medina and Mecca. In Mecca he was arrested, and a speech delivered in Medina after the pilgrimage earned him expulsion as an "instigator."

This renewed conflict intensified the polemical debate over the pilgrimage. The debate itself was not a simple repetition of the old libels but was transformed and made more credible, so that it no longer expressed sectarian distrust so much as it evoked it. This transformation probably reflected the influence of ecumenism upon the intellectual climate of contemporary Islam, a climate now inhospitable to overt sectarian polemics. For most Muslims, it is no longer considered politic to dwell openly on the differences between Sunni and Shiᶜite Islam. Indeed, merely to cite these differences is regarded by many Shiᶜites as an attempt to isolate them, and even as part of an imperialist plot to foment division in Islam. The new sectarianism takes a subtler form: Shiᶜites profess their unity of purpose with Sunnis, but then declare that a major expression of Sunnism (in this case, Saudi Wahhabism) is a deviation from ecumenical Islam. Sunnis declare their acceptance of Shiᶜites as Muslims, but then declare that a major expression of Shi^cism (in this case, Khomeini's revolutionary activism) constitutes a deviation from ecumenical Islam.

In this manner, sectarian prejudice is insinuated, even as the unity of Islam is openly professed. This is precisely how the lines of argument in the new pilgrimage polemic insinuated the libels of yesteryear—most perfectly in the brief correspondence between the late Saudi King Khalid and Imam Khomeini in October 1981, at a time of violent clashes in Mecca and Medina between Iranian pilgrims and Saudi police.[20] Khalid compiled a revealing letter of protest to Khomeini, asking that Khomeini urge his followers to show restraint, but strongly hinting that the Great Mosque had been defiled by blasphemous Iranian pilgrims. According to Khalid, Iranian pilgrims in the Great Mosque had performed their ritual circumambulations while chanting "God is great, Khomeini is great," and "God is one, Khomeini is one." There was no need for Khalid to elaborate on this charge. It was obvious that the Iranian's slogans constituted an excessive veneration of their Imam, a form of blasphemous polytheism. All this had aroused the "dissatisfaction and disgust" of other pilgrims, wrote Khalid to Khomeini.

In fact, Khalid's letter distorted well-known Iranian revolutionary slogans. Iranian pilgrims had actually chanted "God is great, Khomeini is leader." The Saudis had confused the Persian word for "leader" (*rahbar*) with the rhyming Arabic for "great" (*akbar*). And the pilgrims' Arabic chant declared that "God is one, Khomeini is leader." Here, the Saudis had confused the Arabic for "one" (*wahid*) with the rhyming Arabic for "leader" (*qa'id*). There was a vast difference between the slogans as actually chanted by the Iranians and the inadvertent or deliberate misrepresentations of Khalid. In the actual slogans, Khomeini is cast as a leader unrivaled in the world, but subordinate to an almighty God. In the slogans as reported by the Saudis, Khomeini is placed on one plane with God, a verbal pollution of Islam's holiest sanctuary. This familiar but disguised charge of Shi^cite defilement, the Saudis sought to level at Iran's pilgrims. The accusation gained credibility from the formerly widespread Sunni conviction that the Shi^cites are bound to pollute the Great Mosque.

In his reply to Khalid, Khomeini evoked the old Shi^cite libel, charging the Saudis with failing to respect the refuge provided by the Great Mosque. "How is it that the Saudi police attack Muslims with jackboots and weapons, beat them, arrest them, and send them to prisons from inside the holy mosque, a place which according to the teaching of God and the text of the Qur'an, is refuge for all, even deviants?" This was a decidedly Shiᶜite reading of the meaning of the Great Mosque's sanctity, which owed a great deal to the concept of refuge (*bast*) that traditionally applied to Shiᶜite shrines in Iran. Such shrines were indeed absolutely inviolable places of refuge, where any kind of malefactor could find asylum.[21]

Nothing could have been further from the Wahhabi-Saudi concept of the sanctity of the holy places, regarded as sites so sacred that no deviation at all may be allowed in their precincts. Only from a Shiᶜite perspective did this Saudi concern for preserving the purity of the Great Mosque appear as blind disrespect. In 1979, the Saudis had acted in good conscience to clear the Great Mosque of "deviants," relying upon a *fatwa* issued by over thirty other men of religion, who argued that it was permissible to dislodge the defilers even by force of arms. This decision enjoyed wide Muslim support beyond Saudi Arabia, and Khomeini's presentation of the Great Mosque as a place in which even "deviants" enjoyed absolute immunity could only be regarded as peculiarly Shiᶜite, since it relied upon a Shiᶜite concept of inviolable refuge that knows no parallel in Sunni Islam.

Differing concepts of sanctity also affected that part of the pilgrimage controversy played out in Medina. In 1982, Khomeini's representative to the pilgrimage chose the cemetery of al-Baqiᶜ in Medina as the site for a series of demonstrations combined with visitation prayers. After the Saudi demolition of the shrines in the cemetery in 1926, al-Baqiᶜ ceased to serve as a place of Shiᶜite visitation. But after Iran's Islamic revolution, the formal prayers were reinstated against Saudi will and were recited outside the high wall that the Saudis had built to seal off the cemetery.[22] In 1986, in a concession to Iran's pilgrims, Saudi authorities allowed them access to the cemetery itself, and Khomeini's representative to the pilgrimage formally thanked Saudi King Fahd for permitting the return of Shiᶜite pilgrims to the venerated site. This obsessive interest in al-Baqiᶜ and other tombs, and the resort to the cemetery as a rallying point for pilgrims in Medina, reflected an especially Shiᶜite notion of Medina's sanctity and served to evoke past resentment against the Saudis for having defaced the memory of the Imams.

This heightened Shiᶜite interest in Medina also owed a great deal to changes in the spiritual geography of Shiᶜite Islam. After the outbreak of the war between Iran and Iraq, it was no longer possible for Iranians to visit the Shiᶜite shrine cities in Iraq and the tombs of the Imams in their sacred precincts. For the great mass of Shiᶜites, the pilgrimage to these sites in Iraq had taken precedence over the pilgrimage to Mecca and the visitation to Medina. Their inaccessibility greatly enhanced the significance for Iranian Shi^cism of the holy cities of Arabia, and by 1988 over 1 million Iranians had made application to Iranian authorities to conduct the pilgrimage to the holy cities in Arabia.[23] As a result, al-Baqi^c emerged again as a major Shi^cite center of pilgrimage, and mass prayer services were conducted there after Iran's revolution, not by the Saudi men of religion who manage the mosques in Mecca and Medina, but by visiting Shi^cite clerics.

The Pilgrimage Understanding

Such identifiably Shi^cite themes and methods of protest might have blinded other pilgrims to the political message of liberation that Iran wished to convey during the pilgrimage. The fear that Iran's message might simply be dismissed by other Muslims as Shi^cite dissent was responsible for some of the ecumenical intonations of Khomeini's pilgrimage representatives and other Shi^cite clerics. Most notably, Khomeini's representatives instructed Iran's pilgrims to pray with all other pilgrims behind the Sunni prayer leaders in the Great Mosque and the Prophet's Mosque, lest they stand out for their Shi^cism rather than their political activism.

This restraint, matched by a parallel Saudi restraint in dealing with Iran's pilgrims, left the impression that the pilgrimage had been defused. The climate of confrontation dissipated in 1983; although tensions remained high, only minor incidents marred the pilgrimage peace in that and subsequent years. By 1986, it seemed that Iran and Saudi Arabia had reached a compromise permitting Iran to conduct a limited measure of political propaganda during the pilgrimage. By the informal terms of the pilgrimage understanding, Khomeini's pilgrimage representative was permitted to organize two pilgrims' rallies, the first in Medina and the second in Mecca, in areas removed from the holy mosques in each city. A number of understandings restricted the form and content of these demonstrations. Iran's pilgrims were not to import or display printed matter and posters of a political nature, and their slogans were to be directed only against the United States, the Soviet Union, and Israel. Other Muslim governments and the host government were not to be criticized. This understanding allowed Iran's pilgrims to vent their views, but enabled Saudi authorities to confine all demonstrating to two fixed events. It also made possible a sizeable increase in the number of Iranian pilgrims.

In 1986, a group of Iranian pilgrims who opposed the strategy of moderation in dealing with Saudi Arabia arrived in the country with a large quantity of high explosives in their suitcases. Their aim was to destroy the pilgrimage understanding reached between Iran and Saudi Arabia—but they failed. Saudi airport authorities discovered the explosives and arrested over 100 pilgrims upon their arrival. Those Iranian leaders who had assured Saudi Arabia that the pilgrimage peace would be preserved were embarrassed and dissociated themselves from the plot by allowing the Saudis to detain the pilgrims for weeks without protest. But the plotters enjoyed the support of one of the major factions in Iran—that which opposed the pursuit of any opening toward the Saudis and favored the aggressive export of the revolution. In the pilgrimage plot of 1986, it became clear that the pilgrimage peace was an unstable one, affected by the changing balance in Iran's internal power struggle.

Iranian Pilgrims, 1979–1988	
1979	75,000
1980	10,000
1981	75,000
1982	85,000
1983	100,000
1984	150,000
1985	150,000
1986	150,000
1987	150,000
1988	0

The heightened political tensions of 1987 surrounding the introduction of United States naval forces into the Persian Gulf did not immediately threaten the pilgrimage understanding. Nonetheless, Saudi authorities were alarmed by a speech made at the beginning of July by Hujjat al-Islam Musavi-Khoiniha, Khomeini's former pilgrimage representative. Khoiniha had presided over the most turbulent pilgrimage seasons. His replacement as pilgrimage supervisor and his appointment as prosecutor general in 1985 was probably intended to reduce the chances of confrontation in Mecca. But he was still a powerful figure in Iran and a champion of extremists who opposed all limitations on Iran's pilgrims. His speech was plainly provocative.

This year, he declared, "a mere march or demonstration will not suffice." Iran should not simply "gather a certain number of people who might support the views of the Islamic republic." Khoiniha demanded that Saudi Arabia allow Khomeini's pilgrimage representative to enter the Great Mosque in Mecca for one night, and there conduct a referendum among the throngs of pilgrims over the decision of the amir of Kuwait to invite foreign escorts for Kuwaiti tankers. At the same time, Khomeini's representative would explain Iran's case in the war. "All we ask is that the Saudi Government not oppose this, nor send its guards to the Great Mosque. Let us see what happens. We will try it for one year."[24]

Saudi authorities now had grounds to suspect that some of Iran's pilgrims might attempt a takeover of the Great Mosque, as a political maneuver to embarrass Saudi Arabia, Kuwait, and the United States. Khoiniha's statement touched off a raw nerve and immediately elicited a warning from an unnamed official source in Saudi Arabia. The source noted that Saudi Arabia supported numerous other forums for the expression of Muslim opinion on various matters, even during the pilgrimage. But such consultations in the Great Mosque would constitute an innovation in Islam, and "anyone who attempts to innovate in Islam will go to hell." Saudi Arabia would shoulder its responsibility for safeguarding the Islamic shrines in Mecca and Medina.[25] Khoiniha's statement put the Saudi security apparatus on a high state of alert and lent more credence to inevitable rumors that the Iranians planned a violent confrontation.

However, Khoiniha's demand did not figure in the negotiations between the Saudi Ministry of Pilgrimage Affairs and Khomeini's official pilgrimage representative, Mehdi Karrubi. As Khomeini's spokesman, Karrubi asked only that Iran be allowed to conduct its demonstration in Mecca as in past years. An Iranian official even covered the route of the planned demonstration with a Saudi official, and it clearly ended 1.5 kilometers short of the Great Mosque. But, despite this understanding and the absence of any incident during the earlier march in Medina, the Saudi authorities remained deeply suspicious. On the eve of the Mecca demonstration, they pressured Karrubi to cancel the march, lest violence break out. Karrubi refused, and declared that "in the event of disorder and disruption, the responsibility for this will be fully with the Saudi government."[26] Two days before the planned demonstration, the Iranian media published Khomeini's annual message to the pilgrims. Although longer and more high-strung than the messages of recent years, it did not constitute a major departure from the understanding regarding the pilgrimage itself. Khomeini included the customary plea to pilgrims that they "avoid clashes, insults, and disputes" and warned against those intent on disruption "who might embark on spontaneous moves."[27]

The Understanding Destroyed

The atmosphere in Mecca was charged with tension on July 31, the day of the planned demonstration. Many units of Saudi security forces were in evidence throughout the city, and at the Great Mosque, where the usual Saudi "morality" police were replaced by armed soldiers. For the first time, guards at the gate subjected entering pilgrims to full body searches and forbade pilgrims from carrying anything into the Great Mosque, including sun umbrellas and canteens.[28] These measures apparently reflected a Saudi intelligence estimate that an attempted Iranian takeover of the Great Mosque was a real possibility.

In the afternoon, the demonstrations began in the usual fashion, with slogans and speeches. The march commenced upon the conclusion of the speeches; as in the past, it was led by *chador*-clad women and war invalids. At or near the end of the planned route, the march came upon a cordon of Saudi riot police and National Guardsmen who refused to allow the procession to go any further. This dangerous situation became explosive in the wake of two developments. Apparently, some within the crowd of Iranian pilgrims chose this moment to echo Khoiniha's provocative demand and called upon the marchers to continue to the Great Mosque. At the same time (or perhaps even earlier), unidentified persons in an adjacent parking garage began to pelt the Iranian demonstrators with bricks, pieces of concrete, and iron bars. This exacerbated the situation on the confrontation line between the pilgrims and the police, and both sides began to exchange blows, the police using truncheons and electric prods; the demonstrators using sticks, knives, and rocks. Because Karrubi and the other Iranian officials had not positioned themselves at the head of the march, they had no control over the conduct of Iran's pilgrims at the crucial point of contact with Saudi police. During the ensuing confrontation, the Saudis backed down temporarily, and the crowd surged forward. According to American intelligence sources, the tide finally was turned by reinforcements from the National Guard, who fired tear gas shells into the crowd and then opened fire with pistols and automatic weapons.[29] The Saudis have denied firing on the demonstrators or even using tear gas, claiming instead that the demonstrators, once dispersed, surged in retreat. According to the Saudis, those who died were trampled to death. According to official Saudi figures, 402 people died in the clash, including 275 Iranian pilgrims, 85 Saudi police, and 42 pilgrims from other countries. Iran claimed that 400 Iranian pilgrims died and that several thousand were injured.

This reconstruction rests upon a selective reading of the contradictory accounts provided by Iranian and Saudi sources.[30] As no independent investigation will ever be conducted, important details will remain in doubt. But no evidence has been produced by Saudi Arabia or Iran to establish that the other side acted deliberately or with premeditation to provoke violence. The evidence now available indicates that a group of undisciplined Iranian pilgrims, acting under the influence of at least one provocative statement by a leading Iranian official, wished to enter the Great Mosque as demonstrators. Saudi security authorities, who had been alerted to this possibility but lacked self-confidence in the face of provocation, employed deadly force to thwart the Iranian crowd.

Whereas the actual events in Mecca remained shrouded by irreconcilable claims, there could be no doubt about the immediate effect of the deaths at Mecca in revalidating hoary prejudices. The accusations that flew in both directions after the incident had few parallels in their intensity. Saudi Interior Minister Prince Nayif bin cAbd al-cAziz relied upon Sunni prejudice when he charged that the real objective of the Iranian pilgrims was "to spoil the pilgrimage, because, as is known, the pilgrimage is done only if the Great Mosque is entered." Iranian "sedition" inside the Great Mosque would have made it impossible for other pilgrims to have carried out the required circumambulations in the Great Mosque. "The pilgrimage would have been spoilt."[31] There is no evidence that the Iranian demonstrators, even those who wished to carry their protest into the Great Mosque, intended to ruin the rite for other pilgrims. But by his charge Nayif sought to associate the Iranian demonstrators with the legendary Shicite "defilers" of the Great Mosque.

Iranian statements pandered to the belief still held by Shicites that the fanatic Saudis were driven by their own misguided beliefs to kill innocent Shicite pilgrims. Khomeini declared that the Saudi rulers, "these vile and ungodly Wahhabis, are like daggers which have always pierced the heart of the Muslims from the back," and announced that Mecca was in the hands of "a band of heretics."[32] Once more, the

Saudis were transformed into what speaker of the parliament ᶜAli Akbar Hashemi-Rafsanjani called "Wahhabi hooligans." Rafsanjani recalled the nineteenth-century Wahhabi massacres (of Shiᶜites) in Najf and Karbala, the Wahhabi destruction of Islamic monuments in Medina (venerated by Shiᶜites), and the Wahhabi burning of libraries (containing Shiᶜite works). The Wahhabis "will commit any kind of crime. I ask you to pay more attention to the history of that evil clique so that you can see what kind of creatures they have been in the course of their history."[33] This represented a deliberate attempt to fuel a present crisis with the memory of past sectarian hatreds.

Following the Mecca tragedy, both Saudi Arabia and Iran conducted large-scale campaigns to influence Muslim opinion abroad. The Saudi government ordered its principal missionary organization, the Muslim World League, to convene an Islamic conference in Mecca in October 1987. More than 600 supporters and clients of Saudi Arabia from 134 countries attended the conference, which was opened by Saudi King Fahd. As expected, the conference condemned Iran alone for the Mecca violence: the Iranian government — "accustomed to terrorism and a thirst for Muslim blood" — "solely bears the responsibility for the outrage in God's holy mosque." The measures taken by the Saudi authorities "to quell the sedition and to contain the fires of wickedness were legitimate."[34] Iran immediately attacked the conference in Mecca as one more attempt by the Saudis to "buy the religion of Muslims."[35] Saudi Shiᶜite opposition sources charged that the Saudis had spent $470 million on the conference, and that total expenses were liable to reach $700 million.[36] The conference, far from being Islamic, had a narrowly Sunni, Wahhabi, and Saudi orientation, said its Iranian critics; it was a conference of men of religion who served the rulers, not the religion.[37]

The following month, Iran convened an International Congress on Safeguarding the Sanctity and Security of the Great Mosque, under the auspices of the Ministry of Islamic Guidance and the Foreign Ministry. Rafsanjani, in addressing the 300 participants from thirty-six countries, called for the "liberation" of Mecca and the establishment of an Islamic International that would govern Mecca as a free city.[38] Ayatollah Montazeri, who met with the foreign guests, denounced the Saudis as "a bunch of English agents from Najd who have no respect either for the House of God or for the pilgrims who are the guests of God." Just as Jerusalem would be liberated from the "claws of usurping Israel," Mecca and Medina would be liberated from the "claws of Al Saᶜud."[39] A Sunni cleric at the conference apparently took the analogy still further, denouncing the Saudis as Jews. An Iranian pilgrimage official noted that the Iranians themselves had not labeled the Saudis Jews, but "even if we do not agree that you are Jews, your deeds are worse than those of the Jews. What you did to Muslims in the House of God has never been done to Muslims by the Jews."[40] The insinuation that the Saudis were Jews — the worst possible libel — echoed an old piece of Shi'ite bigotry that attributed Jewish origins to the Saudi ruling family.[41] The Tehran resolutions were repeated by Iranian-inspired seminars on the pilgrimage that subsequently met in Beirut and Lahore. The Saudis also convened supporting conferences elsewhere, most notably in London, where Saudi clients declared support for the use of force in quelling Iranian "sedition."[42]

After the initial round of conferences, the polemical debate shifted to the next pilgrimage. The Saudis were reluctant to impose an outright ban on Iran's pilgrims, lest they open themselves to the charge of denying Muslims the chance to meet a fundamental obligation of Islam. But the Saudis clearly sought to translate the tragedy into a far-reaching revision of the informal understanding that had come apart in 1987 and that had become a thorn in the side of Saudi security.

First, Saudi officials, citing wider Muslim support for their version of the 1987 tragedy, made it absolutely clear that no demonstration would be allowed in 1988. The demonstrations that Khomeini had attempted to introduce as part of the pilgrimage ritual — and that the Saudis had tolerated — would no longer be permitted. The Saudis then moved to cut the number of Iran's pilgrims, who at 150,000 per year had come to constitute the largest national group. The move won full endorsement from the foreign ministers' conference of the Organization of the Islamic Conference, meeting in Amman in March 1988. This gathering placed the blame for the tragedy in Mecca squarely on the shoulders of Iran's pilgrims and voiced its support for Saudi measures to prevent a repetition of the violence. But, most important, the conference supported a Saudi proposal to limit the number of pilgrims by establishing national quotas for pilgrims, based upon each country's population.

The ostensible aim was to give Saudi Arabia a three-year interlude to expand and improve facilities in Mecca. Although these facilities needed modernization, the most important effect of the planned quota of 1000 pilgrims per million population would be a drastic cut in the number of Iran's pilgrims, from 150,000 to 45,000. The Saudis, of course, were fully aware of Khomeini's stand that any cut in the number of Iran's pilgrims would result in an Iranian boycott of the pilgrimage. At the same time, Saudi Arabia chose this moment to sever relations with Iran. Saudi Arabia had not severed relations with Iran after the violence of 1987, despite the storming of the Saudi legation building by a Tehran crowd and the resulting death of a Saudi diplomat. Relations were severed only eight months later, when this served the clear purpose of making it impossible for Iranian pilgrims to secure pilgrims' visas. The Iranian government, with the sanction of a ruling by Khomeini, then elected to boycott the pilgrimage altogether. The monarchy had taken the same measure on two earlier occasions in this century: there was nothing revolutionary in this tried and tested Iranian response to the escalation of sectarian tensions.

The intense polemical exchange that accompanied the 1988 pilgrimage also followed precedent. The Saudi Council of Ministers declared that the Iranians, by "causing havoc" during the pilgrimage, had "moved outside the Islamic consensus."[43] The Iranians accused the Saudis of preventing Muslims from fulfilling the fundamental obligation of pilgrimage. Any Muslim with the means to perform the pilgrimage was entitled to do so; the Saudi implementation of a quota system demonstrated their incompetence.[44] In Khomeini's message marking the first anniversary of the "massacre," he accused the "centers of Wahhabism" of "sedition and espionage." At Mecca in 1987, "the sword of blasphemy and divison, which had been hidden in the hypocritical cloak of Yazid's followers and descendants of the Umayyad dynasty, God's curse be upon them, had to come out again from the same cloak of Abu Sufyan's heirs to destroy and kill."[45] Whatever his intention, Khomeini's resort to this historical analogy constituted a sectarian allusion — despite his claim, in the very same message, that it was the United States and the Saudis who tried to portray the Mecca events as a sectarian clash.

Restoring the Pilgrimage Peace

The absence of Iranian pilgrims in 1988 brought an enforced truce to the pilgrimage but not a peace. The polemical debate between Saudi Arabia and Iran did not abate, forcing the Saudis to police the pilgrimage of 1988 to a degree never before witnessed by pilgrims. The cease-fire between Iran and Iraq that followed later in the summer held out the prospect of a future reconciliation, but this would require negotiations almost as delicate and complicated as those between Iran and Iraq.

A political reconciliation conceivably could restore mutual civility during the sacred season of pilgrimage. But the deterioration had not been the sole product of the Persian Gulf crisis. Certainly the evolving rift between Saudi Arabia and Iran over the war determined the timing of the pilgrimage crisis. But the unprecedented intensity of that controversy, culminating in bloodshed, had its roots in sectarian prejudice. Once political differences combined with sectarian bigotries, they interacted as two volatile elements to produce an explosion. It was not simply that the Saudis and Iranians championed two different views of Islam. Beyond present differences, the intensity of their struggle derived from the long history of conflict and mutual intolerance that these rival interpretations of Islam already shared.

Today it seems as though Iran has lost the struggle to redefine the pilgrimage for other Muslims. To the extent that Muslims have tended to interpret the deaths in Mecca within their respective sectarian traditions, the Saudi version of the events has enjoyed the wider credibility in the Muslim world. Iran's marches in Medina and Mecca were devoted to "unity" and "the disavowal of infidels." But the little Muslim unity produced by Iran's pilgrimage policy was directed and orchestrated by Saudi Arabia against Iran's pilgrimage message. The Iranians, keen to disavow the "infidels," have found themselves disavowed and effectively barred from Mecca.

Much more has been lost in the struggle for Mecca than Iran's hopes for mobilizing the masses of Muslim pilgrims against the enemies of Islam. A price has been paid by all Islam. The pilgrimage controversy has torn open the unhealed sectarian wounds on the body politic of Islam. Iranian and Saudi attempts to unite Muslims have only sharpened the divisions among them, particularly along the dangerous fault lines of sectarian bigotry. And the pilgrimage itself, the supposed symbol of Islam's overriding unity, has become a tinderbox.

NOTES

Introduction

1. C. S. Liebman, "Extremism as a Religious Norm," *Journal for the Scientific Study of Religion* 22, no. 7 (1983).

2. Thus when the Salman Rushdie affair erupted in February 1989, *haredi* leaders expressed their sympathy with radical Muslim rage against the "sacrilegious allegations" contained in *Satanic Verses* (London and New York: 1988) "What would we say", demanded Rabbi Abraham Ravitz, "if Moses were said to have associated with prostitutes?" *Ha^{c}aretz* (Tel Aviv), 22 February 1989.

3. S. A. Arjomand, "Iran's Revolution in Comparative Perspective," *World Politics* (April 1986): 406.

4. See H. Tudor, *Political Myth* (London: Macmillan, 1972); L. Thompson, *The Political Mythology of Apartheid* (New Haven, Conn., 1985); D. Kertzer, *Ritual, Politics and Power* (New Haven, Conn., 1988).

5. See E. Sivan, "The Islamic Republic of Egypt," *Orbis* (April 1987): 43–53.

6. For this concept, see A. Kriegel, *French Communists* (Chicago, 1972), Introduction.

7. See M. Kramer, *The Moral Logic of Hizballah*, Occasional Paper, (Dayan Center, Tel Aviv University, August 1987).

Chapter 1

I wish to thank the Olga and William Lakritz Fund, administered by the Hebrew University of Jerusalem, for its generous support in the preparation of this chapter.

1. I. J. Reines, *Sha^{c}arey 'Orah ve-Simḥah* (Vilna, 1899), pp. 12–13. See also Aviezer Ravitzky, "Messianism, Zionism and the State of Israel: The Contemporary Religious Debate," in Aluf Hareven, ed., *Israel Liqrat ha-Me'ah ha-^{c}Esrim ve-'Aḥat* (Jerusalem, 1984), pp. 135–197 [Hebrew].

2. *Ha-Meliṣ* 78 (1900). See Israel Kleusner, "The Beginning of the Mizrah Movement," *Sefer ha-Ṣiyonut ha-Datit* (Jerusalem, 1977), p. 339 [Hebrew].

3. S. I. Rabinovitz, *Ha-Dat ve-ha-Le'umiyut* (Warsaw, 1900), p. 127; Shmuel Almog, *Siyonut ve-Historeyah* (Jerusalem, 1982), p. 45.

4. Reines, *Sha^carey.*

5. Rabinovitz, *Ha-Dat.*

6. Israel Kolat, "Zionism and Messianism," in Zvi Baras, ed., *Meshiḥiyut ve-Eskhatologyah* (Jerusalem, 1984), pp. 419–24 [Hebrew]; Shmuel Almog, "Messianism as a Challenge to Zionism," in Baras, ibid., pp. 433–36 [Hebrew].

7. Gershom Scholem, *Devarim be-Go* (Tel Aviv, 1975), p. 50.

8. See note 31.

9. See below, pp. 19–20.

10. Isaiah 65:17.

11. E. E. Urbach, *HaZal* (Jerusalem, 1969), pp. 649 ff.; Gershom Scholem, *The Messianic Idea in Judaism* (New York, 1971), Chapter 1; Aviezer Ravitzky, "Maimonides on the Messianic Era," in Joel Kraemer, ed., *Studies in Maimonides' Thought and Environment* (Oxford, 1990).

12. Amos Funkenstein, *Ha-Pasiviyyut . . . Mitos u-Meṣi'ut* (Tel Aviv, 1982), p. 10; Uriel Tal, "Jewish Self Understanding and the Land and State of Israel," *Union Theological Quarterly* 26, no. 4 (1971): 357.

13. Menachem Friedman, *Ḥevrah ve-Dat* (Jerusalem, 1978); Norman Lamm, "The Ideology of the Neturei Karta According to the Satmar Version," *Tradition* 13 (1971): 35 ff.; I. Domb, *The Transformation: The Case of the Neturei Karta* (London, 5718); idem, "Neturei Karta," in Michael Selzer, ed., *Zionism Reconsidered* (New York, 1969), pp. 23–48.

14. Yoel Teitelbaum, *va-Yo'el Moshe* (New York, 1960), pp. 84, 18.

15. Shir ha-Shirim Rabbah 2:18; Babylonian Talmud, Ketubot 111a.

16. Amram Blau, "The Idol of Nationalism," in *'Om 'Any Ḥomah* Jerusalem, 1949), pp. 50–52 [Hebrew].

17. Teitelbaum, *va-Yo'el*, pp. 8–13; idem., *^cAl ha-Ge'ulah ve-^cAl ha-Temurah* (Brooklyn, 1967), pp. 8–9.

18. Idem, *va-Yo'el Moshe*, pp. 149, 139, respectively.

19. Y. A. Z. Margulis, *'Ashrey ha-'Ish* (Jerusalem, 1927), p. 65. See also Yehudah Liebes, "The Edah Haredit in Jerusalem," in *Jerusalem Studies in Jewish Thought* 3 (1982): 137–52 [Hebrew].

20. Ibid.

21. Friedman, *Ḥevrah*, pp. 129, 287, 329.

22. Yeshaya Margulis, *Qumy cOry* (Jerusalem, 1925), pp. 24, 62 ff; Teitelbaum, *cAl ha-Ge'ulah*, p. 136; Domb, *The Transformation*, pp. 68, 115, 120.

23. Teitelbaum, *va-Yo'el Moshe*, p. 229.

24. See notes 63 and 64.

25. Teitelbaum, *cAl ha-Ge'ulah*, p. 133.

26. Domb, *The Transformation*, pp. 68, 142, 148, 162.

27. Zvi Yehudah Kook (son of Rabbi A. I. Kook), *li-Netivot Israel* (Jerusalem, 1967), pp. 188–95.

28. Tanhuma, Shofetim 9.

29. Z. Y. Kook, *li-Netivot*, p. 15.

30. Abraham Isaac Kook, *Ḥazon ha-Ge'ulah* (Jerusalem, 1941), p. 199.

31. Babylonian Talmud, 98b; cf. Ketubot 103b. See also Uzi Kalcheim, "The Vision of the Revealed End" *cAderet ha-'Emunah* (Jerusalem, 1936), pp. 237 ff. [Hebrew].

32. Zvi Yaron, *Mishnato shel ha-Rav Kook* (Jerusalem, 1974), pp. 270 ff.

33. Shlomo Avineri, *The Making of Modern Zionism* (New York, 1980), Chapter 14.

34. Ibid., pp. 21–22; cf. *'Iggerot ha-Re'iyah* (Jerusalem, 1974), Vol. 1, p. 148; Vol. 3, p. 158. See also M. M. Kasher, *ha-Tequfah ha-Gedolah* (Jerusalem, 1972), p. 172.

35. A. I. Kook, *'Orot ha-Teshuvah* (Jerusalem, 1966), p. 27; cf. idem., *Ḥazon ha-Ge'ulah*, p. 36.

36. Idem., *'Orot* (Jerusalem, 1963), p. 63.

37. Ibid., p. 135.

38. Ibid., p. 63–64.

39. Eliezer Schweid, *ha-Yehudi ha-Boded ve-Yahaduto* (Tel Aviv, 1974), 178–192.

40. Cf. Rabbi Yehuda Alkalay, *Goral la-Shem* (Vienna, 1957), Chapter 7; idem., *ha-Mevaser* 13 (Nisan, 1866).

41. *'Iggerot ha-Re'iyah*, Vol. 1, p. 143; cf. ibid., Vol. 1, p. 58.

42. Eliyahu Avihayil, *le-'Or ha-Shaḥar* (Jerusalem, 1982), pp. 107, 118–19.

43. Eliezer Waldman, ^c*Al Da^cat ha-Zeman ve-ha-Maqom* (Tel Aviv, 1983), pp. 109–10.

44. Shlomo Aviner, "Our Redemption," ^c*Amudim* 366 (1976): 276–77 [Hebrew].

45. Shalom Ohana, *'Or Ḥadash* (Jerusalem, 1974); Shlomo Goren, *ha-Ṣofeh* (Shevat 14, 1974); Uriel Simon, *Petaḥim* 32 (1975).

46. Uriel Tal, "The Land and the State of Israel in Israel Religious Life," *Proceedings of the Rabbinical Assembly* 38 (1976): 22; Immanuel Jakobovits, "Religious Responses to Jewish Statehood," *Tradition* 20, no. 3 (1982): 194 ff.; Janet O'Dea, "Gush Emunim: Roots and Ambiguities," *Forum* (Spring 1976): 39–50.

47. M. Z. Nehorai, "The State of Israel in the Teaching of Rabbi Kook," *Da^cat* 2–3 (1978–1979): 35–50 [trans. from the Hebrew ^c*Amudim* 360 (1976): 40a].

48. A. I. Kook, *'Orot ha-Kodesh* (Jerusalem, 1971), Vol. 2, p. 544. See also Yaron, *Mishnato*, pp. 270 ff.; S. H. Bergman, "Rav Kook: All Reality is in God," *Faith and Reason* (New York, 1961); idem., "The Theory of Evolution in the Teaching of Rav Kook," *'Anashim u-Derakhim* (Jerusalem, 1967) [Hebrew].

49. A. I. Kook, *'Orot ha-Kodesh*, Vol. 2, p. 134.

50. Ibid., p. 158.

51. A. I. Kook, *Ḥazon ha-Ge'ulah*, p. 183; cf. p. 27.

52. Ibid., p. 187.

53. Zephanya Derori, *Ma^cariv* (July 18, 1984).

54. Maimonides, *Mishneh Torah*, Laws of Kings, 11–12.

55. Hanan Porat, ^c*Amudim* 366 (1976): 276; cf. idem., *Petaḥim* 32 (1975): 3–12.

56. Z. Y. Kook, "Clarifications," ^c*Amudim* 369 (1979): 380 [Hebrew]; Lawrence Kaplan, "Divine Promises—Conditional and Absolute," *Tradition* 18, no. 1 (1979): 41–42; Eliezer Goldman, "Messianic Interpretations of Current Events," *Forum* 26 (1977): 38.

57. See note 42.

58. Shlomo Aviner, "Repentance and Redemption," ^c*Amudim* 376 (1977): 150–53 [Hebrew].

59. Z. Y. Kook *li-Netivot Israel*, p. 381.

60. A. I. Kook, *'Orot.*

61. S. Avineri, *The Making of Modern Zionism*.

62. Jacob Talmon, *ha-Meshihiyyut ha-Medinit* (Tel Aviv, 1968), pp. 9–10; R. S. Werblowsky, *Beyond Tradition and Modernity* (London, 1976), pp. 7 ff.

63. David Sedorsky, "The End of Ideology," *Publications of the Study Circle on World Jewry in the Home of the President of Israel*, 8 no. 4 (1979) [Hebrew] Eliezer Schweid, "The Zionist Enterprise: Between Determinism and Voluntary Decision," *Molad* 8, no. 31 (1980) [Hebrew]; Michael Graetz, "Secular Messianism," in *Meshihiyyut ve-Eshkhatologyah* (Jerusalem, 1984), p. 401 [Hebrew]; Jacob Katz, "Israel and the Messiah," *Commentary* 36 (1982): 34–41.

64. Z. Y. Kook, *li-Netivot Israel*, pp. 103–104; Uzi Kalcheim, in *Peri ha-'Areṣ* (Jerusalem, 1981), Vol. 1, pp. 22.

65. Babylonian Talmud, Sanhedrin 98b; cf. Tanhumah, be-Huqota 13.

66. M. M. Kasher, *ha-Tequfah ha-Gedolah* (Jerusalem, 1972); Arye Morgenstern, "Messianic Expectations toward the Year of 1840," *Meshihiyyut ve-Eskhatologyah* (Jerusalem, 1984), pp. 343 ff. [Hebrew]; Shmuel Weingarten, "The Beginning of the Redemption," in Joseph Tirosh, ed., *Sefer ha-Ṣiyonut ha-Datit* (Jerusalem, 1974), p. 111 [Hebrew]; Yehuda Kill, *Israel u-Ge'ulato* (Jerusalem, 1975), pp. 151 ff.

67. Kalcheim, *Peri ha-'Areṣ*.

68. Aviezer Ravitzky, "Peace" [in Jewish Thought]," in Arthur A. Cohen and Paul Mendes-Flohr, ed., *Contemporary Jewish Religious Thought* (New York, 1986), pp. 685–702, especially pp. 701–702.

69. A. I. Kook, *'Orot*, p. 160.

70. Yitzhak Shilat, *ha-Ṣofeh*, (May 25, 1984); Yoel Bin-Nun, *Zeraᶜim* (Nisan 1984).

71. Meir Kahane, *'Arbaᶜim Shanah* (Jerusalem, 1979), pp. 30–31.

72. Ibid., p. 13.

73. "To Have the Strength to Be Strong," *Jewish Press* 35 (August 1984).

74. M. Kahane, *ha-'Etgar—'Ereṣ Segulah* (Jerusalem, 1973), p. 10.

75. Idem., *'Arbaᶜim Shanah*, p. 2.

76. Idem., *Time to Go Home* (Los Angeles, 1975).

77. Idem., *le-Sikim be-ᶜEyneykhem* (Jerusalem, 1980), pp. 244–45.

78. Relevant publications include Gideon Aran, "From Religious Zionism to a Zionist Religion: The Origins and Culture of Gush Emunim," Ph.D. dissertation. The Hebrew University, Jerusalem 1987 [Hebrew]; David Neuman, ed., *The Impact of Gush Emunim* (London, 1985); Ehud Shprinzak, *Every Man Whatever Is Right In His Own Eyes — Illegalism In Israeli Society* (Tel Aviv, 1986) [Hebrew]; Shubert Spero and Yitzchak Pessin, eds., *Religious Zionism after 40 Years of Statehood* (Jerusalem, 1989); Gideon Samet, ed., *A Religious War?*, *Politica*, no. 24 (Tel Aviv, 1989) [Hebrew].

79. Aviezer Ravitzky, "Exile in the Holy Land: The Dilemma of Haredi Jewry," in Peter Medding, ed., *Israel: State and Society, 1948–1988*, Studies in Contemporary Jewry, Vol. 5 (Oxford and New York, 1989), pp. 89–125. For contemporary developments in the ultra-nationalist camp, see idem., "The Roots of Kahanism: Consciousness and Political Reality," *Publication of the Study Circle on World Jewry in the Home of the President of Israel* 14, no. 8 (1986); *Jerusalem Quarterly* 39 (1986): 90–108.

80. Zalman, Melamed, "An Additional Stage in the Process of Redemption," *Nekudah* 119 (1988) [Hebrew].

Chapter 2

1. On Sunni radicalism, see E. Sivan, *Radical Islam* (New Haven, Conn., 1985). On Shiᶜite radicalism, see R. Khomeini, *Al-Hukuma al-Islamiyya*, (Beirut, 1979); idem., *Islam and Revolution*, ed. H. Algar (Berkeley, Calif., 1981); Ayatollah Taleghani, *Society and Economy in Islam*, ed. H. Algar (Berkeley, Calif., 1982); K. H. Göbel, *Modern Suniitisme Politik und Staatsidee*, (Opladen, 1984), part 3; S. Bakhash, "Sermons, Revolutionary Pamphleteering and Mobilisation" in *From Nationalism to Revolutionary Islam*, ed. S. A. Arjomand (London, 1984), pp. 177–94. Cf. R. Mottahedeh, *The Mantle of the Prophet* (New York, 1985); M. Momen, *Introduction to Shiᶜi Islam* (New Haven, Conn., 1985), chapters 10 and 14.

2. See, in particular, the ecumenical anthology published by the Higher Islamic Committee in Cairo, 1966 *Daᶜwat al-Taqrib min Khilal Risalat al-Islam* ed. M. M. al-Madani, (including contributions by Shaltut, al-Qummi, Kashif al-Ghita', Maghniya). On the Sunni ecumenical position, see also M. A. Zuᶜbi, *al-Sunna wa-l-Shiᶜa* (Beirut, 1961); M. al-Shakᶜa, *Islam bila Madhahib* (Beirut, 1981), pp. 130 ff. On Shiᶜite ecumenism, M. T. al-Qummi, *Qissat al-Taqrib* (Cairo, 1960), pp. 6 ff. Cf. also the speech delivered by the al-Azhar delegates at the ᶜAshura' celebrations in Beirut (*al-Hayat*, March 29, 1969); A. A. Wafi, *Bayna-l-shiᶜa wa-Ahl al-Sunna* (Cairo, 1984).

3. F. ᶜAbd al-Aziz, [Shqaqi] *Khomeini, al-Hall-Islami wa-l-Badil* (Cairo, 1979), pp. 140 ff.

4. On Iranian propaganda see pp. 68–69 and note 53. Radical Shi^cite and radical Sunni views on *ijtihad* in jurisprudence are similar; see ^cA. Najaf, *Al-Shahid Muhammad Baqir al-Sadr* (Tehran, 1985), pp. 37–39; Y. al-Qardawi, *Huda al-Islam: Fatawa Mu^casira* (Beirut, 1986), pp. 5–36.

5. Maybe, but not necessarily so. In Pakistan, for instance, violent clashes erupted on ^cAshura' day (October 1984) due to Shi^cite protest against the imposition of Sunni law by the state. On ecumenical concepts in matters of jurisprudence, see M. H. Maghniya, *al-Fiqh ^cAla-l-Madhahib al-Khamsa* (Beirut, 1960); M. H. Al Kashif al-Ghita', *Asl al-Shi^ca wa-Usuliha*, 10th ed. (Cairo, 1958); A. Salim's article in Madani, *Da^cwat al-Taqrib*, pp. 21 ff.; and articles by Maghniya (ibid., pp. 308–309, 464–69) and al-Qummi (ibid., pp. 205 ff.); Göbel, *Moderne Sunnitisme*, part 2.

6. A. al-Afghani, *Sirab fi Iran* (Beirut, 1982), pp. 35–36.

7. For Khomeini on the Imams, see his *al-Hukuma al-Islamiyya*, pp. 20, 52, 91, 98; Khomeini on Muslim fraternity, see his appeal to Mecca pilgrims, *al-Shahid* (Tehran) (August 22, 1984); Iranian tracts to pilgrims in 1979, 1980 (private collection). Despite the moderate position taken by Khomeini, Arab conservative fundamentalists continue to argue that all the first three caliphs are vilipended in Iran: Z. Berri^c in *al-Ahram* (August 10, 1982); A. S. As^cad, Introduction to *Matariq al-Nur* (Cairo, 1979); M. A. al-Turkmani, *Al-Ta^crif bi-Madhhab al-Shi^ca al-Imamiyya*, (Amman, 1983), pp. 110–25.

8. Turkmani, Al-Tar^cif, p. 118. Cf. (Islamic Association of Gaza), *Jawla fi-l-Fikr al-Shi^ci*, pp. 23–28; S. Ahmad, ed., *Hukm Sabb al-Sahaba* (Cairo, 1978), composed of three tracts, one by Ibn Taymiyya.

9. E. Canetti, *Crowds and Power* (New York, 1973), pp. 168, 171; cf. H. Tudor, *Political Myth* (London, 1972), pp. 137 ff.; M. Vovelle, "Ideologies and Mentalities," in *Culture, Ideology and Politics*, ed. R. Samuel and G. S. Jones, (London, 1982), pp. 2–11; C. Geertz, "Blurred Genres," *Local Knowledge* (New York, 1983), pp. 29–30; L. Thompson, *The Political Mythology of Apartheid* (New Haven, Conn., 1985), chapter 1.

10. Zu^cbi, *al-Sunna*, pp. 42–43; *al-Hayyat* (May 11, 1965). On the Nabatiyya celebrations in 1970 and 1973, see P. Ma^catouk, *La Représentation de la Mort de l'Imam Hussein a Nabatieh*, (Beirut, 1974).

11. Cf. A. A. Arjomand, "The State and Khomeini's Islamic Order," *Iranian Studies* 13 (1980); N. Calder, "Accommodation and Revolution in Imami Shi^ci Jurisprudence," *Middle Eastern Studies* (January 1982): 3–20; M. Bayat, "The Iranian Revolution of 1978–79: Fundamentalist or Modern?" *Middle Eastern Journal* (Winter 1983); W. M. Floor, "The Revolutionary Character of the Iranian Ulama," *International Journal of Middle Eastern Studies* 12 (1980): 501–24; J. Eliash, "The Ithna Asha^cri-Shi^ci Justice Theory of Political and Legal Authority," *Studia Islamica* 29 (1969): 17–30.

12. Khomeini, *al-Hukuma al-Islamiyya*, pp. 70–76, and 91. Cf. J. Murtada, "Wilayat al-Faqih," *al-Tawhid* (Tehran) 9–10 (1983): 66–75.

13. See, for instance, A. N. ᶜUlwan's *The Heirs of the Prophets* [Arabic], 6th ed. (Beirut and Aleppo, 1983).

14. *Haqa'iq Hawla Harakat al-Ittijah al-Islami* (Tunis, 1983), pp. 8, 9, 43, and 46. Of the 601 Muslim Brethren arrested in Egypt in 1954 only 3 were ulama. Of the 303 members of the Jihad group in Egypt (1981) only 6 were ulama (5 of them students of theology). Of the 296 members of the Syrian Islamic underground arrested or killed during 1979–1981 18 were ulama (none of them in the higher ranks). The same is true of the radical Islamic movement in Morocco, see M. A. al-Jabiri's article in *al-Yaqza al-ᶜArabiyya* (Cairo) (September 1985).

15. Sayyid Qutb, *Maᶜalim fi-l-Tariq*, pp. 152, 160.

16. *Asl al-Shiᶜa wa-Usuliha*, p. 128. Critique in Afghani, *Sirab*, p. 35 ff.

17. *Al-Hukuma al-Islamiyya*, pp. 20, 23, 25, 39, 82. Cf. M. H. Fadlallah *Maᶜna al-Quwwa fi-l-islam* (Beirut, 1979), pp. 236–37.

18. Sheikh Hasan Maᶜtuk, *al-Marjaᶜiyya al-Diniyya al-ᶜUlya inda-l-Shiᶜa al-Imamiyya* (Beirut, 1970); Muhammad Baqir al-Sadr, *Lumha Tamhidiyya an Mashruᶜ Dustur al-Jumhuriyya al-Islamiyya* (Najf, 1979); M. H. Fadlallah, "The Islamic Revolution and Its Lessons," *al-Hikma* (Beirut) no. 8 (January 1981); idem., *Ma Huwa Hizb Allah* (January 1984).

19. M. Mutahhari, *Nahdat al-Mahdi* (Arabic trans.) (Beirut, n.d.), Introduction, p. 3. See the radical Sunni critique in *Jawa fi-l-Fikr al-Shiᶜi* (Gaza, 1985), pp. 15–19.

20. See A. al-Liwasani, "Studies in the New Iranian Constitution," *al-Hikma* no. 5 (1980). Cf. *al-Hukuma al-Islamiyya*, pp. 26, 47, and 144; S. Abbud, "Wilayat al-Faqih: Theory and Constitutional Practice," *al-Wahda* (Beirut), 2 (1983): 104–12.

21. For example, his speech on the *Mahdi*'s birthday, 1980, which enlisted sharp reactions in the Sunni world (p. 90–91); cf. al-ᶜAhd (Beirut) (May 3, 1986).

22. Shqaqi, *Khomeini*, pp. 39–40 and 59–60; cf. A. Banni Sadr, "Imammat," *Peuples Mediterrannéens* (October–December 1982); critique in A. Mughniya, *al-Khumayni fi Aqwalihi wa-Afᶜalihi* (Beirut, 1979), p. 167; M. al-Khalidi, *Naqd Kitab al-Hukuma al-Islamiyya* (Amman, 1983), pp. 4–6, and 9.

23. Hanafi in introduction to the Egyptian edition of *al-Hukuma al-Islamiyya* (Cairo, 1979), pp. 15, 17, 24, and 26–27. Cf. Maᶜtuq, *al-Marjaᶜiyya* (on the *marjaᶜ* as a religious and not politico-religious authority).

24. Interview with *al-Watan al-ᶜArabi'* (April 19–25, 1982).

25. Interview with *al-Shiraᶜ* (November 21, 1983). Cf. D. B. Bawwab, "Introd. a l'étude des mouvements islamistes sunnites," Ph.D. dissertation, Paris, 1985.

26. Rashid al-Ghanushi, "The Iranian Revolution," *al-Maᶜrifa* (Tunis), (February 12, 1979); idem., "The Leaders of the Contemporary Islamic Movement," ibid. (April 1, 1979). Cf. his book, *Maqalat* (Paris, 1984), pp. 77–79, 87, and 101 ff. On tensions between Sunni and Shiᶜite radicals in the Gulf see J. A. Bill, "Resurgent Islam in the Persian Gulf," *Foreign Affairs* (Fall 1984).

27. M. al-Shibaᶜi, *al-Sunna wa-Makanatuha fi-l-Tashriᶜ al-Islami*, 2d ed. (Beirut, 1976), Introduction cf. Turkmani, *Al-Tarᶜif*, pp. 103–104; Afghani, *Sirab*, p. 48 ff.

28. Cf. B. al-Ghanushi, "The Spiritual Barricade," *al-Maᶜrifa* (June 2, 1979).

29. Abu Muᶜawiya Muhammad, *Hukm Sabb al-Sahaba*; I. I. Zahir, *al-Shiᶜa wa-l-Sunna*.

30. *Matariq al-Nur*, ed. M. Matallah; cf. *Jawla fi-l-Fikr al-Shiᶜi*, pp. 30–37.

31. M. A. Ibn al-Tiyani, *Fada'il al-Sahaba*; M. Malallah, *Ihya' al-Shariᶜa fi Naqd Kitab Limadha Ihtartu Madhab al-Shiᶜa*; S. M. Nasih, *Mawqif al-Khomeini mina-l-Shiᶜa wa-l-Tashayyu*; cf. A. Shalabi, *Harakat Farisiyya Mudammira* (Cairo, 1988).

32. *Al-Ahram* (August 14, 1980); M. M. al-Tayr, "The Hidden Imam," *Majallat al-Azhar* (November 1980): 1635–48. Cf. *Ruz al-Yusuf* (November 19, 1979); al-Turkmani, *Al-Tarᶜif*. Text of the speech in *al-Mujtama'* (Kuwait) (August 7, 1980).

33. *Haqa'iq Hawla Harakat al-Ittijah al-Islami*, pp. 21 and 18. Cf. R. al-Ghanushi, "Islamic Thought between Ideals and Reality," *al-Wahda* (Tunis) (May 29, 1982); idem., "Westernization and Tyranny," *al-Ghuraba'* (Paris) (September 1980).

34. *Jawla fi-l-Fikr al-Shiᶜi*, pp. 29–30.

35. A. S. Ahmad, Introduction to *Matariq al-Nur*, p. 4; M. J. Maghniya, *Al-Khumayni wa-l-Dawla al-Islamiyya* (Beirut, 1979). As a historian, Maghniya contributed to the new myth of Husayn (discussed later) in works that also were translated into Persian.

36. A. ᶜUlwan, *al-Uhuwwa al-Islamiyya* (Amman, 1981). The author is a Syrian.

37. G. Thaiss, "Religion, Symbolism and Social Change—the Drama of Hussein," in *Scholars, Saints and Sufis*, ed. N. Keddie (Berkeley, Calif., 1972), pp. 349–66; Mottahedeh, *The Mantle*, p. 353 ff. M. Hegland, "Two Images of Hussein," in *Religion and Politics in Iran*, ed. N. Keddie (New Haven, Conn., 1983), pp. 218–35; W. Ende, "The Flagellations of Muharram and the Shiite Ulama'," *Der Islam* 55 (1978). On the traditional concept of ᶜAshura', see M. R. a-Muzaffar, *Aqa'id al-Imamiyya* (Najf, 1968), p. 118 ff.; C. Virolleaud, *La Passion de l'Imam Hossein* (Beirut, 1927); M. Ayoub, *Redemptive Suffering in Islam* (The Hague, 1978).

38. For instance, see A. al-Sharqawi, *al-Husayn Tha'iran* (Cairo, 1969); A. H. al-Kharbutli, ᶜ*Asharat Thawrat fi-l-Islam* (Beirut, 1970), pp. 170 ff; A. M. al-Aqqad, "Hussein b. Ali—Father of the Martyrs," *Islamiyyat* (Cairo, 1959).

39. See M. J. Maghniya, *al-Islam maᶜa-l-Hayat* (Beirut, 1959), pp. 57–59; idem., *Maᶜa Batalat Kerbela'* (Beirut, 1960); idem., "Extremist Shiᶜa Viewed by the Imamiyya," *Risalat al-Islam* (1954), pp. 379–81; "The Shiᶜa Viewed by Dr. Taha' Husayn," *al-ᶜIrfan* (July 1953): 379–81. On ecumenical notables' assemblies on ᶜAshura' see *al-Fikr al-Islami* (Beirut, November 1983): 4–17; *al-Hayat* (Beirut, April 9, 1968; March 29, 1969; February 27, 1971; and February 26, 1972); *al-Nahar* (Beirut, February 14, 1973; November 20, 1981; and October 29, 1982; *al-Anwar* (Beirut, January 23, 1975; and December 22, 1977).

40. Maᶜatouk, *La Représentation*, pp. 21–26, 37, and 43–44; W. Chrara, *Transformations d'une Manifestations religieuse sans un village du Liban sud* (Ashura), (Beirut, 1968), pp. 33–57.

41. M. M. Shams al-Din, "The Husayn Revolution in History and in Popular Consciousness," *al-Hayat* (April 15, 1969) (text of a lecture); idem., *Thawrat al-Husayn* (Beirut, 1969). Expanded versions of this book were published in 1974 and 1979. Cf. M.H. Fadlallah, *Afaq Islamiyya* (Beirut, 1980) (sermon delivered in 1976); and Qadiyat al-ᶜIzz wa-l-Dhull (Beirut, 1972), p. 9ff.

42. On similar attempts (in Iran and in Arab lands), see H. Enayat, *Modern Islamic Political Thought* (Austin, Texas, 1981), pp. 190–94; W. Ende, *Arabische Nation und Islamische Geschichte* (Beirut, 1977), pp. 153 ff.; Mottahedeh, *The Mantle*, p. 353; S. Irfani, *Revolutionary Islamic Iran* (London, 1983), pp. 82, and 122–33.

43. W. Chrara, *Transformations*, pp. 94–100. Cf. H. Nur al-Din, ᶜ*Ashura' fi-l-Adab al-Amili al-Muᶜasir* (Beirut, 1988).

44. *Al-Nahar* (February 3, 1974; January 23, 1975).

45. Cf. *al-Anwar* (December 22, 1977); *al-Amal* (organ of the movement) (October 29, 1983); *al-Nahar* and *al-Anwar* (October 5, 1984); *Liberation* (Paris) (September 26, 1985).

46. *Al-Nahar* (August 26, 1974).

47. *Al-Nahar* (December 11, 1978; November 30, 1979).

48. Al-Hakim's speech, *Thawrat al-Husayn*, booklet edited by Jama°at al-°Ulama' al-Mujahidin fi-l-Iraq, 1982 (speech delivered in exile, in Tehran). Cf. by same author and same publisher, *al-Kifah al-Musallah Limadha? wa-Kayfa?*, 1981; Munazzamat al-Amal al-Islamic fi-l-Iraq, *Warathat al-Husayn*, same publisher, *Iraq al-Yawm wa-l-Bahth ani-l-Husayn*, 1982; M. K. Sulayman, *al-Idiyulujiyya al-Shi°iya fi Ritha' al-Imam al-Husayn* (Beirut, 1981); M. H. Fadlallah, *Mantiq al-Quwwa*, p. 243.

49. Leaflet of *al-Amal al-Islami* (January 12, 1984) (private collection); cf. Sheikh Raghib Harb, *al-Minbar al-Muqawim* (Beirut, 1988), p. 139 ff. (sermon delivered on October 7, 1983).

50. *Al-Liwa' al-Sadr* [Organ of the Islamic Revolution in Iraq] (June 16, 1982), p. 5.

51. Cf. editorial, °Ashura', *al-Hikma* no. 8 (1981), p. 3.

52. See al-Hakim, *al-Kifah al-Musallah*; speech of a Sidon qadi quoted in *Risalat al-Thawra al-Islamiyya* (Tehran) (April 15, 1983), p. 13; interview of Iraqi radical leader, al-Husayni to *al-Shahid* (Tehran) (June 3, 1981), p. 21; *al-Liwa' al-Sadr* (June 16, 1982), p. 8; Lajnat Ihya' al-Munasabat al-Islamiyya (Lebanon, no. 4), *Yawm al-Quds - Yawm al-Wahda wa-l-Jihad*, 1983. Cf. *Mazzarat Makka* (Beirut, 1988), published under the auspices of the Iranian embassy.

53. For instance, A. Hasan, "Islam and the Question of Unity, Nationalism and Minorities," *al-Hikma* no. 3: 41–43; and the attack on Arab nationalism in *al-Shahid* (June 3, 1981), p. 57. Cf. R. Harb, *al-Minbar*, p. 110.

54. M. B. al-Sadr, *Lumha Tamhidiyya*; idem., *al-Tashayyu°* (Cairo, 1977); idem., *Khilafat al-Insan wa-Shahadat al-Anbiya'* (Beirut, 1979), pp. 23–26 and 46–50. [The latter two include a selection of his writings in the 1960s and early 1970s that may have influenced Khomeini]. Cf. Mumazzamat al-Amal al-Islami fi-l-Iraq, *al-Qiyada al-Islamiyya*, 2d ed., Tehran, 1980. For a broader analysis of Sadr's contribution to Khomeini's thought, see Baram's essay in this volume.

55. On the debates in Iran in the 1960s and their historical background, see K. S. Lambton, "A Reconsideration of the Position of the *Marja' al-Taqlid" Studia Islamica* 20 (1964): 115 ff; J. Eliash, "Misconceptions Regarding

the Juridical Status of the Iranian Ulama," *International Journal of Middle Eastern Studies* 10 (1979): 9–25. On the new concept of Marja°iyya, see sources in note 49 and A. Najf, *Wilayat al-Faqih*, ed. Jama°at al-Ulama'(al-Ulama' al-Majahidin fi-l-Iraq, 1980). For a good presentation of the traditional concept see H. Ma°tuq, *al-Marja°iyya al-Diniyya al-°Ulya* (Beirut, 1970, between the death of al-Hakim and the election of al-Khu'i).

56. *Ya Mahdi, Adrikna!* (Beirut, 1983); A. al-Liwasani, "New Iranian Constitution," p. 17 (and the sequel to his article in *al-Hikma* no. 6).

57. J. M. al-°Amili, "Infallibility of Prophets and Imams," *al-Hikma* no. 5, pp. 35–36; A. Najf, *Dawr al-°Ulama' fi Qiyadat Hadhihi-l-Umma*, ed. Jama°at al-Ulama' al-Mujahidin, 1982; interview of al-Husayni to *al-Shahid* (June 3, 1981), p. 21; interview of Sheikh Mahir Mahmud to *al-Liwa'* (Beirut) (March 16, 1984). Cf. *Risalat al-Thawra al-Islamiyya*, (RTI) (February 1984); Islamic Da°wa Party, The Form of Islamic Government and the *Wilayat al-Faqih* (Bethesda, Md., 1981).

58. Published in Tehran: *al-Tawhid* (bimonthly, ecumenical publication of the Iranian Ministry of Education); *Risalat al-Thawra al-Islamiyya*, (monthly, publication by the Revolutionary Guards); *al-Shahid* (fortnightly, "Organ of the Iranian Revolution,"). Published in London: *al-Basa'ir* (weekly, pro-Khomeini); al-Adwa' (Qom); *al-Thawra al-Islamiyya* (monthly publication of the Islamic Studies Institute, pro-Khomeini); *al-Jihad* (Iraqi weekly, Tehran); *al-Fajr* (Office of Islamic Information, Qom); *Turathuna* (Qom).

59. Same sources in note 58. Cf. H. Rafsanjani, *Injazat al-Thawra al-Islamiyya fi °Amiha al-Khhamis* (Tehran, 1984); M. T. al-Mudarresi, *Ba°th al-Islam*, ed. of the Islamic Studies Center (the author is head of the Coordination Committee of the Iraqi Islamic Revolution); M. B. al-Sadr, *Khutut Tafsiliyya°an Iqtisad al-Mujtama° al-Islami* (Beirut, 1979).

60. M. Mutahhari, *Nahdat al-Mahdi* (Beirut, 1982); cf. Mutahharri in *Risalat al-Thawra al-Islamiyya* (RTI) (April 15, 1983), pp. 44–45; A. Qasim, ed., *al-Hajj—Bay°a wa-Jihad* (Beirut, 1983); Lajnat Ihya', *Ya Mahdi, Adrikna!*; °Ali Husayni, "The Legal Background for the Iranian Constitution," *al-Fajr* (Qom), 2 (1983): 9–10, 21–221, and 37–38.

61. *RTI* (March 16, 1983), p. 11; *al-Shahid* (August 22, 1984), p. 24. Cf. report on a pan-Islamic conference of imams of mosques in *al-Tawhid* no. 1 (1982), especially the speech by Ayatollah Mudarresi (pp. 38–40).

62. "On the birthday of Husayn," *al-Shahid* (May 11, 1983), pp. 32–33; (April 15, 1983), p. 45; M. T. al-Mudarresi; *Thawrat al-Husayn: Durusuha wa-Ab°aduha*; idem., *°Ashura'—Istimrar li-Harakat al-Anbiya'*; Kashif al-Ghita' quoted and commented upon in *al-Tawhid* no. 1 (1982): 82–97.

63. Quoted by H. Hanafi, in *al-Watan* (Kuwait) (November 29, 1982).

64. Speech by Ahmad Zayn, Shi^cite qadi of Sidon, in *RTI* (April 15, 1983), p. 13; see *al-Shahid* (August 22, 1984), pp. 3 and 13; M. H. Fadlallah, "The Concept of Madhahib as a Means for Islamic Unity," *al-Tawhid* 7 (1984). A. Husayn, "Islam," pp. 29–30; and his article on Jihad in *al-Fajr* (Qom) 3 (1983): 5 ff; M. Hammud in *al-Muntalaq* 21 (1983).

65. Fadlallah *art.cit.* A.S. ^cAli, "Ijtihad in Islam," *RTI* (April 15, 1983), pp. 38–39; see Mudarresi, *Ba^cth al-Islam*; speech by Ayatollah Muntazzeri in *al-Tawhid* no. 1: 31–33.

66. "Wilayat al-Faqih," *al-Tawhid* nos. 9–10 (1983); H. al-Haydar, "Wilayat al-Faqih," *al-Fajr* 1 (Qom); ^cAli al-Husayni, legal commentary in the Iranian constitution, *al-Fajr* 2: 29–30.

67. *RTI* (February 15, 1983), p. 39; *al-Shahid* (April 9, 1980), p. 54; (August 22, 1984), pp. 10–11, and 24.

68. Publisher's introduction to *Nahdat al-Mahdi*, p. 3; see the text of the dedication to Khomeini in the booklet *Ya Mahdi, Adrikna!; al-Shahid*, (February 13, 1980).

69. K. Siddiqi, *al-Harakat al-Islamiyya — Qadaya' wa-Ahdaf* (London, 1981). This is also the position taken by the organ of the Islamic Studies Institute headed by Siddiqi, *al-Thawra al-Islamiyya*.

70. The quotation is from *al-Nadhir*, (Syrian underground) (August 11, 1980). Cf. *al-I^ctisam* (Cairo) (January 1980), pp. 28–29; (March–April 1980), p. 5; *al-Muslimun fi Suriya wa-l-Irhab al-Nusayri* (1980): 20–21; M. ^cAnbar, *Nahwa Thawra Islamiyya* (Cairo, 1979), pp. 86–90.

71. Proceedings of the trial in *al-Safir* (May 28, 1982); on the impact of Iranian use of cassettes, see Ansari's article in *International Journal of Middle Eastern Studies* (March 1984): note 40.

72. Interview of A. Babti with *al-Shira^c* (Beirut) (December 5, 1983).

73. Sa'd al-Din interview with *al-Watan al-^cArabi* (April 16, 1982). *Al-Nadhir* (May 2, July 17, 1981; March 27 and May 8, 1982); *al-I^ctisam* (February 1980), pp. 6–7; *al-Shira^c* (November 21, 1983).

74. Quoted in H. Hanafi, "The Contemporary Islamic Movement" *al-Watan al-^cArabi* (Kuwait) (November 29, 1982).

75. Interview with the movement's leaders in *al-Ushu^c al-^cArabi* (January 14, 1985); *al-Liwa'* (Beirut) (March 16, 1984); *al-Bilad* (Beirut) (September 23, 1984); *al-^cAlim* (London) (January 26, 1985); and their publication *al-Hajj-Bay^ca wa-Jihad* (Beirut, 1983). On ulama and revolution, cf. K. Siddiqi's two articles in *al-^cIrfan* (September and October 1984).

76. *Al-Wahda al-Islamiyya* no. 1 (1983): 32–34; (Qutb); no. 5 (1984): 16–22; (Mutahheri) no. 3 (1983): 31–34, article on Sadr by Fadlallah; no. 4 (1983): 16–18, synthesis by Dr. Nafisi, a Kuwaiti Sunni.

77. M. Hammud, "Islamic Unity," *al-Muntalaq* 21 (May 1983): 16–27. Note the overlapping of participants in the two organs (notably Hammud and Fadlallah).

78. M. H. Fadlallah, *Muntalaq* no. 23 (1984): 4–7; Sheikh J. Khalisi in *Muntalaq* no. 26 (November 1984): 9–22; Fadlallah, ibid., pp. 4–8; Z. A. Zaji, ibid., pp. 23–29. Cf. M. H. Fadlallah, "The Contemporary Reasons for Islamic Disunity," *al-Wahada* (Beirut) 3 (1983): 4–19; idem., "Present Problems in Iran," *al-Hikma* 11 (1982): 6–12.

79. Sheikh S. A. Dan in *al-Muntalaq* 23: 30–34; cf. in the same issue the articles by I. Salim and M. H. Fadlallah, Fadlallah's article in *al-ᶜIrfan* (January 1984); also M. Hammud's article in *al-Muntalaq* 21 (1983).

80. *Liberation* (Paris) (September 26, 1985); cf. Fadlallah's interview with *al-Hawadith* (Beirut) (May 24, 1985).

81. *Al-Sharq al-Awsat* (London) (September 10, 1984); Shaᶜban's interview with *al-Mukhtar al-Islami* (Cairo) (July 1986).

82. Cf. A. Yasin, "Propaganda and State," *al-Jamaᶜa* (Marrakesh) 1, no. 3 (1982); *al-Dustur* (London) (November 14, 1985); interview of Sheikh ᶜUmar ᶜAbd al-Rahman in *al-Shaᶜb* (Cairo) (November 5, 1985); *al-Thawra al-Islamiyya* (Saudi radicals) (May 1985); anon., *Jawla fi-l-Fikr al-Shiᶜi* (Gaza, 1985); M. A. al-Lawi, "Nationalism in Contemporary Islamic Thought," *al-Muntaqa* (Paris) 9 (1986). For a firm rejection of these views by a Syrian radical fundamentalist, who had been an early admirer of Khomeini but was disabused by the latter's "blatant Shiᶜism," see Saᶜid Hawwa, *Al-Khumayniyya* (Cairo, 1987).

Chapter 3

I wish to thank Amiel Ungar, Giora Goldberg, Bernard Susser, and Benny Kraut for their helpful comments. This is a revised version of the Louis Feinberg Memorial Lecture, published by the University of Cincinnati's Program in Judaic Study. This is the original version read at the conference that led to this volume.

1. I am indebted to Dr. Mina Zemach for permission to use this and other sample data reported here.

2. A. Fishman, "Tradition and Renewal in the Religious Zionist Experience," in *Bishvilei Hatikhiya*, ed. A. Rubinstein (Ramat Gan, 1983), pp. 127–146 [Hebrew].

3. Israel's first Ashkenazi chief rabbi, Isaac Halevi Herzog (1888–1959), father of the current president of the State of Israel, felt it necessary to justify the provisions of religious tolerance in Israeli law. Writing shortly before the state was established and sensitive to *haredi* criticism, he explained that Israel had to grant religious freedom to non-Jews, otherwise the United Nations would not have supported the establishment of a Jewish state. This apologetic tone is also found in the famous letter sent by the Jewish Agency leader to Agudat Israel in 1947, promising them that basic Jewish religious rights would be safeguarded in the new state. That same letter explained that the United Nations would not tolerate denying religious rights to non-Jews. Among the *haredi* "doves," one hears the argument that Israeli sovereignty over Judea and Samaria is pointless from a Jewish point of view since Israel dares not act as it is enjoined to act by religious law; that is, to expel the non-Jews or at least destroy their places of worship.

4. Z. Y. Kook, "The Sanctity of the Holy People in the Holy Land," in *Religious Zionism: An Anthology*, ed. Y. Tirosh (Jerusalem [World Zionist Organization], 1978), pp. 140–46 [Hebrew].

5. Ibid., p. 141.

6. Y. Shilhav, "Interpretation and Misinterpretation of Jewish Territorialism," (Paper presented to the Harry S. Truman Research Institute colloquium on Religious Radicalism and Politics in the Middle East, May 13, 1985).

7. Kook, "The Sanctity," p. 144.

8. Statement made in a television broadcast in October 1984.

9. M. Ben-Yosef (Hagari), "Gush Emunim May Become a Sect," *Nekudah*, no. 71 (March 1984): 9 [Hebrew].

10. Y. Ariel, "Love Disrupts Order," *Nekudah*, no. 79 (November 2, 1984): 24 [Hebrew].

11. M. Friedman, "The NRP in Transition—Behind the Party's Electoral Decline," in *The Roots of Begin's Success*, ed. D. Caspi et al. (London, 1984), pp. 141–68.

12. Ibid.

13. E. Don-Yehiya, "Religion and Coalition: The National Religious Party and Coalition Formation in Israel," in *The Elections in Israel, 1973*, ed. A. Arian (Jerusalem, 1975), pp. 255–84.

14. M. Keren, *Ben Gurion and the Intellectuals: Power, Knowledge and Charisma* (De Kalb, Ill., 1983).

15. Y. Bin-Nun, *Koteret Rashit*, 114, no. 2 (1985): 36–37 [Hebrew].

16. A. Hourani, "Conclusion," in *Islam in the Political Process*, ed. J. Piscatori (Cambridge, 1984), pp. 228–29.

17. M. Shamir and A. Arian, "The Ethnic Vote in Israel's 1981 Elections," in *The Elections in Israel, 1981*, ed. A. Arian (Tel Aviv [Ramot], 1981), pp. 91–111.

18. Y. Peres and S. Shemer, "The Ethnic Factor in the Elections to the Tenth Knesset," *Megamot*, no. 28 (March 1984): 316–31 [Hebrew].

19. E. Yuchtman-Yaar, forthcoming.

20. C. Liebman, "Myth, Tradition and Values in Israeli Society," *Midstream*, 24 (January 1978): 44–53.

21. H. Herzog, "Political Ethnicity in Israel," *Megamot*, 28 (March 1984); 332–54 [Hebrew].

22. C. Liebman and E. Don-Yehiya, *Civil Religion in Israel: Traditional Religion and Political Culture in the Jewish State* (Berkeley, Calif., 1983).

23. Y. Shapiro, *An Elite without Successors: Generations of Political Leaders in Israel* (Tel Aviv, 1984), p. 30 [Hebrew]. See idem., "Jewish Youth Movements in Eretz Israel and the Elite," *Jerusalem Quarterly*, 36 (Summer 1985): 17–30.

24. *An Elite without Successors*, p. 30.

25. D. Henshkeh, "What Happened to the 'Lights' of Rav Kook," *Nekudah* 79 (November 2, 1984): 12 [Hebrew].

26. A. Sugarman, "Attitudes toward Minorities in the State of Israel," *Niv Hamidrashia* 18–19 (1984); 267 [Hebrew].

Chapter 4

I am indebted to E. Kohlberg, H. Lazarus-Yafeh, E. Sivan, and M. Ma^{c}oz, for their comments on the manuscript. Research for this article was assisted by a grant from Stanley M. Bogen of New York and The Harry S. Truman Institute, Jerusalem. The final version of this article was written during my stay as a fellow of the Institute for Advanced Studies, at The Hebrew University of Jerusalem. The first section: "Shi^{c}ite Opposition Organizations" is based on a separate study.

1. One issue over which there is no such convergence, for example, is Islamic social justice (which is not discussed herein). On another, that of Arabism, al-Sadr remains silent; and there are still other, less central issues. Apparently for lack of source material, the few existing studies that deal with

the radical Shi^cite organizations of Iraq leave their ideology essentially untouched, settling instead for an account of some of the more salient aspects of Sadr's thought (see H. Batatu, "Iraq's Underground Shi^ca Movements: Characteristics, Causes and Prospects," *Middle East Journal* 35, no. 4 (1981): 578–94; and his "Shi^ci Organizations in Iraq: al-Da^cwa . . . and al-Mujahidin", in ed. Juan R. I. Cole and Nikki R. Keddie *Shi^cism and Social Protest*, (New Haven and London, 1986), pp. 179–200; Ofra Bengie, "Shi^cis and Politics in Ba^cthi Iraq," *Middle Eastern Studies* 21, no. 1, (January 1985): 1–14; R. H. Dekmejian, *Islam in Revolution, Fundamentalism in the Arab World*, (Syracuse, N.Y., 1985), pp. 127–36; Pierre Martin, "Le Clergé Chi'ite en Irak hier et aujourd'hur," *Maghreb-Machreq* (Paris).

2. See, for example, quotations from an article by Hassan al-Bana that appeared in 1934, in Muhammad Amara, "al-Jami^ca al-^carabiyya wal-jami^ca al-islamiyya," in *Qawmiyya al-arabiyya wal-islam*, the Centre for Arab Unity Studies (Beirut, 1981), p. 172.

3. Abd al-Rahman al-Kawakibi, *Umm al-Qura* (Mecca and Cairo, 1931), quoted by Sylvia Haim, ed., *Arab Nationalism*, (Berkeley, Calif.: 1967), p. 80. For Rashid Rida and others, see Israel Gershuni, *Egypt between Particularism and Unity*, (Tel Aviv, 1980), pp. 103–104, and 126–6 [Hebrew].

4. The families of Hasan al-Shirazi and his brother, Muhammad al-Husayni al-Shirazi, leaders of the al-^cAmal al-Islami, and Muhammad Mahdi Asifi, of al-Da^cwa, for example, originated in Iran.

5. *The Da^cwa Chronicle* (henceforth *D.Ch.*) no. 10 (February 1981): 4; see also no. 8 (December 1980): 8.

6. *D.Ch.* no. 10 (February 1981): 10.

7. *D.Ch.* no. 22 (February 1981): 1.

8. *D.Ch.* no. 29 (September 1982): 4; no. 25 (May 1982): 3.

9. See, for example, *Tariq al-Thawra* (henceforth *TTH*) no. 25 (Rajab 1402): 37–8. *D.Ch.* no. 1 (May 1980): 6; no. 16 (August 1981): 5; no. 25 (May 1982): 1.

10. *TTH* no. 25 (Rajab 1402): 22.

11. *Sawt al-Iraq* (July 1982): 4.

12. *D.Ch.* no. 17 (September 1981): 7. See also 5 (September 1980): 2; no. 37 (May 1983): 4 and 6; no. 38 (June 1983): 6; no. 39 (July 1983): 6; *Saddam Husayn warith al-shah* (Saddam Husayn, Heir of the Shah), a publication by al-^cAmal al-islami, 1981.

13. See, for example, *D.Ch.* no. 6 (October 1980): 5; no. 24 (April 1982): 2; no. 25 (May 1982): 2–3; no. 29: p. 3; no. 30: 1; *TTH* no. 25: 18–19, 34, and 38; *Sawt al-Iraq* no. 42 (December 1, 1983): 1.

14. *D.Ch.* no. 30: 1.

15. *D.Ch.* no. 25 (May 1982): 4.

16. *D.Ch.* no. 18 (October 1981): 2; no. 4 (August 1980): 1; *TTH* no. 29 (Jamadi 1–2, 1403): 5–6.

17. *Sawt al-Iraq* (July 1982): 1.

18. *D.Ch.* no. 40 (August 1983): 6.

19. *al-Jihad* no. 52 (September 6, 1982): 1, 3, 8, and 9; see also *D.Ch.* no. 30: 1, 2, and 8; no. 40: 8; no. 33: 6.

20. *Al-Jihad* no. 105 (October 3, 1983): 8.

21. See, for example, *D.Ch.* no. 2 (June 1980): 7; no. 3: 1; no. 8: 7; no. 25: 3; *TTH* no. 3, Sha^cban 15, 1400: 3 and 6; no. 25: 12, 15, and 20–21; *Saddam Husayn warith al-shah*, pp. 12 and 29.

22. *D.Ch.* no. 26 (June 1982): 2. This approach is close to that of Khomeini regarding the Ottoman Empire. See *al-Hukuma al-islamiyya* (Beirut, 1979), pp. 34–35. The book was first published in 1969 or 1970.

23. *Al-Nadhir* no. 62 (November 10, 1983): 8–9 and 12.

24. *Al-Nadhir* p. 12; see also no. 61: 3; no. 59 (August 1, 1983): 29; no. 23 (September 28, 1980): 3.

25. Sa^cid Hawwa, *al-Islam* (Beirut, 1969), vol. 2, pp. 70–71 and 204, demands that the Muslim's first allegiance be to Islam. In *Fi afaq al-ta^calim* (Cairo, 1980), pp. 20–27, 34–35, and 62–64; *Min ajli khutwa ila al-amam ala tariq al-jihad al-mubarak* (n.p., 1978), pp. 85–87; and *Jund allah thaqafa wa akhlaq* (n.p., n.d.), pp. 44–45, he expresses hope that the Arab world or some of its states will form the nucleus of the pan-Islamic state.

26. *Al-Jihad* (January 2, 1984): 7.

27. *Al-Jihad* no. 52: 3–4; *Liwa al-sadr* (February 9, 1983): 1, 7, 8, and 13; *TTH* no. 3: 3, 6, and 13; no. 25: 4, and 8; *al-Qadiyya al-iraqiyya*, a booklet issued by the Movement of Muslim Masses at an international Islamic Conference in Tehran in 1980, see quotations in *TTH* no. 3: 6; *Yawm al-quds al-alami*, a publication in Europe (July 16, 1982); *D.Ch.* no. 2: 1; no. 5 (September 1980): 1; a communiqué by the supreme council in *al-Jihad* no. 105 (October 3, 1983); *al-Muqatilun* no. 3 (1980): 4, 6, and 39.

28. *Liwa al-Sadr* (February 9, 1983): 11; Mahdi al-Hakim in an interview with *Impact International* (April 24–May 8, 1980): 6.

29. *Al-Jihad*, no. 52: 3–4. In his speeches, al-Nasiri often addresses the "noble Iraqi people."

30. *D.Ch.* no. 22, (February 1982): 4.

31. *Imam* 3, no. 1 (January 1983): 31. See also the interview with his brother, Mahdi, in *Impact International*.

32. *TTH* no. 29: 52; *D.Ch.* no. 40 (August 1983): 8.

33. *D.Ch.* no. 21 (January 1982): 6.

34. *Yawm al-Quds*, op. cit.

35. *Sawt al-Iraq* (July 1982): 1.

36. *D.Ch.* no. 23 (March 1982): 1.

37. *D.Ch.* no. 19 (November 1981): 4 and 6.

38. *D.Ch.* no. 3: 2.

39. See Shaykh Muhammad Baqir al-Nasiri in *al-Jihad*, no. 103 (September 17, 1983): 2; see also *D.Ch.* no. 40: 8. An *imam* (small *i*) is a prayer leader, leader; an *Imam* (capital *I*) is one of the Twelve Imams of the *Ithna ᶜashariyya*, Shiᶜa.

40. *Al-Massar* (London) (September 4, 1986): 2.

41. A letter from an Iraqi exile in Qom, Iran, ibid., p. 7. For more on the Najf-Karbala tug-of-war also see ibid. (August 29, 1986).

42. Hawwa, *Fi afaq al-taᶜalim*, p. 20; also pp. 31–32, and 62–63.

43. An interview with a senior figure in the movement, ᶜAdnan Saᶜd al-Din, *al-Nadhir*, no. 59: 21.

44. *Al-Nadhir*, appendix no. 1 (n.d.): 4 and 7; see also no. 62: 12.

45. *Al-Nadhir* no. 9: 17.

46. *Al-Nadhir* no. 3: 16; no. 61: 3.

47. See his speech to "the noble nation of Iraq," *D.Ch.* no. 2: 7. See also *al-Jihad* (September 28, 1982): 4.

48. *TTH* no. 13: 11.

49. Ibid.

50. *D.Ch.* no. 3 (July 1980): 2. For other late writings where all the first four caliphs appear in a positive context, see, for example, al-Sadr's *Khilafat al-insan wa shahadat al-anbiya* (Beirut, 1979), p. 48; *Manabiᶜ al-qudra fi al-dawla al-islamiyya* (Beirut, 1979), p. 23.

51. See E. Kohlberg, "The Evolution of the Shiᶜa," *The Jerusalem Quarterly*, no. 27 (Spring 1983): 116–117.The Shiᶜites, for their part, made use of an early all-Islamic concept according to which a "Muslim" is one who believes only externally, while a *"mu'min"* is a true believer.

52. *Iqtisaduna; Falsafatuna* written in 1959–1960 and reprinted in the late 1970s and early 1980s in Beirut; and *al-Madrasa al-islamiyya*, a collection of essays (Beirut, 1973). See also Sadr's *al-Bank al-La rabawi fi al-islam*, 8th ed. (Beirut, 1983); *al-Usul al-mantiqiyya lil-istiqra*, 3rd ed. (Beirut, 1981). Both books were first published in the early 1970s.

53. *Al-Masa'il al-mutajaddida, wa-hiya alf mas'ala islamiyya* (1st ed. (Beirut, 1977). Muhammad al-Shirazi, the elder brother of Hasan, founder of al-ᶜAmal al-Islami, is still connected with that organization, although not in an official capacity; see *al-Massar* (September 4, 1986): 10. According to one source, most members of this organization are Shirazi's religious followers (*muqallidun*) (ibid., p. 7).

54. *Al-Imam ᶜAli b. abi Talib . . . sira wa ta'rikh* (Beirut, 1978).

55. Ibid., pp. 43–48.

56. Ibid., also pp. 40–42. This attitude is clearly different from the traditional Shiᶜi approach that saw in ᶜUmar the driving force behind the attempt to strip ᶜAli of his rights and that brought Shiᶜites to burn ᶜUmar's image on the anniversary of his assassination (see Kohlberg, "Evolution," p. 115).

57. *D.Ch.* no. 22 (February 1982): 1.

58. *D.Ch.* no. 23 (March 1982): 3.

59. Sura 3 (*Al-Imran*), ayah 103. *D.Ch.* no. 24: 3. See also *D.Ch.* no. 1: 2; no. 40: 3; *Sawt al-Iraq* no. 39 (September 1983): 3.

60. See Hava Lazarus-Yafeh, "The Shiᶜi Aspect of Khomeini's Political Theory," in *Hamizrah Hehadash* 30, nos. 1–4 (1981): 99–106.

61. See, for example, Ghassan R. Atiyyah, *Iraq 1980–1921* (Beirut, 1973), pp. 79–86.

62. Ibid., pp. 311–38; P. W. Ireland, *Iraq* (London, 1937), pp. 262–64; Amal Vinogradov, "The 1920 Revolt in Iraq . . .", *International Journal of Middle Eastern Studies*, 2, (April 1972): 134–35.

63. Vinogradov, ibid., p. 136. See also Peter Sluglett, *Britain in Iraq 1914–1932* (London, 1976), pp. 77–79, 82–86, 150–170, and 303–304. For more on Sunni-Shiᶜite cooperation, before and during the monarchy, see Muhammad al-Basir, *Ta'rikh al-qadiyya al-iraqiyya* (Baghdad, 1924), Vol. 1, pp. 33, 75, 99–111, 149 and 156–57. Abd al-Razzaq al-Hasani, *al-Iraq fi*

dawray al-ihtilal wal-intidab (Syria, 1935), Vol. 1, pp. 98–100; A. T. Wilson, *Mesopotamia, A Clash of Loyalties, 1917–1920* (London, 1931), p. 255.

64. U. Dann, *Iraq under Qassam* (Jerusalem, 1969), pp. 300–302.

65. *al-Hayat* (Beirut) (January 19, 1961): 1.

66. It is true that in his book, Khomeini does not curse or criticize directly any of the first three caliphs (nor does he curse even Mu^cawiya; see pp. 74 and 82). But, in fact, he refrains from mentioning them altogether: whenever he discusses past proper Muslim governments, he mentions only those of the Prophet and ^cAli and remains silent about Abu Bakr, ^cUmar, and ^cUthman (see pp. 26–27, 33, 37, 41, 47, 49–51, 61, 71, 75, 79, 81, 84, and 85). Also, by repeatedly stressing the fact that ^cAli was the only legitimate heir of the Prophet and that this was a God-ordained legacy, Khomeini implies that the three first caliphs, in fact, were usurpers (see pp. 23, 25, 43, 75, 81, and 131). There is only one place where the first three heirs of the Prophet are shown in a more positive light, although they are not mentioned by name (see pp. 123–124). Whatever the case, Khomeini does not even try to approach the issue directly, as do Sadr and Al Yasin.

67. See, for example, *al-Nadhir* no. 9 (January 8, 1980): 15; no. 2: 24; no. 24: 25–28; no. 21: 39–41. See a similar approach in *al-Thawra islamiyya,* organ of the Saudi Muslim opposition, no. 45 (January 1984): 6–10.

68. *Al-Nadhir* no. 3: 16.

69. *Al-Nadhir,* no. 62: 12.

70. *Al-Muslimun fi surya* (The Muslim in Syria) (n.p., n.d.), p. 6.

71. Ibid., pp. 6 and 8.

72. *Al-Nadhir,* no. 4: 16. See also no. 4: 16; no. 7: 1; no. 19: 19; and "a warning to the evil sect," *al-Nadhir* no. 25: 15; no. 59: 21.

73. There is evidence that in negotiations between the Shi^cite and the Kurdish opposition groups power-sharing, indeed, was discussed (interviews), but the subject found no expression in publications.

74. *D.Ch.* no. 4: 3–4. See also al-Da^cwa's letter to the Communist party, *al-Ghad* no. 13 (May–August 1982): 14–18.

75. See Sheikh al-Nasiri's lecture, *al-Jihad* no. 52: 1. According to one interview, within the Da^cwa and al-^cAmal al-islami there is opposition to the principle of "the rule of the jurist." However, no trace of such opposition is in the public records of any Shi^cite group.

76. Da^cwa letter in *al-Ghad.*

77. Sura 28 (*al-Qisas*), ayah 5. *Rahe enqelab*, no. 29 (Jamadi 1–2, 1403): 7.

78. *TTH* no. 28 (Rabi^c 1, 1403): 15–16.

79. *Al-Jihad* no. 55 (Setember 1982): 5. See the demand for applying the principle of *wilayat al-faqih* throughout the Islamic world despite the author's recognition that this principle is alien to the Sunna, in al-Da^cwa treatise *Shikl al-Hukm al-Islami wa wilayat al-faqih* translated and reproduced by the Islamic Revival Movement (Falls Church, Va., August 1982), pp. 5–6.

80. *TTH* no. 31 (Ramadan 1403): 5–6; also pp. 7 and 9.

81. Cf. *al Hukuma al-islamiyya*, pp. 59, 69–70, 72–75, 80, and 88. For "*ulama ummati kasa'ir al-anbiya' qabli*" and more importantly "*al-ulama warathat al-anbiya*" see pp. 93–100. Khomeini regarded the jurists as the legitimate heirs of the twelve Imams, although of lower rank, and endeavored to prove that the Imams themselves were active political leaders and not just religious authorities. See, for example, pp. 103, 116, 127, 129–30, 132, and 141–42.

82. Sadr *Ikhtarna Laka* (Beirut, 1975), pp. 57, 60–62, and 65–68.

83. Sadr's introduction to Dr. Abd Alla al-Fayyad, of Baghdad University, *Ta'rikh al-imamiyya wa aslafihim min al-shi^ca* (Baghdad, 1970), pp. 32–33.

84. Sadr, *Lamha tamhidiyya 'an mashru' dustur al-jumhuriyya al-islamiyya* (Beirut, 1979), pp. 13 and 20.

85. *Liwa' al-Sadr* (February 9, 1983): 11.

86. *TTH* no. 25: 8–11.

87. *Al-Jihad* (January 2, 1984): 13; A. Najaf, *Al Shahid al-Shahid*, (Tehran, 1981), pp. 5–47.

88. *D.Ch.* no. 4 (August 1980): 5; no. 37 (May 1983): 7.

89. Roger M. Savory, "The Problem of Sovereignty in a Twelver Shi^ci State," in *Religion and Politics in the Middle East*, ed. M. Curtis (Boulder, Colorado, 1981), pp. 131–36; Hamid Algar, *Religion and State in Iran, 1785–1906* (Berkeley, Calif., 1960), pp. 4–9; W. G. Millward, "Aspects of Modernism in Shi^ca Islam," *Studia Islamica* 37 (1973): 114–15; A. K. S. Lambton, "A Reconsideration of the Position of the *Marja al-Taqlid* . . .," *Studia Islamica* 20 (1964): 116–30; E. Kohlberg, "The Evolution of the Shi^ca," *The Jerusalem Quarterly* no. 27 (Spring 1983): 125; Nikki R. Keddie, "Iran: Change in Islam; Islam in Change," *International Journal of Middle Eastern Studies* no. 2, (1980): 527–42.

90. Sayyid Qutb, *Ma'alim Fi al-tariq*, (Dar dimashq lil-taba^ca wal-nashr, n.d.), p. 82.

91. Hasan al-Banna, founder of the Muslim Brethren society, and Sayyid Qutb, its leading ideologue since the 1950s, were not ulama. For the continual battle between the Muslim radicals in Egypt and the ulama who tried to legitimate the rulers, see Gilles Kepel, *The Prophet and Pharaoh* (London, 1985), pp. 52, 57–67, and 183–90.

92. *TTH* no. 30 (Rajab-sha^cban 1403): 8–11.

93. This, no doubt, refers to the Koranic verse *"jahidu bi-amwalikum wa anfusikum fi sabil allah"* which also is the motto of the Movement of the Muslim Masses.

94. *TTH* no. 30: 8–11.

95. Sura 2 (*al-Baqara*), ayah 195.

96. Sura 3 (*Al Imran*), ayah 169.

97. *Al-Jihad* no. 52 (September 6, 1982).

98. *TTH* no. 28: 17–21. See also *al-Jihad*, no. 105.

99. *TTH* no. 30: 24–26. See also a similar story about the confrontation between Sa^cid n. Jubayr and al-Hajjaj n. Yusuf in *TTH* no. 25: 35–36.

100. See, for example, a publication by the Movement of the Muslim Masses, *al-Afkar al-Salbiyya*, (Tehran, n.d.), pp. 28–30.

101. E. Kohlberg, "Some Imami Shi^ci Interpretations of Umayyad History," in *Studies on the First Century of Islamic Society*, ed. G. H. A. Juynboll (Carbondale, Ill., 1982), p. 153. And see Sadr, *Manabi^c al-qudra*, p. 23.

102. For total rejection of both the Umayyads and the Abbasids, see *al-Kashif* no. 45 (Muharram 1403): 16; *TTH* no. 28: 44; *D.Ch.* no. 12: 8. For Yazid and al-Hajjaj, see, for example, *TTH* no. 25: 35; *Sawt al-Iraq* (July 1982): 6; *D.Ch.* no. 12 (April 1981): 8.

103. *TTH* no. 32 (Dhu al-Hijja 1403): last page.

104. Muhsin al-Amin, *A^cyan al-Shi^ca*, (Damascus, 1366/1947), pp. 524–526; Encyclopedia of Islam, 2d ed., (henceforth: EI II), vol. 2, p. 993a; Muhammad n. Ali n. Shaharashub (d. 588h), *Manaqib Al abi Talib*, (Najf 1376/1956), vol. 2, p. 224. For Shi^ci poetry regarding the event of Ghadir Khumm, see ibid., pp. 225–27, and 230–44.

105. *Al-Jihad* no. 105: 4. Khomeini, in his *al-Hukuma*, said: "In Ghadir Khumm . . . the Prophet appointed him as a governor after him [and not as just a *mufti*]," p. 131.

106. Al-Fayyad, *Ta'rikh*, pp. 3–26. See also Sadr's lecture in 1969 in *al-Mihna*, (Qom, 1986), p. 31. The attitude toward most of the companions

(those who failed to support ᶜAli) is another major area of traditional Shiᶜite-Sunni controversy.

107. *Al-Ghad* (May–August 1982): 16–17. See also belief in the *imama* as one of the five articles of faith, Sadr, *Muqaddimat fi-al-tafsir al-mawduᶜi lil Kur'an*, (Beirut-Kuwait, 1980), pp. 163–65.

108. *D.Ch.* no. 12 (April 1981): 8.

109. Sadr's introduction to al-Fayyad, *Taᶜrikh*, pp. 24–26.

110. Sadr, *Ikhtarna Laka*, pp. 68–69.

111. Ibid., pp. 61–62. Although al-Sadr mentions the difference in the mode of action between al-Hasan and al-Husayn (pp. 58–59), he does not dwell upon the latter's example and prefers to bring as examples of political and military activism other imams and Shiᶜite leaders, notably ᶜAli. This is probably due to al-Husayn's failure to defeat Yazid, which casts doubt on his omniscience or wisdom. Khomeini, on the other hand, strengthens his call for activism when he calls for the creation of "a new ᶜashura," an acute one of *jihad*, different from the sad one, and uses the example of al-Husayn to educate toward active sacrifice (pp. 127–29).

112. *Al-Jihad* no. 105 (October 3, 1983): 11. See also *Liwa' al-Sadr* (February 9, 1983): last page.

113. On Sayyid Talib's activity near Basra, see, for example, ᶜAbdalla al-Fayyad, *al-Thawra al-ᶜiraqiyya al-kubra*, (Baghdad, 1963), pp. 75–76; and on the Sheikh of Banu Malik to a Turkish officer regarding Turkish hate for the Arabs, which proves Turkish deviation from Islam, see Fariq Al Mazhar Al Firᶜawn, *al-Haqa'iq al-nasia fi ta'rikh al-thawra*, (Baghdad, 1952), pp. 39–41.

114. For example, Muhammad Ali Kamal al-Din, *Thawrat al-ishrin fi dhikriha al-khamsin . . .* , (Baghdad, 1971), pp. 78–79. The black, white, green, and red flag was that of the Arab revolt in the desert under the Sharif Husayn of Mecca.

115. See ibid., p. 135, for the historic communiqué.

116. See, for example, a poem by Muhammad Mahdi al-Basir, in Muhammad Ali Kamal al-Din, *Thawrat*, p. 328; also pp. 312, 333–34, and 338.

117. See the attitude of Grand Ayatollah Muhsayn al-Hakim of Najf to this kind of pan-Arabism in his interview in *al-Hayat* (Beirut) (January 19, 1961).

118. Elie Kedourie, "Refléxions sur l'histoire du Royaume d'Iraq, 1921–1958," *Orient* no. 11, (1959): 55–79.

119. See, for example, Sadr's *al-Mihna* (1984), p. 63; *Khilafat al-insan* (1979), p. 48; and his lecture of 1966 in *Ikhtarna Laka*, (Beirut, 1980), pp. 62–70.

Chapter 5

1. G. Herbert, *Fundamentalism and the Church* (Philadelphia, 1957); R. Hofstadter, *Anti-Intellectualism in American Life* (New York, 1963).

2. Neturei Karta (Guardians of the City, in the religious-spiritualistic sense) emerged against the backdrop of the confrontation between the Zionists and anti-Zionists in Palestine under British mandate during the *yishuv* period (1917–1948). See M. Friedman, *Society and Religion: The Non-Zionist Orthodoxy in Eretz-Israel* (Jerusalem, 1978), especially pp. 365–66 [Hebrew]. See also N. Lamm, "The Ideology of Neturei Karta According to the Satmar Version," *Tradition* 13 (1971).

3. Amram Blau died on July 5, 1974.

4. Aharon Katzenelbogen died on December 13, 1978.

5. A community in Jerusalem, which incorporates within it those who do not recognize the State of Israel as a legitimate Jewish political entity. Founded in 1918, the Edah Haredit evolved into an isolationist religious community representing the religious elements that rejected the aspirations of Zionism in Palestine.

6. Agudat Israel initially was organized in 1912 as part of the struggle against the processes of change and secularization undergone by the Jews in Europe since the second half of the eighteenth century. Chiefly represented in this movement were traditional-religious groups that objected to any change in the traditional Jewish way of life. After the establishment of Israel this movement adopted a more moderate political stance, and it now takes part in the country's political life.

7. For an expanded treatment of this subject, see M. Friedman, "Haredi Jewry Confronts the Modern City," in *Studies in Contemporary Jewry*, ed. P. Medding, vol. 2 (Bloomington, Ind., 1985).

8. Numbers 25:1–15.

9. *Babylonian Talmud*, Sanhedrin 81a, 82b.

10. Ibid.

11. *Der Id* (Yiddish weekly of Satmar Hassidim, published in New York City) (May 11, 1984).

12. Many illustrations of this can be found in J. Katz, *Exclusiveness and Tolerance: Jewish-Gentile Relations in Medieval and Modern Times* (London, 1961; New York, 1962).

13. For a detailed treatment of this subject, see M. Friedman, *Society and Religion*, pp. 146–84.

14. Hamizrahi (short for "spiritual counter" in Hebrew), founded by Rabbi Isaac Reines in 1902, expressed the desire of Orthodox circles in Judaism to be integrated into the activity of the Zionist movement and to adapt to the values and ways of life of modern society, while also maintaining a binding affinity to *halakhah*.

15. Rabbi Kook served as the first chief rabbi of Palestine (1921–1935). On his philosophical outlook see especially Z. Yaron, Mishnato shel ha-Rav Kook (Jerusalem, 1974).

16. For a detailed treatment of this subject, see M. Friedman, "The NRP in Transition: Behind the Party's Decline," in *The Roots of Begin's Success: The 1981 Israeli Election*, ed. D. Caspi et al. (London and New York, 1984), pp. 141–68.

Chapter 6

1. Unless otherwise quoted, material on Fathi Shqaqi's life and activities is derived from police records of his interrogation on October 7, 1983, Military Court File 1201/83, Gaza.

2. ^cAbd al-^cAziz, Fathi, *al-Khumayni, al-hall al-islami wal-badil* (Cairo, 1979), p. 6.

3. Ibid., pp. 10–30.

4. During the 1970s, al-Qardawi wrote at least four essays on the necessity of the Islamic Solution. Excerpts were published during the early 1970s in the Beirut magazine, *al-Shihab*. Between 1973 and 1975, four volumes were published there by Muasasat al-Risala in a series entitled *Hatmiyat al-hall al-islami* (The Definitiveness of the Islamic Solution): (1) *al-Hulul al-mustawrida wa-kayfa jannat ^cala ummatina* (The Imported Solutions and the Way They Have Driven Our Nation Crazy); (2) *al-Hall al-islami, farida wa-darurah* (The Islamic Solution, a [Religious] Duty and Necessity); (3) *A^cda' al-hall al-islami* (Enemies of the Islamic Solution); (4) *Shubahat al-mushakkikin wal-murtabin* (The Doubts of the Skeptics and the Doubters). Qardawi, who has made Duha, Qatar, his base of operations, enjoys substantial popularity among devout Muslims.

5. ^cAbd al-Aziz [Shqaqi], *al-Khumayni*, pp. 46–48.

6. Ibid., pp. 51–60.

7. ᶜAbd al-Aziz, *al-Khumayni*, p. 122.

8. See Israel Altman's chapter on Egypt in *The Middle East Contemporary Survey*, vol. 4, *1979–1980* (New York and London, 1981), p. 332 (hereafter cited as *MECS*).

9. Susser, Asher, "Jordan," in ibid., vol. 5, *1980–1981*, p. 641.

10. Cf. Khalifa's interview in *Le Monde* (Paris) (February 26, 1980); Tilmisani's interview in *al-Wadi* (Cairo) (July 1982): 36–37.

11. *MECS*, vol. 5, p. 641.

12. *Al-Majalla* (Saudi Arabia) (July 9, 1983): 7.

13. *Al-Musawwar* (Egypt) (June 28, 1985): 26–27.

14. In an interview with *Yediᶜot Aharonot* (Tel Aviv), Ruth Beloy (formerly Ruth Ben David, *nee* Madlene Lust), the widow of the late leader of Neturei Karta, described Khomeini as "a genuine leader, a man of principles, like de Gaulle. I sympathize with him and wish we [Jews] would have such a leader who would turn us all religious. Then the Messiah would surely come." See Amos Nevo, "Ruth Beloy Awaits the Messiah," *Yediᶜot Aharonot, Shivᶜa Yamim* (December 13, 1985), pp. 16–18.

15. Al-Hay Zahir Ihsan, *al-Shiᶜa wal-sunna* (Cairo, 1979) *silsilat ma anaᶜalayhi wa-ashabi*, no. 2: 3–67.

16. I am grateful to Sheikh Khalid Ahmad Mihnah from Umm al-Fahm for this information.

17. This episode suggests that, after Sadat's assassination in October 1981, the security services in Egypt reviewed their files as far back as 1979 and that a number of these files were incomplete.

18. The role of Palestinians or other nationalities in radical Islamic movements in Egypt has not received proper attention. Notably, the Islamic Liberation Organization that stormed the Military Technological Academy in Egypt in April 1974 was headed by Salih Siriyya, a Palestinian by birth who carried a Jordanian passport. Many Palestinian Muslims in the Gaza Strip suspect that Sheikh Tawfiq Hasan al-Kurd, head of the Islamic Piety Society there, was chosen as one of the heads of the Muslim group known in Egypt as Jamaᶜat al-takfir wal-hijra after the execution of its leader Shukri Mustafa in 1977.

19. For a list of periodicals published by the Iranians in Arabic, see the chapter by Sivan in this book, n. 58.

20. Cf. *al-Tali^ca al-islamiyya* no. 4 (April 1983): 1–13.

21. For names and further details on the group, see: MCF 1156, 1157/83, Gaza; 814/84, Gaza.

22. For details, consult Martin Kramer, "The Divided House of Islam," in *MECS*, Vol. 3, *1982–1983*, pp. 242–43.

23. This cooperation became evident during the Syrian siege and bombardment of Tripoli in the second half of 1985.

24. Text of ^cUbaydat's speech on May 15, 1984, as transmitted by Radio Amman, in *Foreign Broadcast Information Service* (MEA) (May 16, 1984), pp. F1–F3; the quotes are from F3. It is noteworthy that ^cUbaydat cited "documents, interrogation reports and trial transcripts," which remained classified, as the sources of his claim.

25. Al-Sattar Qasim, ^cAbd, *Suqut malik al-muluk* (n.p. [the West Bank], 1981), pp. 172–73.

26. Ibid., pp. 211–43.

27. H. K. al-islami, *Bayan hawl al-majzara al-jadida* (n.d. [July 1983]). The pamphlet was issued following the assassination of several Palestinian students and the wounding of others in the Islamic Academy (*Kulliyat al-shari^ca*) in Hebron by Jewish terrorists.

28. *Al-Bayan* no. 4 (April 1985): 2–3.

29. *Al-Bayan* no. 6 (May–June 1985): 5–8.

30. Cf. *Al-Quds* (Jerusalem) (June 6, 1985), on the appearance of *al-Bayan* no. 6.

31. Shqaqi and the Imam ^cAbd al-Aziz ^cAbd al-Rahman ^cAwda were sentenced to eleven months in jail in addition to a small fine and a suspended sentence. Other members received two- to four-month jail terms in addition to small fines and suspended sentences.

Chapter 7

1. G. Aran, "From Religious Zionism to a Zionist Religion: The Origin and Culture of Gush Emunim," Ph.D. dissertation, The Hebrew University of Jerusalem, 1987.

2. See, for example, D. Newman, ed., *The Impact of Gush Emunim* (Beckenham, Kent, 1985), an anthology of studies on the various aspects of GE, with an extensive bibliography of Hebrew and English articles.

3. A. I. Kook, *Orot* (Jerusalem, 1975); *Orot Hakodesh* (Jerusalem, 1969); Z. Y. Kook, *Li-Netivot Israel* (Jerusalem, 1968) [Hebrew].

4. G. Aran, "The Roots of GE" in *Studies in Contemporary Jewry*, vol. 2 (Bloomington: Indiana University Press, 1986).

5. See Z. Werblowsky, *Beyond Tradition and Modernity* (London, 1976), especially Chapter 3.

6. On Jewish mysticism in general and the messianic Kaballah of Rabbi Luria in particular, see G. Scholem, *Major Trends in Jewish Mysticism* (New York, 1961); *On the Kaballah and Its Symbolism* (New York, 1969); *Kabbalah* (Jerusalem, 1974); *Writings on Jewish Heritage and Renaissance* (Tel Aviv, 1976) [Hebrew].

7. In the argument presented in the following pages, I have relied heavily on the works of Gershom Scholem, whose historical and theological studies contain revealing sociological insights that have been further developed here to apply to GE and its religion. I am aware that since Scholem's monumental pioneering work other research, supported by newly revealed data and updated analytical methods, has been published which differs from his theses. It could be claimed that in some cases Scholem's argument does not stand up to the historical test. I nonetheless find his general sociological model eminently applicable to the issue here.

8. For a short, elementary, and systematic survey of institutional religious attitudes toward Israeli nationalism and statehood, see E. Don-Yehiya, "Jewish Orthodoxy, Zionism and the State of Israel," *The Jerusalem Quarterly* no. 31 (Spring 1984).

9. On messianism in theory and practice, see M. Weber, *The Sociology of Religion* (Boston, 1964), Chapters 9–12; Z. Werblowsky, "Messiah and Messianic Movements," *Encyclopedia Britannica*, 1974; J. Talmon, "Pursuit of the Millennium" and "Millenarian Movements," *European Journal of Sociology* (1962, 1966). On Jewish messianism, see G. Scholem, *The Messianic Idea in Judaism and Other Essays* (New York, 1971); Z. Werblowsky, "Messianism in Jewish History," in *Jewish Society through the Ages*, ed. H. Ben-Sasson and S. Ettinger (New York, 1973); S. Sharot, *Messianism, Mysticism and Magic* (Chapel Hill, 1982); J. Katz, "The Messianic Component in Modern Jewish Nationalism," *Commentary* 73, no. 1 (1982).

10. See L. Festinger et al., *When Prophecy Fails* (Minneapolis, 1956). For a summary of various classical and updated theses and research on this theory, see J. Tedeschi et al., *Introduction to Social Psychology* (St. Paul, Minn., 1985), Chapter 6.

11. See G. Scholem, *Sabbatai Sevi: The Mystical Messiah* (Princeton, N.J., 1973).

12. See the works of G. Scholem mentioned earlier and his introduction to *Sabbatai Sevi: The Mystical Messiah* (Princeton, N.J., 1973).

13. Y. Ben-Nun, *Nekuda* no. 53 (1983) [Hebrew].

14. M. Ben-Yosef, *Nekuda* no. 80 (1984) [Hebrew].

15. Y. Etzion and other "Messiah Men," quoting the relatively unknown teachings of S. Ben-Dov.

16. H. Porat, *Ptahim* (March 1975) [Hebrew].

17. See, for example, H. Cox, *The Secular City* (New York, 1965).

18. Personal interview with Y. Michaelowitz.

19. See the works of G. Scholem, especially *Mitzva Haba'a Be^{c}avira*," *Knesset* 2 (1937) [Hebrew].

Chapter 8

1. Khamene'i sermon, Radio Tehran (August 6, 1987); quoted in *BBC Summary of World Broadcasts: The Middle East and Africa* (hereafter, *BBC Summary*) (August 7, 1987).

2. On the doctrinal shift from pilgrimage to visitation, see Said Amir Arjomand, *The Shadow of God and the Hidden Imam* (Chicago, 1984), pp. 168–70.

3. Richard Burton, *Narrative of a Pilgrimage to Mecca and Medina* (ed. London, 1893), p. 168; John Lewis Burckhardt, *Travels in Arabia* (ed. London, 1829), pp. 168, and 251–52.

4. Burton, ibid.

5. On these taxes, see H. Kazem Zadeh, "Relation d'un pèlerinage à la Mecque," *Revue du Monde musulman* (Paris), no. 19 (1912): 159–60.

6. C. Snouck Hurgronje, *Mekka in the Latter Part of the 19th Century* (Leiden, 1931), p. 141.

7. A general history of Wahhabi-Shi^{c}ite relations is provided by ^{c}Ali Asghar Faqihi, *Vahhabiyan* (Tehran, 1352/1973–1974).

8. Quoted by H. St. J. B. Philby, *Arabia of the Wahhabis* (London, 1928), p. 67.

9. On the special place of Medina in Shi^{c}ite Islam, see Dwight M. Donaldson, *The Shi^{c}ite Religion* (London, 1933), pp. 142–51. On the cemetery's history, see *Encyclopaedia of Islam*, 2d ed. (Leiden), q. v. "Baki^c al-Gharkad" (A. J. Wensinck-[A.S. Bazmee Ansari]), vol. 1, pp. 957–58.

10. For the text of the *fatwa* that sanctioned the demolition, see Hasan Sadr al-Din Kazimi, *al-Radd ᶜala fatawa al-wahhabiyyin* (Baghdad, 1344/1925-1926). For a description of the demolition, see Eldon Rutter, *The Holy Cities of Arabia* (London, 1930), pp. 562-64.

11. This and other episodes in modern Saudi-Iranian relations are discussed on the basis of original documents in a publication of the Iranian Ministry of Foreign Affairs, *Ravabit-i dowlat-i Shahanshahi Iran ba-doval-i khavar-i mianeh* (Tehran, 1976), pp. 61-89.

12. *Oriente Moderno* 6 (1926): 310, 513-14, and 600.

13. *Oriente Moderno* 7 (1927): 99 and 111-12.

14. *Oriente Moderno* 10 (1930): 105-106.

15. The evolution of this policy is detailed by Jacob Goldberg, "The Shiᶜite Minority in Saudi Arabia," in *Shiᶜism and Social Protest*, ed. Juan R. I. Cole and Nikki R. Keddie (New Haven, Conn., 1986), pp. 230-46.

16. As reported by James S. Moose (Jidda), dispatch of February 24, 1944, National Archives, Washington, Record Group 59, 890 f. 404/55.

17. Ali Shariati, *Hajj*, 2d ed. (Bedford, Ohio, 1978), p. 109.

18. Khomeini's message to the pilgrims (February 6, 1971), in *Islam and Revolution: Writings and Declarations of Imam Khomeini*, trans. Hamid Algar (Berkeley, Calif., 1981), pp. 195-99.

19. A full treatment of the pilgrimage since Iran's revolution may be found in M. Kramer's essays in the annual *Middle East Contemporary Survey*, beginning with volume six (covering 1981-1982). For a very different approach, see R. K. Ramazani, *Revolutionary Iran: Challenge and Response in the Middle East* (Baltimore, 1986), pp. 91-100 and 111-12.

20. Full text of Khalid-Khomeini exchange is in *al-Nashra al-ᶜarabiyya li'l-hizb al-jumhuri al-islami* (Tehran) (21 Dhu al-Hijja 1401/October 19, 1981); and in *Sawt al-umma* (Tehran) (October 31, 1981).

21. *Encyclopaedia of Islam*, 2d ed. (Leiden), q.v. "Bast" (R. M. Savory), vol. 1, p. 1088.

22. For a description of the site's desolation as late as 1974, see Wa'il Saᶜid ᶜAli al-Wa'ili, *Mi'a sura wa-sura ᶜan istiqhlal duyuf al-rahman* (n.p., c. 1981), pp. 524-25.

23. The figure was given by Mehdi Karrubi, Tehran television (June 16, 1988) in *Foreign Broadcast Information Service Daily Report: The Middle East and South Asia* (henceforth, *FBIS*) (June 21, 1988). The same need explains Iranian Shiᶜism's rediscovery of the mausoleum of Sayyida Zaynab, the Imam Husayn's sister, near Damascus. A minor site of Shiᶜite visitation in the

past, it has now been transformed into a major shrine, visited by thousands of Shi^{c}ites from Iran and Iranian-backed Shi^{c}ites from the Lebanese Hizballah. Iran has also invested large resources in restoration of the still lesser shrine of Sayyida Raqiya, Husayn's daughter, near the Umayyad Mosque in Damascus. On these sites, see Biancamaria Scarcia Amoretti, "A proposito della comunità imamita contemporanea di Siria," *Oriento Moderno*, new series, 3, no. 7–12 (July–December 1984): 193–201.

24. Text of speech, Radio Tehran (July 2, 1987), in *BBC Summary* (July 4, 1987).

25. Saudi Press Agency (July 3, 1987), quoted in *BBC Summary* (July 6, 1987).

26. Radio Tehran (July 30, 1987), quoted in *BBC Summary* (August 1, 1987).

27. Text of speech, Radio Tehran (July 29, 30, and 31, 1987), quoted in *BBC Summary* (July 31, August 1 and 3, 1987).

28. Fahd al-Qahtani, *Majzarat Makka: Qissat al-madhbaha al-Sa^{c}udiyya li'l-hujja* (London, 1988), pp. 27–28.

29. Report on the assessment of American intelligence sources, *New York Times* (September 6, 1987).

30. The most detailed eyewitness accounts from a pro-Iranian perspective include that of the Pakistani Shi^{c}ite journalist Mushahid Hussain, which appeared in the *Washington Post* (August 20, 1987), and the several reports collected by Qahtani, *Majzarat Makka*, pp. 77–107. Qahtani's book is an extensive survey of the event and the worldwide reaction to it. The Saudi director-general of public security, General ^{c}Abdallah bin ^{c}Abd al-Rahman Al Shaykh, provided the most comprehensive Saudi account in a statement, which prefaced a special Saudi documentary film on the incident, aired on Saudi television on August 20, 1987.

31. Nayif press conference, Saudi Press Agency (August 25, 1987), quoted in *BBC Summary* (August 27, 1987).

32. Khomeini's message to Karrubi, Radio Tehran (August 3, 1987), quoted in *BBC Summary* (August 5, 1987).

33. Text of Rafsanjani's speech to protest march in Tehran, Radio Tehran (August 2, 1987), quoted in *BBC Summary* (August 4, 1987).

34. Text of communiqué, Saudi Press Agency (October 15, 1987), quoted in *FBIS* (October 16, 1987).

35. *Al-^{c}Ahd* (Beirut) (October 23, 1987).

36. *Al-Thawra al-Islamiyya* (London) (October 1987).

37. *Ibid.*

38. Rafsanjani's speech, Radio Tehran (November 26, 1987), quoted in FBIS (November 28, 1987).

39. Montazeri's speech, Radio Tehran (November 27), quoted in *FBIS* (November 29, 1987).

40. Report of speech by Emami-Jamarani (April 29, 1988), quoted in *FBIS* (May 2, 1988).

41. For a Shiᶜite compendium of alleged proofs of the Jewish origins of the Saudis, see Nasir al-Saᶜid, *Tarikh Al Saᶜud* (Beirut, n.d.), vol. 1, pp. 392–403. I am indebted to Werner Ende for this reference.

42. Report of conference, *al-Sharq al-awsat* (London) (July 4, 1988).

43. Saudi Council of Ministers statement, Saudi Press Agency (June 28, 1988), quoted in *FBIS* (June 30, 1988).

44. Mehdi Karrubi, Tehran television (June 16, 1988), quoted by *FBIS*, (June 21, 1988).

45. Message of Khomeini on occasion of the Mecca "massacre" and Iran's acceptance of U.N. Resolution 598, Radio Tehran (July 20, 1988), quoted in *FBIS* (July 21, 1988). Abu Sufyan was a member of the Prophet Muhammad's tribe who had originally opposed Muhammad; his son, Yazid, was responsible for killing the Imam Husayn; and another son, Muᶜawiya, founded the Umayyad dynasty. The family and the dynasty are deemed usurpers in the Shiᶜite reading of early Islamic history.

INDEX

229

Husayn, 153; and Iran, 151; Islamic Revolution, 147, 152; Neturei Karta, 36
Palestinian Arabs: Iranian revolution, 146, 151; in Israel, 155; and Gush Emunim, 172; and Jews, 152; and leaders (Arab), 153
pan-Arabism: Baᶜth, 100; and Muslim Brethren, 102
pan-Islam: conferences, 70; movement, 48; and Palestinian nationalism, 152; opposition in Iraq, 95
Peres, Y., 87
Persian Gulf, 67, 177, 178, 187, 194
Porat, Hanan, 26
propaganda: Iran revolution, 68, 70; Khomeinistic, 42, 68; Shiᶜite, 68, 69, 148; mentioned, 46, 68, 74
Prophet Muhammad: companions of, 45, 120; mentioned, 65, 110, 117, 119, 120, 121, 122

qa'id al-Umma, 66
al-Qardawi, Yusuf: and Shqaqi, 145; teaching of, 145
Qasim, ᶜAbd al-Karim, 96
Qasim, ᶜAbd al-Sattar, 151
al-Qassam, Sheikh ᶜIzz al-Din, 145
quietism, 14
Qur'an. *See* Koran
Quraysh tribe, 44
Qutb, Sayyid: execution, 110; rebellion, 49; teachings, 52; thought, 39; writings of, 39, 115; mentioned, 4, 149 153

rabbinical court (BaDaṣ): Neturei Karta, 36
racism: crimes against Jews, 92; inherent sanctity of Jews, 93
radicalism, Islamic (*see also* Shiᶜism, Sunnism): 75; in Morocco,

202n.14; Muslim movements, 68, 195n.2; rise of, 41
Shiᶜism: in Iraq, 40; in Lebanon, 40; movements, 75; and al-Sadr, 67; Shiᶜite writing, 67; mentioned, 3, 48, 182, 201n.4
Sunnism: interpretation, 56; movements, 39, 51, 75; terminology, 74; thought, 39; writing, 39; mentioned, 3, 40, 48, 58, 72, 200n.1, 201n.4
radicalism, Jewish (*see also* Gush Emunim, Kach, Neturei Karta, and zealotism): and Gush Emunim, 139–140; Neturei Karta, 139–140; trends in Jewish radicalism, 36; ultra-Orthodox, anti-Zionist, 32
radicalization: Iranian Islam, 40; of Qutb, 39; Gush Emunim and religious, 160
radicals, Islamic (*see also* Shiᶜism, Sunnism): Muslim, 44, 155; in Egypt, 148
Shiᶜites: in Iraq and Lebanon, 66; organizations, 67; successor to Husayn, 65; mentioned, 49, 73, 203n.26
Sunnis: decentralized, 51; and Gaza, 57; and Iranian revolution, 71; and Khomeini, 57; and Palestinians, 45, Shiᶜite-Sunni theorists, 74; and ulama, 51; mentioned, 58, 67, 203n.26
radicals, Jewish: in Neturei Karta, 130; religious and establishment, 141; religious and Six Day War, 140
Rafah, 148
Rafsanjani, ᶜAli Akbar Hashemi, 191
al-Rahman, Sheikh ᶜUmar ᶜAbd, 51
Rajᶜa: return of Imam, 52, 57
Rashidun, 44